New Yorkwalks

This is the
Henry Holt Walks Series,
which originated with
PARISWALKS, *by Alison and Sonia Landes.*
Other titles in this series include:

LONDONWALKS *by Anton Powell*
JERUSALEMWALKS *by Nitza Rosovsky*
FLORENCEWALKS *by Anne Holler*
ROMEWALKS *by Anya M. Shetterly*
VIENNAWALKS *by J. Sydney Jones*
VENICEWALKS *by Chas Carner and Alessandro Giannatasio*
BARCELONAWALKS *by George Semler*
RUSSIAWALKS *by David and Valeria Matlock*
BEIJINGWALKS *by Don Cohn and Zhang Jingqing*

NEW YORKWALKS

The 92nd Street Y

edited by
Batia Plotch
with
John Morse

Photographs by
Glenn Wright

An Owl Book

Henry Holt and Company · New York

Published by Henry Holt and Company, Inc.,
115 West 18th Street, New York, New York 10011.
Published in Canada by Fitzhenry & Whiteside Limited,
91 Granton Drive, Richmond Hill, Ontario L4B 2N5.

Library of Congress Cataloging-in-Publication Data

New Yorkwalks / the 92nd Street Y; edited by Batia Plotch;
Photographs by Glenn Wright. — 1st ed.
p.   cm. — (Henry Holt walks series)
"An Owl book."
Includes index.
1. New York (N.Y.)—Tours.   2. Walking—New York (N.Y.)—
Guidebooks.   I. Plotch, Batia.   II. 92nd Street Y (New York,
N.Y.)   III. Title: New Yorkwalks.   IV. Series.
F128.18.N475   1992
917.47'10443—dc20   92-4847
                                                    CIP

ISBN 0-8050-1660-0

Henry Holt books are available at special discounts for bulk
purchases for sales promotions, premiums, fund-raising, or
educational use. Special editions or book excerpts can also be
created to specification.
For details contact:
Special Sales Director, Henry Holt and Company, Inc.,
115 West 18th Street, New York, New York 10011.

First Edition—1992

Designed by Claire Naylon Vaccaro
Maps by Jeffrey L. Ward
Printed in the United States of America
Recognizing the importance of preserving the
written word, Henry Holt and Company, Inc.,
by policy, prints all of its first editions
on acid-free paper. ∞

1   3   5   7   9   10   8   6   4   2

Contents

Acknowledgments

This book has been a dream of mine since the inception of the Tours and Talks Program at the 92nd Street Young Men's and Young Women's Hebrew Association fourteen years ago.

Although I was born in Tunisia and spent many years in Israel, I consider myself a New Yorker. I have an insatiable desire to learn and absorb every facet of this spectacular metropolis. I love its people, its art, its history, its music, and, above all, the feeling of ebullience in the air—which I still sense after nearly thirty years. New York City exudes an intoxicating energy, an energy that we've tried to capture in each walk presented here.

This dream could not have been realized without the help and advice of many people. I owe the biggest debt of gratitude to John Morse, for his devoted assistance with the manuscript and for walking with each of the contributors. I'd like to thank the contributors themselves for their enthusiasm and knowledge over the years, and especially for giving up their weekends to be included in this book. I'd also like to thank my editor, Theresa Burns, who was always so generous with her time and comments; and my literary agent, Carla Glasser, for her patience and cooperation.

There wouldn't be a Tours and Talks Program without my staff at the 92nd Street Y—Maryanne Reilly, Melissa Golub, Shelley Sheinin, and Clara Keita—as well as the many wonderful volunteers who help us out. Special thanks for their support of the program go to the Y's management: Daniel Kaplan, President; Sol Adler, Executive Director; and Helaine Geismar Katz, Director of the Center for Adult Life and Learning, who recommended the first tour. And, of course, to all the thousands of 92nd Street Y patrons who take our tours each year.

Last, but not least, my gratitude and love go to my family. To my children, Adam and Dina, who have walked with me (even before their birth!) all over this city, and to my husband, Stephen, for his unending support throughout the trials and tribulations that go hand in hand with my love of New York.

> —Batia Plotch, Director
> Tours and Talks Program
> 92nd Street Y
> May 1992

New Yorkwalks

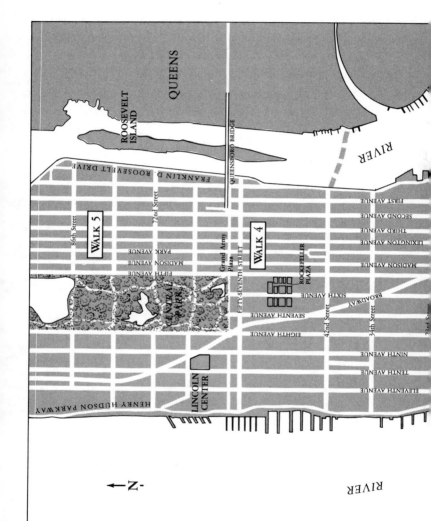

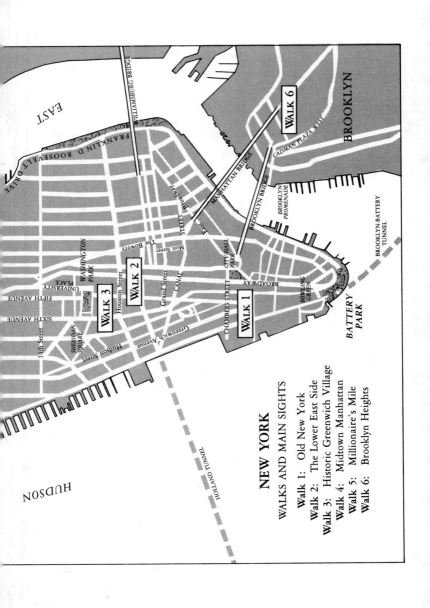

NEW YORK

WALKS AND MAIN SIGHTS

Walk 1: Old New York
Walk 2: The Lower East Side
Walk 3: Historic Greenwich Village
Walk 4: Midtown Manhattan
Walk 5: Millionaire's Mile
Walk 6: Brooklyn Heights

Introduction

Not everything you've heard about New York City is true, but most of it is. It's the city of big dreams and desperate living, the land of opportunity and squandered fortunes. It is home to the United Nations, the Metropolitan Opera, the Museum of Modern Art, Rockefeller Center, Lincoln Center, the Statue of Liberty, and Nathan's Famous Hot Dogs. It's an international center of fashion, media, insurance, retailing, banking, transportation, culture, and trade. And it all serves as home to about eight million New Yorkers who can insult the place better than any outsider and will defend it to any who try. Despite detractors and difficulties—and there are plenty of both—New York is undeniably a world-class city, a reputation in development since the city's founding in 1664.

New Yorkers are a special breed who have pretty much learned to get along because they have to. This is the nation's most crowded city. Chicago, with less than half the population of New York, has about twice the land area. In Manhattan, not the most populous of New York's five boroughs, there are more people *on the*

The Empire State Building, symbol of New York

street at any given moment during the day than *live* in the entire city of San Francisco. If the sleek, 110-story twin towers of the World Trade Center were placed in Vermont, its daytime population of 50,000 employees—that is, not those who merely visit or come to do some business and leave, but who work there every day—would constitute one of the state's largest cities. Pulling it all together are the city's streets and avenues, the threads of New York's tapestry.

To the uninitiated, the streets of the city are a chaotic, frantic mess. But to those who live here, they're a chaotic, frantic mess. It is here you may best observe the refined New York art of getting from one place to another on foot. Look closely. Notice how people come within millimeters of each other as they walk, yet rarely collide. They may disregard traffic signals, but instinctively know how to cross the street as bicycles, taxis, buses, cars, and trucks pass within a whisker. The sidewalk ballet that is walking in New York requires agility, concentration, a sense of adventure, and an outward show of determination to get where you're going.

New Yorkwalks is designed to show you a side of the city that many visitors—and even New Yorkers themselves—seldom see. The six intimate walking tours presented here avoid the obvious, the overcrowded, and the overrated, and focus instead on little-known details about historically and culturally stimulating pockets of town.

The walks have been selected from the Tours and Talks Program developed thirteen years ago by the 92nd Street Y, one of New York's preeminent cultural centers. The tours have become a favorite not only of the city's many visitors but of residents, too. These six walks in particular rank among the most popular offered through the program, and draw large crowds each time they're placed on the calendar. But you won't need to wait until the tours are scheduled. You can begin anytime you want, and *New Yorkwalks* will be your guide.

Each of the walks has been contributed by one of the

actual guides who have led the tours over many years. The total amount of time that these contributors—all native New Yorkers—have lived here is over 350 years—longer than the city has been a city!

So put on some comfortable walking shoes and discover with us the many secrets of New York.

Information
and Advice

GETTING HERE

Many people first arrive in New York via one of the three main airports that serve the city. **John F. Kennedy International Airport**, also known as "Kennedy" or "JFK," is located about one hour away from Manhattan and serves mostly international flights. **La Guardia** is much closer and serves domestic flights. **Newark**, located in New Jersey but as close as JFK, serves a mix of domestic and international flights.

Transportation possibilities from each of the airports include bus services that will take you from the airport to a variety of locations in Manhattan, including the World Trade Center (near the tip of Manhattan), Grand Central Terminal (42nd Street and Park Avenue), the Port Authority Bus Terminal (42nd Street and Eighth Avenue), and a variety of Midtown hotels. Prices range from $9 to $11. Consult the ground transportation counters near the baggage checkouts at each airport.

Taxis will also be able to take you into town. Taxis from JFK or Newark into Midtown will cost from $30 to

$45. La Guardia, because it is so much closer, costs from $15 to $25. Sharing a taxi ride is a way to get into town at less cost, but that option is not always available. Ask at the ground transportation counter.

If you need passport information, the U.S. Passport Office is located at 630 Fifth Avenue, telephone (212) 541-7700.

American Express offers its cardholders travel services at a series of offices located around the city. Here's a list:

65 Broadway
150 East 42nd Street
125 Broad Street
822 Lexington Avenue
199 Water Street at South Street Seaport
The New York Hilton Hotel at 1335 Avenue of the Americas (Sixth Avenue)
Bloomingdale's department store at Lexington Avenue and 59th Street
Macy's department store at 34th Street and Broadway

SPEAKING THE LANGUAGE

Of the scores of languages and dialects you might encounter in this city, sometimes the hardest to understand is English—at least the way New Yorkers speak it. What follows is an abbreviated guide to a few of the more common words and phrases.

Geography

The Park	Central Park
The Garden	Madison Square Garden
The Met	The Metropolitan Museum of Art (also used for the Metropolitan Opera)

Outer Boroughs	Bronx, Queens, Brooklyn, Staten Island
Lex	Lexington Avenue
Sixth Avenue	What real New Yorkers call Avenue of the Americas
SoHo	The artsy neighborhood SOuth of HOuston, north of Canal and west of Broadway
NoHo	Less defined, but roughly that area immediately north of SoHo
The Village	Greenwich Village. The city's first suburb remains a desirable neighborhood
Alphabet City	Avenues A through D in the East Village; a mix of punk, bohemia, The Ukraine, Puerto Rico, avant-garde art, music, drugs, and crime. Not for the squeamish, but still pretty good fun
Hell's Kitchen	Officially known as Clinton, the area stretches roughly from Broadway to the Hudson River and between 34th and 57th Streets
The Bowery	The down-and-out street of restaurant suppliers, flophouses, soup kitchens, and the homeless, stretching from Canal Street to Cooper Square. For all its troubles, it still has a certain appeal

Harlem	A centerpiece of African-American history. Parts of the old, grand neighborhood have fallen victim to crime and decay, but Harlem still thrives as a fascinating home of art, culture, and politics
Midtown	Manhattan's business district that stretches approximately from 34th to 59th Streets
Downtown	Manhattan below 14th Street
Wall Street	The core of the Financial District with Wall Street as its center
Uptown	Manhattan above 59th Street
Way Uptown	Harlem and above
Upper East Side	East of Central Park, between 59th and 96th streets
Upper West Side	West of Central Park, between 59th and 110th streets
Upstate	Anywhere in New York other than the city or the Island
The Island	Long Island
The Hamptons	The beach resort towns at the tip of Long Island
Jersey	New Jersey
The Shore	The New Jersey coast
The Coast	California

Food

A slice	A single slice of pizza; for example, "Give me a slice with extra cheese"

Ray's	What Webster's is to dictionaries, Ray's is to pizza in New York. Not a chain, just a nontrademarked name that's become synonymous with a decent slice
Regular	A cup of coffee with a moderate amount of cream. If you'd like sugar, now's a good time to say, "With one [or more] sugar"
Dark	Coffee with just a touch of milk
Light	Coffee with lots of milk
A schmear	A spread of cream cheese; for example, "I'll have a bagel with a schmear"
Egg cream	A beverage of club soda, milk, and chocolate syrup; contains no egg, no cream
Nosh	To eat (verb) or a bite to eat (noun), as in "Let's nosh" or "Let's get a nosh"
Dairy restaurant	Kosher restaurant that serves no meat products
Glatt kosher restaurant	Restaurant that sticks to the highest standards of Jewish food-preparation laws

Transportation

Subway lines:

IRT	Interborough Rapid Transit
BMT	Brooklyn-Manhattan Transit

| IND | Independent Subway Lines |

Roads:

LIE	Long Island Expressway
BQE	Brooklyn-Queens Expressway
FDR	Franklin D. Roosevelt Drive, Manhattan's east-side highway

Trains:

Metroliner	Amtrak's commuter trains to Washington and Boston, leaving from Penn Station
LIRR	The Long Island Rail Road, leaving from Penn Station
PATH Trains	Trains from Manhattan's west side to New Jersey
Metro-North	Trains from Grand Central Terminal to Connecticut and upstate New York

Planes:

| Shuttle | From La Guardia Airport, the hourly commuter flights to Washington and Boston |

Airports:

| La Guardia | The small but busy Queens airport that's convenient because it's so close to Manhattan |

JFK	The large and busy Queens airport about an hour from Manhattan; the airport for most international flights. Some terminals are notable for their incredible architecture
Newark	New Jersey's airport serving the metropolitan region; convenient and comfortable

Taxis

Yellow cab	The familiar yellow taxis, which operate mostly below 96th Street in Manhattan
Gypsy cabs	Private cars that operate as taxis all over the city, particularly in neighborhoods not frequented by yellow cabs
Checker cab	The bulky oversized cabs that used to be the mainstay of the yellow cab fleets. Now a rarity, but a great ride if you can find one

People

New York's Finest	The police
New York's Bravest	Firefighters
Bridge and Tunnel Crowd	Those who live outside of Manhattan but enter to go to the clubs, bars, and

| | restaurants; for example, "That place is really fun on weeknights, but on weekends it's strictly bridge and tunnel" |
| Yankees, Mets, Knicks, Jets, and Giants | Respectively, New York's two baseball teams, its basketball team, and its two football teams |

CLIMATE

Like the city itself, New York's weather is varied and a bit unpredictable. From blizzards to heat waves, torrential downpours to droughts, anything is possible. Each season (and there are four distinct ones here) has its own appeal.

Winter days, with average temperatures between 25° and 36° Fahrenheit, can be brutally cold, but often are crisp and fresh, especially when it's sunny. To see the city beneath a blanket of fresh snow (a rarity in recent years) is one of the more exquisite urban experiences. Layers of clothing usually work well, with sweaters and sports coats covered by a good winter jacket. Boots, gloves, muffler, and hat will help you enjoy being outdoors. Also, watch for the terrific gusts of wind that can greet you as turn corners onto the avenues or near the rivers. On a chilly March day, for example, the Wall Street area can seem like one giant wind tunnel.

Spring has temperatures that average between 43° and 60° Fahrenheit. Once the sun sets, temperatures often drop considerably, so be prepared with a jacket, and maybe a scarf. Springtime in New York can be breathtakingly beautiful.

Summer is often humid, but activities never stop. With average daytime temperatures of 85° Fahrenheit in July and humidity that can reach 95 percent, the city has

11

all the appeal of a steam bath. These may be good days to visit waterfront attractions such as South Street Seaport, Brighton Beach, or the Staten Island Ferry, or seek shade in Central Park. Dress light, but be warned: Many bars and restaurants like to crank up the air-conditioning in summer, and while it's sweltering outside you may find yourself freezing at lunch. A sports coat or wrap is recommended.

One particularly nice feature of summer in the city is that many New Yorkers flee during the months of June, July, and August to seek cooler climes along the many beaches of Long Island. As you're strolling down the tranquil streets, particularly in SoHo and Greenwich Village, it can feel as though you have the whole place to yourself.

Fall in New York, like spring, is generally comfortable and crisp, with temperatures ranging from 50° to 66° Fahrenheit. A light coat or sweater is usually sufficient to stay warm.

New York's annual rainfall is about 42 inches, not much less than that of Seattle; but instead of an occasional drizzle, the rain here tends to descend in buckets. It's a good idea to keep a small, folded umbrella with you while you're touring. If you're caught in a rainstorm (commonplace in summer), take cover until it's over, which shouldn't be long. You may also get to meet someone interesting as you huddle beneath an awning.

HOTELS

No other city in the United States has as many hotel rooms as New York; but, while there are many to choose from, prices are not so varied, with about $100 a night considered the threshold for decent accommodations.

At the least expensive end are rooms at the **92nd Street Y** at 1395 Lexington Avenue (at 92nd Street), **McBurney YMCA** at 215 West 23rd Street (near Seventh Avenue), **Vanderbilt YMCA** at 224 East 47th Street (near

Grand Central Terminal), and the **West Side Y** at 5 West 63rd Street. Rooms range from $33 to $36 per night. The 92nd Street Y requires a minimum of a one-week stay, which costs $245.

The **American Youth Hostel**, at 891 Amsterdam Avenue (103rd Street) offers dormitory-style rooms beginning at $18.75 per night, plus a $3 fee per night for nonmembers. Despite the name, all ages are welcome. Farther downtown, the **International Student Hospice** at 154 East 33rd Street (near Lexington Avenue) welcomes those between eighteen and twenty-eight years old and costs $30 per night, with discounts for those who stay longer. During the summer, it's a good idea to make reservations in advance.

At the other end of the scale are the ultraluxurious hotels that dot Midtown near Fifth Avenue. The newly refurbished **St. Regis** boasts that it is the city's most expensive hotel, with standard rooms at from $350 to $450. Louis XV furnishings, crystal chandeliers, and 22-karat gold leaf molding give the hotel an aristocratic air, as does the service, which includes personal room attendants wearing white ties and tails.

Between these two extremes is the **Gramercy Park Hotel**, at 2 Lexington Avenue, a charming European-style hotel that's moderately priced. The hotel faces Gramercy Park, the only private park in the city, to which guests have access.

Three new hotels started in part by the late Studio 54 impresario Steve Rubell have recently made a pleasant mark on the city's accommodation scene. **The Royalton** (44 West 44th Street), **Morgan's** (237 Madison Avenue), and the **Paramount** (235 West 46th Street) each have quietly elegant service and stylish settings. The Paramount has furnishings designed by Phillipe Starck, including designer toothbrushes in every room. The Royalton and Morgan's begin in the $220 range, but the Paramount is relatively reasonable, starting at about $120 a night.

For those who must stay in the quintessential New York hotel, there are essentially two choices: The **Waldorf-Astoria**, at Park Avenue and 49th Street, and the **Plaza**, at Fifth Avenue and Central Park South, both provide enough glitz to justify their rates (beginning at $250 at the Waldorf-Astoria and $225 at the Plaza) and enough honest-to-goodness class to justify their reputations.

There's also a list of hotels in the back of this book, page 297.

RESTAURANTS AND CAFÉS

It is no exaggeration that the more than 25,000 bars and restaurants in the city cater to every budget, every cuisine, and every taste. You want Ethiopian, we got Ethiopian. You want Basque, we got Basque. You want Chinese, we got Chinatown (although you'll find good Chinese restaurants throughout the city).

Meeting and schmoozing in New York restaurants is a time-honored tradition. Greenwich Village has many quaint and cozy restaurants. The Upper East Side features a slew of elegant establishments that can be expensive, but tranquil, with a heavy emphasis on service. The Upper West Side is home to an array of restaurants equal in quality to the East Side, but much more relaxed. Mexican, Cuban, and Chinese restaurants—even a Native American restaurant—dot the culinary landscape and manage to please the very particular tastes of the tweed and blazer crowd that populate this neighborhood.

Look in the back of this guide on page 291 for an extensive list of some New York favorites. Many New York restaurants are open late and some are open all night. For the more popular restaurants, be sure to make reservations, especially on weekend nights.

TRANSPORTATION

No American city is served by mass transit like New York. Whereas most of the country is tied to automobiles, New York, especially Manhattan, has managed to provide real transportation alternatives to owning a car. In fact, only about one out of four households in the city even owns a car.

Buses

Blue-and-white city buses run 24 hours a day, with less frequent service at night and extra buses at rush hours. Buses are generally modern, safe, clean, and efficient and allow riders to watch the street as they travel. On certain routes at certain times, though, you might wait an interminably long time for a bus—only to have several arrive simultaneously. In addition, during rush hours especially, buses can get mired in the same stop-and-go pace of the rest of the traffic, and that can mean getting nowhere slowly.

Bus fare at the time of this writing is $1.25, all in coin. The bus driver won't make change, but sometimes another passenger may be able to help you out. Don't try this during rush hour, though: The glare of other passengers just isn't worth it. You may also use tokens, which also cost $1.25 and can be purchased at subway stations and some newsstands, and most recently, McDonald's.

Subways

Subways are often the fastest way to get around town, especially at rush hour and particularly for journeys from one end of town to the other. Like buses, they operate 24 hours a day. A vigorous effort in the mid-1980s removed almost all of the subway's fabled graffiti, improving the image of the subways, a standard bearer of New York denigration. Work has also been under way to improve service and more police officers have been added to subway patrols on the platforms and trains, and new cars have been added to the fleet. During summer, most cars have air-conditioning.

Subway entrances and exits should be treated with extreme caution, especially at night. As always, use common sense: Travel with other passengers and stay out of empty cars; at night, ride in the center car with the conductor, and wait for the train at the designated area on each platform.

To know which entrances are open, look for the lighted globes at street level. A green light indicates the entrance is open and a token seller is inside. A yellow light means that no token booth is open, but those who already have tokens may enter through metal gates. (These don't always work, though, and if you lose your token, there's no one to refund your money.) A red light means the entrance is closed.

If all routes were laid end to end, the subway system would stretch halfway to Detroit. The trains can take you from Coney Island to the Bronx Zoo, from Yankee Stadium to Jamaica Bay. At a $1.25 per token, it can still represent quite a bargain.

Taxis

One of the city's most enduring symbols is the New York yellow cab—cars that dart and dare with seemingly little regard to potholes, pedestrians, passenger safety, or police. Most taxi drivers are, however, experts at getting you where you're going with courtesy and for a relatively inexpensive price. Taxis charge $1.50 upon entering the cab, and 25 to 75 cents for every one-fifth mile (four street blocks), depending on how fast traffic is moving.

After 8:00 P.M., cabs are allowed to tack on an additional 50 cents. A 15-percent tip is standard. There is no per-passenger charge.

You may notice that each taxi has three lights on the roof. If the center light is on, the taxi is available. If the center light is off, but the two lights on either side are on, the taxi is occupied. All lights on means the taxi is off duty. The law permits four passengers per cab, and an extra tip is generally expected if the driver has to open the trunk for you. To hail a cab, step into the street and raise your arm—just like they do in the movies.

Once you're in the taxi, the driver is required by law to take you anywhere in the city you want to go, including the worst section of town, the outer boroughs, or the airports, although there is an additional charge for going to Newark (New Jersey) International. Passengers must pay any tolls. Remember to always get a receipt—if you should have a complaint, it will give the city's Taxi and Limousine Commission the information it will need to follow up. Furthermore, if you lose something in the taxi, it will help you track it down. Believe it or not, people who have lost purses or expensive cameras in New York taxis have had them returned.

Personal Automobile

In the outer boroughs a car is sometimes helpful, particularly in Staten Island, but in Manhattan they are basically a hassle. If you must drive into Manhattan, there are many parking garages where you can safely leave your car and avoid break-ins, or other disappointments that can ruin a vacation. A few good locations include:

148 West 48th Street (between Sixth and Seventh avenues)

240 Albany Street (in Battery Park City)
443 East 49th Street (off the FDR Drive, near the UN)
201 West 75th Street (enter on Amsterdam Avenue)
121 East 80th Street (between Park and Lexïngton avenues)
122 West 3rd Street (in Greenwich Village)

These are all covered garages and are open from 7:00 A.M. to 2:00 A.M., with West 3rd Street and West 75th Street open 24 hours. Prices range from $11.50 to $18.75 per day, with most offering "early bird" specials for those who arrive before 10:00 A.M.

To encourage visitors to the **Theater District** (on the West Side around Times Square), the city recently added 900 new parking spaces along the street, so parking there is much easier than it had been previously.

For those who would like to know where every parking garage and lot in the city is, a series of parking maps, called "Your Move Neighborhood Parking Maps," are available in bookstores for $4.95 per neighborhood or $34.95 for the entire city.

Bicycle

Bicycling in New York can be insanity, especially on crowded streets during rush hours. On lighter traffic days, however, and in Central Park (particularly on weekends when automobile traffic is barred), bicycling can be an exhilarating experience. Bicycle rentals are available in Central Park at **Loeb Boathouse**, near the East 72nd Street entrance. For information, call (212) 861-4137. A major credit card will serve as a deposit.

Other locations include:

14th Street Bicycles, 332 East 14th Street (between First and Second avenues). Telephone (212) 228-4344.
6th Avenue Bicycles, 546 Sixth Avenue (corner of 15th Street). Telephone (212) 255-5100.

Midtown Bicycles, 360 West 47th Street (at Ninth Avenue). Telephone (212) 581-4500.

Canal Street Bicycles, 417 Canal Street (near Sixth Avenue). Telephone (212) 334-8000.

Metro Bicycles, 1311 Lexington Avenue (corner of 88th Street). Telephone (212) 427-4450.

West Side Bicycles, 231 West 96th Street (corner of Broadway). Telephone (212) 663-7531.

At each location, bicycle rentals are $25 for four hours. Locks can be rented for an additional $5. Remember, though, that the best way to keep your bike safe is to always keep it in sight.

Walking

This is the true way to see New York. Be sure to dress comfortably, and wear soft-soled shoes that can take a day of walking.

A walk in New York is its own reward. Not only will you get to where you're going (and often faster than in a car), you will experience the essence of the city. And isn't that why we're here?

For all the push and shove of the city, probably nothing brings out the friendliness in New Yorkers like being asked for directions. If you don't know how to get somewhere, ask for help. People here take pride in their city and fancy themselves experts. Don't let shyness cause you to walk in circles. One caveat: Not everyone who gives directions is accurate, so if you're not confident, ask again.

SHOPPING

A good rule of thumb for shopping in the city is to remember this: If it costs money, you can buy it in New York. As a world commercial center, New York shops

Quiet elegance on the Upper East Side

feature a continuous flood of imported and domestic items in every price range.

For a taste of the truly international, visit the gift shop of the **United Nations** (42nd Street and First Avenue), beneath the General Assembly building. This emporium sells an eclectic collection of toys, books, and other fine merchandise from around the world. Because the UN is on international, not U.S., property you do not have to pay New York's 8.25 percent sales tax. Postcards sold at the store can be mailed at the UN's post office, another international entity with its own stamps (prices for the stamps are the same rate as American postage).

Along Madison Avenue, shoes can cost a thousand dollars. On Fifth Avenue, you can buy jewelry that costs hundreds of thousands of dollars. But window shopping is free—and this is the shopping district in which merchants have perfected the art of displaying their goods. Virtually every major designer has a boutique here and the world's most famous jewelers have showrooms. Come and look, even if you can't buy. You won't be disappointed. In fact, even here it's possible to find bargains. **Tiffany's** (57th Street and Fifth Avenue), the world-renowned jeweler, for example, has a remainder table at the northwest corner on the third floor. It's a good place to pick up an espresso cup and saucer for $15 and, at the same time, experience the luxury of Tiffany's service. These are people who know how to wait on you (and the elegant baby-blue gift wrap is free).

More reasonably priced are the boutiques of the Upper West Side. Although many of these specialty shops closed at the end of the booming 1980s, there are still plenty of smart clothing and shoe stores, particularly on Columbus Avenue and Broadway from the 60s to the 80s.

On humble Orchard Street in the Lower East Side, you can stroll from one end of this venerable bargain zone to the other, filling bags with clothing and accessories. The stores are closed on Saturdays, the Jewish Sabbath, but things come alive on Sundays when streets are blocked off and the area becomes a giant shopping mall.

West of Union Square on 14th Street, bargain hunters looking for classic kitsch, such as velvet paintings of Elvis and watches featuring pictures of Jesus, peruse the wares of sidewalk vendors in a string of stores with names like **Tango, Dee & Dee**, and **Robbins**. It's a hustle-bustle shopping affair, but it can be a bonanza whether you're looking for quality clothes or quality junk. It's also a good spot to buy some inexpensive and surprisingly hip accessories. Geoffrey Beene was once asked to create a "designer" outfit using only $100 and a trip down 14th Street. It worked.

For something more eccentric, try the shops of the East Village. You may see a lampshade in a shop window being touted as a hat with only a trace of irony. Rose's Vintage Men's Store at 350 East 9th Street has an outstanding collection of antique yet hip fashions. The T-shirt shops on St. Marks Place between Second and Third avenues are probably the best in New York.

For shoppers craving the ultimate department store experience, **Macy's** at 34th Street and Broadway is the grande dame. The sign outside claims it's the world's largest store, and after wandering through nine floors (and a basement!) of clothes, electronics, housewares, and gourmet foods, you will not likely argue the point. Macy's is more than a shopping emporium. It is a New York icon that sponsors one of the world's most famous holiday events—the Macy's Thanksgiving Day Parade—and has been used as an integral part of such movies as *Miracle on 34th Street* and *Mame*.

Bloomingdales, at 59th Street and Lexington Avenue, is a bit more snobby, but has won over many New Yorkers. If Macy's has any competition, this is it. Seemingly endless floors of perfumes, furs, furnishings, and everything else a grand department store should have. It, like Macy's, is open daily until 6:00 P.M. and on Monday and Thursdays until 9:00 P.M.

Gourmands from some of the best New York kitchens enjoy shopping at the Farmer's Markets that sprout up around the city on various days of the week. Here, farmers from New Jersey, upstate New York, Pennsylvania, and Connecticut bring their fruits, vegetables, cheeses, ciders, and fresh cut flowers to city folk who yearn for delectables, such as a tomato that doesn't taste like cardboard. The market at Union Square (Broadway and 17th Street) operates year-round and is open Wednesdays, Fridays, and Saturdays. Another at 10th Street and Second Avenue is open May through November on Tuesdays. These are just two of the many locations around the city where you can taste the country.

For a more urban food-shopping experience, **Balducci's** at 424 Sixth Avenue provides groceries for the rich and sophisticated. A loaf of bread can cost $9.50 here, but as their fans attest, "It's really great bread." Produce is polished to a luster and the bakery provides delectables made all the more inviting by the delicious aroma that fills the store.

Uptown, **Zabar's** is a shopping legend. Located at 80th Street and Broadway, it began as a simple grocery store and grew into a food and housewares bazaar. Wade through the shoppers on a Saturday morning and pick out selections of cookies, breads, caviar, pate, salmon, cheese, coffees, and kitchen items such as wicker baskets, cutlery, food processors, and juicers from all over the world. Fighting for a table at the espresso bar can be more fun than sitting down. The bakery next to Zabar's is a good place to stock up for Sunday brunch. Saturday night shoppers can be found lining up here, early editions of the Sunday *New York Times* under their arms, waiting for freshly baked bagels.

If you're fortunate enough to be in the city during the holiday season, strolling Fifth Avenue from 34th Street to Central Park South can be an exhilarating experience. The legendary windows of **Lord & Taylor**, **Saks**, **Tiffany's**, and **F.A.O Schwarz** toy store—dressed to delight—draw crowds of excited children of all ages.

POPULAR . . . FOR GOOD REASON

Sometimes tourists avoid a New York landmark because it is so popular—so *cliché*—that it's left off the travel itinerary on general principle. That sometimes make sense when visiting New York, but not always. Here are some well-known yet thoroughly worthwhile New York attractions. Like the Grand Canyon or Niagara Falls, once you've been there, you'll know why people talk about them.

Perhaps a good place to start is at the base of Manhattan with the **Staten Island Ferry**. For 50 cents round-trip, you can ride these enormous ferries that pull out from the Battery (at the southern end of Whitehall Street) and travel to Staten Island. The idea isn't to go to Staten Island, it's just to take the ride. The trip provides a stunning view of lower Manhattan as the ferry plies the **New York Harbor** past **Governors Island**, **Ellis Island**, and the **Statue of Liberty**. Round-trip takes about one hour, and beverages and snacks are served on board. The ferry operates 24 hours a day. Take the number 1 subway train to its final stop, South Ferry, to get there.

From sea level to a quarter-mile high is a big jump, but worth it to have cocktails at the bar of **Windows on the World** on the 110th floor of the **World Trade Center**. Next to the bar is a restaurant that critics praise as being an exception to the rule of thumb that restaurants at the top of skyscrapers can't be good. The restaurant is very expensive, but if you want to make it the centerpiece of a day on the town, you will be pleased. For a much more reduced cost, make the trek to the bar at sunset to catch the drama of flickering city lights. From here you can actually watch the moon rise *below* you. Service is proper, but not stiff, and before 7:30 P.M. there is no minimum charge. Prices are reasonable, too. Men must wear sports coats or suit jackets, but ties are not required. No jeans allowed. By the way, people really *do* look like ants from up here.

Another quarter-mile-high icon is the observation deck of the **Empire State Building** (Fifth Avenue and 34th Street). Although the view is inevitably spectacular, a trip up at 11:00 P.M. or 6:30 A.M. is particularly special, since it can seem as if you have the whole place to yourself. Purchase some classic tourist kitsch such as key chains and felt pennants adorned with the skyscraper's image at the tiny gift bar, have a hot dog, or remember the day with a picture taken in the photo booth for two dollars.

At **Rockefeller Center**, skating beneath the statue of Prometheus has been a favorite New York pastime since the Center opened in 1931. With the tall Christmas tree standing above the ice and surrounded by joyous holiday throngs leaning over the upper-level railing, it feels as if you're in the middle of a Currier and Ives painting come to life.

Up in the Bronx, a certain zoo has been entertaining millions since it opened in the late nineteenth century. Laid out on 252 acres, **The Bronx Zoo** was one of the first major zoos of the world that stressed a natural setting for animals in captivity. The Safari Train, Aquatic Bird House, and World of Darkness (where day and night are artificially switched so that nocturnal animals are active during visitor hours) are only a few of the myriad attractions.

Farther south in the Bronx, the New York Yankees do their thing from spring to fall at **Yankee Stadium**. Whether the team is winning or losing, an afternoon in the park with hot dogs, peanuts, and—yes—Crackerjacks can be a great way to observe a distinct New York personality: the Yankees fan.

At the other end of the city, ride the F, B, or D trains to a world of early-twentieth-century New York, **Coney Island**. Although much of the polish is gone, Coney Island still has its beach, its pier, and its boardwalk. The hot-dog stalls (this is the home of **Nathan's Famous**) stand next to the shells of carnival attractions from the 1920s and '30s along a boardwalk that extends for miles along the Atlantic Ocean. For the intrepid, there is the Cyclone, which some consider the world's scariest roller coaster. (A word to the wise: Keep your hands inside the car).

Back in Manhattan, **Central Park**—the world's most famous, and sometimes infamous, park—still provides

Skaters at Rockefeller Center

New Yorkers with the closest thing to country for many miles around. More than twice the size of the principality of Monaco, it has rocks to climb, birds to watch, a lake for rowboating, horses to ride, paths for jogging, and lots of space in which to do nothing. In New York, that can be an attraction in itself.

SAFETY

Those who say that crime in New York is awful are right. Statistically speaking, though, this is far from the most dangerous city in the country. Of the nation's largest ten cities, for example, New York consistently ranks number ten for murders per capita.

That said, there are still plenty of ways to find trouble in New York, particularly if you're looking for it; but with a little common sense, you can avoid most problems. It may sound simplistic, but be careful. Don't flash jewelry or money. Carry your wallet in the front pocket or, better, don't carry a wallet at all. Don't carry too much cash. When you walk around the city, don't daydream to the point of distraction and don't look helpless. Don't take the subways alone late at night.

At **Grand Central Terminal**, **Penn Station**, and the **Port Authority**, be on the lookout for hustlers who ask if you want a cab. The scam involves putting you in a cab while taking a piece of your luggage. Politely but firmly refuse offers of help. Look for a registered yellow cab or an official dispatcher to assist you. Police officers are often at the exits to these locations, so ask for help if you need it.

Be alert. Streets that look deserted and dangerous may well be. If someone you're approaching looks suspicious, cross the street. If you feel the sidewalk is too dark or dangerous, walk in the street itself along the path of traffic. But be polite: Nobody in New York likes to be insulted, especially criminals—and chances are the person you're passing is not a criminal and is just as concerned with safety as you are. New York has a lot of weirdos, but they're usually just weirdos. In general, if you mind your own business you can stay out of most trouble.

If you are a victim of a crime, contact the police immediately. New York may seem like a huge, faceless city, but the police are sensitive and will treat you seriously and with respect. In an emergency, dial 911.

HEALTH AND EMERGENCIES

Just in case, here are some numbers that can get you through an emergency:

24-hour pharmacy—Kaufman-Beverly Pharmacy at 557 Lexington Avenue (at 50th Street). Telephone (212) 755-2266.

24-hour dentist—telephone (212) 679-3996 before 8:00 P.M. Sponsored by the First District Dental Society of New York, the Dental Emergency Service plays a recording listing three or four doctors who are immediately available for emergency dental care. The recording will give you the doctor's name, address, and phone number. (For emergencies after 8:00 P.M., the dental society recommends requesting a doctor using the service outlined below, or going to an emergency room.)

If you need a doctor, dial 0 and tell the operator, "This is an emergency, I want a doctor." You'll be connected to an emergency doctor service.

If you should need it, here is a list of five respected New York hospitals:

Mount Sinai Medical Center, Fifth Avenue and 100th Street. Telephone (212) 241-6500.
St. Vincent's Hospital and Medical Center, Seventh Avenue and 11th Street. Telephone (212) 790-7070.
St. Luke's–Roosevelt Hospital Center, 428 West 59th Street. Telephone (212) 523-4000.

New York University Medical Center, 550 First Avenue.
  Telephone (212) 263-7300.
Beth Israel Medical Center, First Avenue and 16th Street.
  Telephone (212) 420-2000.

One thing you don't have to worry about in the city is drinking the water. Consistently, New York's water ranks among the world's best for an urban center. Last century, the city's leaders—displaying incredible foresight—bought up vast tracts of land in upstate New York to create freshwater reservoirs to supply New York City. So you may stroll the streets with a bottled water imported from another continent, but you certainly don't have to.

One final note: There is a dearth of public restrooms in New York, and the ones that do exist are not always clean. Restaurants and bars make good spots to stop in emergencies, and by simply asking the maitre d' or bartender for permission, you may be accommodated. McDonald's, which has many locations throughout the city, also has restrooms available for public use.

Walk · 1

▚▚▚▚▚▚▚▚▚▚▚▚▚▚▚▚▚▚▚▚▚▚▚▚▚▚▚▚▚▚

Old New York

FROM BATTERY PARK
TO CITY HALL

FELIX CUERVO

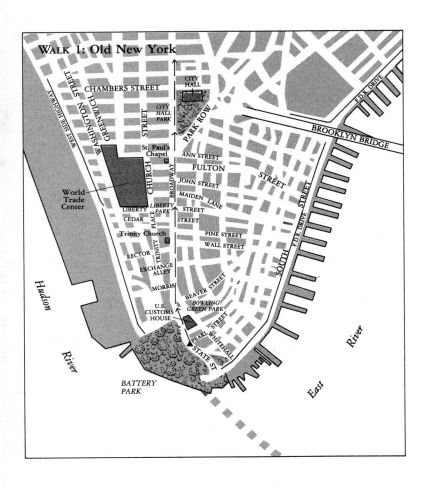

Walk 1: Old New York

Starting Point: 7 State Street, one block north of the entrance to the Staten Island Ferry, at the Watson House
Walk Length: About 2 hours
Subway Stop: South Ferry (1 train) Whitehall Street (R train)

Compared to European capitals, New York is relatively new. While Paris, London, and Rome were dating themselves by the millennium, New York was just beginning. But compared to the rest of the United States, New York is ancient history.

When Giovanni da Verrazano sailed into what is now New York Harbor in 1524, the "city" was a green island heavily populated by Canarsie Indians. The explorer reported to his financial backer, France's King Francis I, that the natives were extremely friendly, but a sudden storm prevented his landing. Verrazano was eaten by cannibals in South America before he could return, but he became the first of a long line of visitors smitten with this patch of real estate.

Hundreds of years of development have followed Verrazano's visit to New York, although most of what surrounds us today are creations of the very recent past.

Some survivors from the early centuries, however, remain.

Your walk, from the tip of Manhattan to the old City Common, threads in and out of a long-ago New York. These are gloriously historic steps you will be taking. Native Americans launched their birchbark canoes from here. Peter Minuit bought Manhattan Island here (thus instituting a commercial rhythm that has become the neighborhood's heartbeat). George Washington slept here—really. He also fought the British here, became president here, went to church here, and walked the very streets you will be walking. This is where Alexander Hamilton was buried after he was killed by Aaron Burr. Here is the canyon that has welcomed returning armies, astronauts, and a string of other heroes with showers of confetti in New York's legendary ticker-tape parades. And today, lower Broadway and Wall Street—reverberating with commerce and tourism—emit such an energy that visitors cannot help but feel the excitement of so much power and history.

As you walk, ghosts of the past may stroll with you, too, if the numerous sightings regularly reported by New Yorkers are to be believed. Charwomen, stockbrokers, and federal guards have all seen them, or so they say. As you prowl those haunts you'll also see some tangible fragments of the seventeenth, eighteenth, nineteenth, and early twentieth centuries.

This relatively brief tour delves into New York's long roots. No other part of the city packs so many years into so few steps. But this is also modern New York. Battery Park, the embarkation point for Ellis Island and the Statue of Liberty, is a cornerstone of the city's vital tourist industry. Wall Street and the Financial District are perhaps the most critical foundations of the world's economic infrastructure. Farther north, nearly two hundred years after its opening, City Hall is still the center of New York City's government, a political entity with a $30-billion-plus annual budget.

To really get the *rush* of what this powerful corridor is all about, a midday, weekday stroll is recommended. The swirling, frenetic pace during business hours delivers a pure glimpse of why this piece of real estate still commands the world's attention.

We begin our walk at the quaint two-story town house and church at 7 State Street, the **Watson House**. The house is at the foot of the stunningly curved, blue-mirrored skyscraper that looms over Battery Park at 17 State Street, near the intersection of State and Water streets. The entrance to the **Staten Island Ferry** is one block to the south. **Battery Park**—the only significant stand of trees in all of lower Manhattan—is on your left.

The Watson House, unique for its curved facade, features a redbrick construction offset by a second-story colonnade. This was the home of Elizabeth Ann Seton, who, in 1975, became the first American-born saint. Seton lived here from 1801 to 1803, during which time she gave birth to her daughter, Rebecca. A plaque on the building indicates that she was a "wife, mother, educator and foundress of the Sisters of Charity." The building today serves as the Roman Catholic Church of Our Lady of the Rosary.

This delicate town house, designed by master Federal architect John McComb, was built about 1800. The second-story columns are thought to have been hewn from ships' masts. This building is all that remains of what once was the city's most elegant string of homes. Around the corner (where the blue-mirrored skyscraper at 17 State Street stands) was where Herman Melville lived. To your right, at what was once 1 State Street, Peter Stuyvesant, the first governor of Dutch New Amsterdam, resided. One hundred years later, inventor-artist Robert Fulton lived at the same address.

About two centuries ago, a resident of 6 State Street decided that he would plant hundreds of trees in front of his home, along what was then the harbor's edge, to add to the real estate value and pleasure of the neighborhood. It worked only too well. Today, long after most of the homes have disappeared, consumed by the towers of commerce, the park remains. Being careful of the traffic, cross now at Water Street to **Battery Park**. (There's a dearth of street signs in the neighborhood, but at the intersection in front of the Watson House follow the pedestrian lanes that lead directly to the park.)

Virtually all of the park is on landfill. Peter Stuyvesant's home, for example, was on a tiny peninsula that stuck out into the harbor. Lower Manhattan's Water Street was so named because it was at the water's edge. The street one block to the north was lined with so many mother of pearl shells that it was called Pearl Street. Hundreds of years of landfill, however, have placed these streets far from today's waterfront.

Entering the park, you come upon a tiny, corroded cannon sitting in a small, fenced-off plot. A Heritage Trail marker is nearby. The cannon was exhumed in 1892 at 55 Broadway (which we'll see later) and was part of a British fortification wall, known as "Oyster Pasty," that was built in 1695 and lasted until the end of the Revolutionary War, when it was demolished to make way for an expanding New York.

Turning now toward the harbor and walking to the waterfront, you come to the white **flagpole** that resembles the mast of a ship (it stands next to the park's public restrooms and an indoor/outdoor concession stand). This is the latest in a long series of flagpoles that have stood at the city's edge since the time New York was still a colony. When the British fled New York on Evacuation Day—November 25, 1783—the embittered troops decided to grease that era's flagpole, with their own Union Jack still flying, to prevent anyone from raising the American flag.

However, sailor boy Johnny Van Arsdale outfoxed them. Picking up a hammer and an armful of wooden cleats and nailing the cleats as he climbed, the young man reached the top and installed the American flag, which has flown there ever since. Ghost watchers say that late at night a light sometimes appears at the top of the flagpole, the apparition of Van Arsdale.

Now proceed to the waterfront, to the mighty New York Harbor. The stretch of asphalt that curves along the park's edge is called **Admiral Dewey Promenade**, named after an American hero of the Battle of Manila Bay who commanded the "Asiatic squadron" during the brief flex of American military muscle known as the Spanish-American War. There's a plaque and monument to Dewey at Gangway 2 (gangway signs are at even intervals at the water's edge all along the park).

Walking along the waterfront, you are strolling near the area where Aaron Burr spent many of the last years of his life, bemoaning the loss of his daughter. Burr, the U.S. vice president who shot Alexander Hamilton in 1804 at their infamous duel in Weehawken, New Jersey, spent the last years of his life here pining for his daughter, Theodosia. Burr developed an extremely close relationship with his daughter after the death of one wife and divorce from another, and relied on Theodosia for political advice and counsel. In 1813, thirty-year-old Theodosia set sail from the Battery for an ocean voyage.

Burr wore a beard on the day his daughter was due to return, the first time he had ever publicly appeared that way. It was a bad omen. Theodosia's ship had disappeared, believed captured by pirates who killed all on board. Some years after Theodosia's disappearance, a piece of her jewelry was found in a slave cabin in Virginia, but that was as close as Burr would ever come to knowing what had happened to his beloved daughter. Ghost watchers say Burr still returns here, wearing his tricornered hat and calling her name.

Looking out over the harbor, you see a host of historic sites. The round, redbrick fort visible on the far left is **East Battery**, once part of the early American defenses and now part of the U.S. Coast Guard facilities on **Governors Island**. Looking to the right, you see the **Verrazano Narrows Bridge**, which joins Brooklyn to Staten Island, **Staten Island**, the **Statue of Liberty**, **Ellis Island**, and, across the harbor in New Jersey, the old station for the New Jersey Central Railroad at Communipaw Junction.

Looking out to the Statue of Liberty and Ellis Island, you will see two of New York's most revered—and haunted—locations. Ellis Island, to the right of the Statue of Liberty, is perhaps the largest haunted house in America. The newly opened and refurbished Great Hall, easily distinguished by its enormous Victorian turrets, from 1892 received millions of immigrants during its use as a holding and processing facility for the world's yearning masses. It's estimated that about half the U.S. population is descended from immigrants who passed through Ellis Island. Now a major tourist attraction, federal rangers stationed there report that they hear sounds of moving furniture, children weeping, and an aching voice that pleads, "Help me!"

These are possibly the sounds and cries of some of the 3,000 suicides who shot, poisoned, or hanged themselves as they waited for permission to enter America, permission that was sometimes refused. Often, those who were rejected had to undergo the pain of seeing their entire families accepted for admission while they were kept out due to things such as even minor diseases, including glaucoma. For these unfortunates, taking their own lives became the final refuge. It's unlikely that any of these island spirits will ever enter New York, though, since—as everyone knows—ghosts cannot cross running water.

Behind Ellis Island is the Statue of Liberty and Liberty Island. Originally called Bedloe's Island, the island and statue are supposedly haunted by the ghosts of pirates hanged on gallows when the island was a favorite execution site in the seventeenth century. One particularly

New York Harbor from Battery Park

vindictive spirit is said to be Hicks, a pirate hanged here. Hicks publicly placed a curse on the island before the noose ended his life.

Walking north along the waterfront you can see the old firehouse at **Pier A** on the edge of Battery Park, built in 1895, with its clocktower at the pierhead. The tower was added after World War I to memorialize the war dead. Today the building serves as the repair shop for the marine division of New York's fire department.

Just before the firehouse, and to your right, lies the round, single-story brick fort known as **Castle Clinton**. This is the counterpart to Governors Island's East Battery, which you saw earlier. The two forts were built around 1811 to fire cannons across the harbor and protect New York City in case of a British invasion during the tense times that led up to the War of 1812. Neither fort ever fired a shot in anger, though. Castle Clinton was erected through the efforts of students from Columbia College (now Columbia University) and local laborers who came to dig foundations or lay stones after a day of classes or work. The word "moonlighters," to describe those who work a second job, was coined to describe Castle Clinton's workers.

Castle Clinton

When Castle Clinton was built, it stood on pilings far into the harbor and was connected to the land by a catwalk. Eventual landfills, however, have made it a high and dry fort. Note the thickness of the walls and the openings for cannons that point from all waterfront sides of the building. At the end of the War of 1812, the battery was renamed for former New York mayor and New York governor DeWitt Clinton. It served as military district headquarters, but by 1821 had outlived its purpose and the building was ceded to the city.

The fort's next incarnation was as a place of public entertainment, calling itself "Castle Garden." The shell of mortar and stone we see today is only a frail indication of the grand hall that once occupied these ruins. On the top floors was an awning-covered walkway, and inside the hulking building fireworks, band concerts, balloon ascensions, and displays of the latest scientific achievements were featured. It was here that Lafayette began his triumphant return to America in 1824. He was the first of many dignitaries who would be honored at the fort, including Presidents Jackson, Tyler, and Polk.

By the 1840s, the building was roofed over and became a grand entertainment house. *The Barber of Seville* opened in 1845 with a full audience who could enjoy the opera as well as the "most inspiring mint juleps," according to one newspaper of the day. Perhaps the most auspicious event occurred on September 11, 1850, when showman P. T. Barnum presented Jenny Lind, "the Swedish Nightingale." At $3 a ticket, more than 6,000 eager New Yorkers crowded the theater beneath a banner that read "Welcome Sweet Warbler."

By the mid-1800s, though, Castle Garden's days as an entertainment palace were ending. It was at about this time that the fort was joined to the mainland by landfill. In 1855, New York State began using the building to advise newly arrived immigrants. The building helped newcomers with information about boarding houses, travel routes, and fares, and helped to protect them from unsavory types who preyed on unsuspecting visitors and immigrants. (Some things never change.)

When Ellis Island opened, the fort was ready for a new role. In 1896, the building became the New York City Aquarium, a repository for the exotic, living marine specimens from around the world that ship captains based in the city collected for display. Over 30,000 visitors came on the first day. The aquarium soon became part of the city's personality. By the 1930s, a favorite April Fools' Day ploy was to give someone a message that "Mr. Fish" had called and to leave the number "WHitehall 4-1560," the aquarium's number.

In 1941, the aquarium moved to Coney Island (where

it is today) and the fort was ready for its next life, although it was almost to be its death. When the aquarium moved, powerful voices in the city argued that the building should be razed to make way for a new traffic tunnel under the park. World War II, however, cooled real estate development enough to give preservationists enough time to save the structure. In 1946, Castle Clinton was declared a national monument and in 1975 it became the New York headquarters for the National Park Service, which administers the Statue of Liberty, Ellis Island, and several other sites in the city.

Entering Castle Clinton, you see a unique view of lower-Manhattan skyscrapers, framed by the fort's roof. Note the pyramid top of the Standard Oil Building in the middle. Inside to the rear is a small but extraordinary set of dioramas that provide easy-to-understand models of how this part of Manhattan has developed over the centuries. The fort has several pamphlets on Park Service sites and you may purchase tickets here for the ferries to Ellis Island and the Statue of Liberty. The ferries leave regularly during daylight hours. Tickets are $6 for adults, $5 for seniors, $3 for those under eighteen, and free for children under three. One ticket allows you to visit one or both of the islands. Traveling early in the day will give you sufficient time to see both Ellis and Liberty islands, as well as an opportunity to climb to the crown of the Statue of Liberty.

Exiting at the rear of Castle Clinton, toward the skyscrapers, walk now up the promenade that stretches in a straight line to the corner of Battery Park. You will pass by Luis Sanguino's 1981 statue **The Immigrants** in the middle of our path. As you walk out of the park you may notice some homeless people. They've had some pretty good company. When Rudolph Valentino came to America to seek his fame and fortune, he spent many of his pre-Hollywood days living in the park and sleeping on these benches.

At the park's edge you are standing at the intersection

of Battery Place/Merchant Marine Veterans Place and State Street. Across the street is the Beaux Arts masterpiece the **U.S. Customs House**, with its statue of a reclining lion at the front of the building. Carefully crossing the street (this is a heavy-traffic intersection) you arrive at the plaza in front of the Customs House, with Bowling Green Park behind us.

It was here, or somewhere nearby, that the Dutch settler Peter Minuit swapped beads and trinkets worth $24 with the local Indians in exchange for Manhattan Island. The often-told story is rich in legend. One version has it that the Indians who sold the land were actually residents of the uplands, who had sold the same property to European settlers several times. Another tale relates how the Dutch showed the natives a piece of cowhide and indicated that they only wanted an equal-sized piece of property for the beads. After making the sale, the Dutch then took a pair of scissors to the cowhide and cut a ribbon which they used as a lengthy tape measure to mark off a large parcel of land next to the harbor.

Several ghosts are said to haunt this site, including some Indians. One notable spirit reported seen on the stairs in front of the Customs House is that of Edward Hyde, also known as Lord Cornbury. The profligate Cornbury, who served as New York's British governor from 1702 to 1708, was a thieving rascal who put himself and the colony in debt. The governor is probably best known as a cross-dresser who fancied himself as bearing a great resemblance to his cousin, Queen Anne. Dressing in the elegant women's fashions of his day, Lord Cornbury would parade along the walls of the old fort that used to stand here. His embarrassed wife, Lady Cornbury, would order soldiers to haul her husband back home. A painting of what is allegedly Lord Cornbury in full drag may be seen at the New-York Historical Society on Central Park West.

The Customs House is a stunning example of architecture meant to serve the people. It was built with a grand purpose and it shows. Currently serving as a U.S. Bankruptcy Court, the upstairs is slated to open as the Museum of the American Indian by early 1993. On the outside are four statues that dominate the facade. The four, carved by Daniel Chester French—creator of the Abraham Lincoln statue in the Washington, D.C., memorial—represent the four major continents. From left they are *Asia* (note the Buddha in the lap), *America*, *Europe*, and a sleeping *Africa*.

Several forts stood on the site of the Customs House, beginning with the first Dutch fort in 1626. Here, inside the fort's walls, the first church services in the city were held. The site then became an English fort, then a Dutch fort, then an English fort, and, finally, an American fort.

Turning your back to the Customs House and looking north, you see one of the great boulevards of the world: **Broadway**. To your left and right we see the two lanes of this historic highway that merge on the north side of Bowling Green to form Broadway. On your left, at 1 Broadway, is the site of what was George Washington's, then General Howe's, headquarters during the Revolutionary War. A large plaque on the building explains the history of the corner. The building that stands here today is the **International Mercantile Marine Building**. Note the "First Class" entrance on the building's south side and the city seals of the world's great ports rendered in mosaic on the facade. Benedict Arnold, the Revolutionary War traitor, lived next door at **no. 3**.

Walk north now into **Bowling Green**, New York's—and perhaps the nation's—oldest park. Its first recreational use dates from 1633, when it was established for the "beauty and ornament" and "recreation and delight" of the city. The park was a cattle market from 1638 to 1647. Later, it became popular as a place for lawn bowling and was rented for the charge of one peppercorn a year. A statue of King George III was installed in the mid-1700s and a fence built in 1771 to protect the statue. The fence, still standing today, had small crowns on its posts.

When George Washington personally read the Declaration of Independence from the City Common on July 9, 1776, revolutionary fever swept the city, with New Yorkers destroying the crowns (note the ragged tips of the fence posts) and toppling the statue, which stood where the fountain is today. Most of the statue was melted down for bullets, and legend has it that forty thousand were made, from which four hundred Redcoats were killed.

Proceeding north through the park, be sure to take a look at the small, ground-level plaque to our left just before the north gate: It commemorates one of the nation's earliest tests of freedom of religion. In 1707, Francis Makemie, an Irish-born Presbyterian, was holding private services in the home of William Jackson, which stood nearby. Lord Cornbury issued a prohibition on the services, which he described as "pernicious" and contrary to the officially-sanctioned teachings of the Church of England. Makemie was indicted and a spirited trial ensued with the preacher making his own defense. The jury acquitted him in a decision that set the tone for American religious freedom.

Leaving the park, you pass an oversized statue of a bull. Originally intended as an icon for Wall Street, the financial community rejected it and it somehow found a home here. Even though its size and subject are pointedly garish, tourists seem to enjoy crawling over the bull and having their pictures taken with it.

On your left as you stand in front of the bull, you see the U.S. Post Office at **27 Broadway**. This is the former Cunard Building, completed in 1921 for the great ocean travel company. From the outside you can notice the faces that represent various climates and weather. Inside is a marvel of early twentieth-century interiors. Designed in part by Carrère and Hastings, who were responsible for the New York Public Library at 42nd Street, the interior was meant to convey the lavishness of a first-class berth on a Cunard ship. Even though the post office has awkwardly filled this space, many of the exquisite touches of the original building remain, including the intricately detailed Italian travertine marble floors. The centerpiece is a grand, vaulted rotunda with ceiling murals that depict the great sailing ships of Columbus, Drake, Erikson, and Cabot.

Returning now to Broadway, you will see across from the post office, at 26 Broadway, the **Standard Oil Building**. Completed in 1926, again with a design team that included Carrère and Hastings, the building dramatically curves to take advantage of its prestigious location and views of Bowling Green and New York Harbor. Inside at the no. 26 entrance, the lobby carries the names of the board of directors of Standard Oil when the building was erected and the Rockefellers were fully in charge (note how many of the names are Rockefeller). What we can't see from street level is the 27-story pyramid-topped skyscraper that sits atop 26 Broadway. This was the building we were looking at when we stood inside Castle Clinton. After New York's precedent-setting zoning law of 1916, buildings were required to use setbacks. In compliance with that, Carrère and Hastings erected a building that looks restrained at street level, while it soars out of the view of the masses.

Next door at **32 Broadway** is a small deli with inside seating, a nice place to take a break.

Heading farther up Broadway, you pass by **no. 39** on your left, which was the site of the second presidential mansion. George Washington lived here in a house designed by John McComb in 1790 (after living at a home near where the Brooklyn Bridge stands today) before Philadelphia and then the District of Columbia became the nation's capital. In 1613, when British skipper Samuel Argall sailed up the Hudson, he reported seeing four small houses on what are now 39 and 45 Broadway, probably the homes of Dutch fur traders.

Today, **45 Broadway** is a skyscraper, but its lobby offers a beautiful oasis from the outside. Enter the building and note the six-story waterfall that cascades gently into an immense tropical pool.

On the north side of 45 Broadway is **Exchange Alley**. This small, stepped street is where "Oyster Pasty," the British defense wall that led to a fortification at the Hudson River, once stood (remember the cannon from Battery Park?).

Across the street, on the northeast corner, is the venerated **Irving Trust Company Building**, completed in 1931. Clad in white limestone, the building soars over 650 feet through a series of setbacks that create a dramatic presence on the street and the skyline.

Crossing Broadway at Exchange Alley (the street signs are only on Broadway's west side), walk two blocks down Exchange Place toward **Broad Street**. It was here—in an area now so dominated by skyscrapers that the sun rarely touches the pavement—that a Dutch family, the Van Dycks, had their farm. The farm consisted mainly of a peach orchard, which the Indians living in the area considered to be fruits of the land, free for the picking. Van Dyck, attorney general of the New Netherlands, didn't appreciate this type of open access. In 1655, he caught a young Indian woman attempting to steal a peach, so he shot and killed her. What followed became known as the Peach War. A severe Indian uprising led to the deaths of many settlers, wiped out with bows and arrows, and the Dutch fort, now site of the Customs House, was regularly attacked in revenge, with several soldiers being shot. The attacks eventually subsided, but ghost watchers say this street is still haunted by the young Indian girl.

At Exchange Place and Broad Street, turn left. Broad Street was once split by a canal that led to the East River. Because the canal was eventually filled in (yellow fever epidemics led the city slowly to choke off mosquito breeding grounds during the 1700s and 1800s), the street that remains today is one of the widest in the neighborhood, hence its name.

As you walk north on Broad Street, you are entering one of the most compactly historic areas in the United States. On your left is the **New York Stock Exchange**. On your right is the two-story J. P. Morgan Bank. And across the street is Federal Hall, the site where George Washington took the oath of office.

The Stock Exchange was begun when the U.S. government offered $80 million in bonds to cover the country's consolidated debt from the Revolutionary War. Small markets to deal with the trading sprung up in the coffee houses of Wall Street. Eventually, the traders met under a buttonwood (sycamore) tree on Wall Street and developed a brief set of rules and guidelines for trade. The now-famous Buttonwood Agreement was the framework that led to what is today probably the most important stock exchange in the world. Tours of the exchange are offered during business hours on weekdays on a limited basis. Enter at **20 Broad Street**. If you take the tour, notice as you cross the bridge that takes you over the exchange floor that you are separated from the action by a wall of glass. This was installed in the late 1960s after hippies entered the building and caused total chaos by tossing dollar bills onto the exchange floor.

Next door at **18 Broad Street** is a plaque commemorating Dr. Alexander Corolus Cursius Curtius, the appropriately-named Latin schoolmaster hired by Peter Stuyvesant who began the nation's first Latin school at this location in 1659.

Across from the Stock Exchange, on the southeast corner of Broad and Wall streets, is the very discreet headquarters of the J. P. Morgan Bank, now known as **Morgan Guaranty Trust**. While other financial institutions were interested in showing their power on Wall Street with immense skyscrapers, J. P. Morgan took the quiet-money route, erecting a tasteful two-story bank. Don't even look for the Morgan name, it's not displayed. In the bank's mind, either you know where the bank is or you don't. That's not to say the bank doesn't welcome new customers; it's just that a minimum deposit of $10 million is required to open an account.

To get a tangible idea of just what kind of power this bank represents, walk to the north (Wall Street) side of the building. Those deep chunks missing from the facade are not the effects of weather. On September 16, 1920, a horse-drawn wagon stuffed with explosives was detonated outside the building. No one was ever caught, but it's suspected that this was the work of anarchist radicals intent on toppling the capitalism they saw as destroying American workers. The blast killed thirty-three people and injured four hundred more. So mighty was the impact that a horse's ass was embedded into the facade of the Stock Exchange. To this day, the bank is surrounded by concrete barriers.

From capitalist and anarchist tyranny, now cross the street to one of the cradles of true democracy: **Federal Hall**, 26 Wall Street. Guarded by the oversized statue of George Washington, which stands on the spot where the first president took his oath of office, the building is reminiscent of the Acropolis. Completed in 1842, this building stands where earlier city and federal buildings stood since 1701. This is also where the first Congress met. It was here that the national government made provisions to settle what would eventually become Indiana, Ohio, Illinois, Michigan, and Wisconsin.

It was also on this site that John Peter Zenger, a young apprentice of William Bradford, was tried for sedition. Zenger's newspaper, the *New York Weekly Journal*, reported the undemocratic aspects of a political campaign in 1733 for what was then the Provincial Assembly of New York. Royal Governor Cosby objected to the reports (he favored the undemocratic slate) and had Zenger jailed. But, in a now famous decision, the jury ruled in 1735 in favor of Zenger and laid the foundation for America's freedom of the press.

Federal Hall is a national monument and features regular lectures and concerts during weekdays. Inside are also some interesting memorabilia of Washington's era, such as his dagger. Careful as you go inside, these are terrifically steep stairs.

Returning to Wall Street, proceed up the left side of

the street toward Broadway. On your left, about halfway along the Stock Exchange building, is a plaque marking the location where *The Wall Street Journal* was begun in 1889 at **15 Wall Street**. What started as a trade paper for a small business community is now the largest-circulation newspaper in America, with 1.9 million subscribers.

Continuing up Wall Street, you are walking toward the sleek, slender steeple of **Trinity Church**, one of the earliest churches founded in America. Chartered in 1697, the church received a land grant from Queen Anne in 1705 that included a parcel extending from Fulton Street to Christopher Street and from Broadway to the Hudson River, making it one of the greatest New York landowners of all time. Only about 5 percent of the property remains in church hands, but it creates enough income to assure it the funds to do its work.

When the church was built, it was just outside the famous Dutch wall that was laid between the Hudson and East rivers and was intended to keep out Indians and land-based British attackers. This is how Wall Street got its name. By the time the church was started, much of the wall had fallen into disrepair and had been dismantled by settlers looking for firewood and building materials.

The present church building, with its 280-foot steeple, is the third to be built on this site. It was erected in 1840 and replaces an earlier structure that had been demolished because of faulty construction. That church had been built to replace the original structure, which burned in the great fire of 1776. The fire, which apparently began by accident, was used as a propaganda tool by church leaders who insisted (wrongly) that it was the work of revolutionaries disloyal to the crown. As might be expected of a church with such an extensive endowment, the crown had its defenders in Trinity Church.

Today, Wall Street money-makers come here to seek

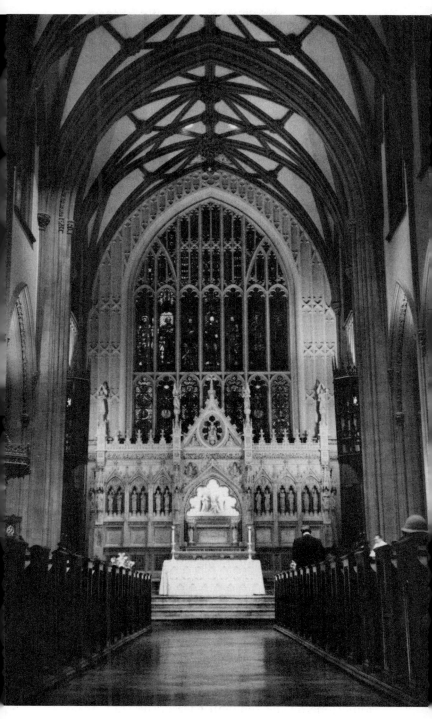

Trinity Church

solace from their earthly pursuits. During hot summer days, the church offers a cool refuge from city streets; during the winter, a warm place to rest. Everyone is welcome here and services are held daily. A brief lecture tour is given weekdays at 2:00 P.M. and meets in the front pews of the sanctuary. The church has some interesting artifacts in a small museum entered next to the altar, including the original 1697 Church of England charter and duplicates of the dueling pistols used in the Hamilton-Burr duel.

Hamilton, America's first secretary of the Treasury, was a bitter opponent of Burr. Their fatal encounter followed years of political enmity between Founding Father Hamilton and Burr, whose loyalties during the revolution were questionable. When Burr accused Hamilton of spreading malicious rumors about him, he challenged Hamilton to the duel. This wasn't the first Hamilton to meet his end in such a barbaric fashion. Alexander Hamilton's son, Philip, was also killed on the very same spot as his father in another duel four years earlier.

At the duel, Hamilton supposedly shot into the air, but Burr went for the heart and won. After Hamilton was shot, a vestryman of Trinity Church was at his side as he lay dying at 2 Jane Street in Greenwich Village. Hamilton promised the clergyman that if he survived he would become an advocate against dueling; but he never had an opportunity to make good on his promise.

After his death, New York children went around chanting this haunting rhyme:

Burr, oh Burr! What hast thou done?
You shooted the great Hamilton
You hid behind a clump of thistle
And shooted him dead with a great horse pistol!

Hamilton is buried beneath the tall, pyramid-shaped tombstone on the southern edge of the churchyard. His ghost is said to haunt the graveyard, particularly around the nearby grave of Matthew Davis, who stood as Aaron Burr's second, or witness, in the duel.

Besides Hamilton, **Trinity Churchyard** has the graves of several significant historic figures. William Bradford, who started the nation's first newspaper, is buried here. Robert Fulton, who has a large monument dedicated to him near the southern fence of the graveyard, is buried nearby.

The tombstones of the churchyard represent some of the earliest forms of European-American folk art and often portray death in a most morbid sense. Common embellishments are death's heads, skulls and crossbones, and winged cherubs, known in these parts as "soul effigies." Inscriptions on the tombstones do little to soothe the nervous visitor. Several markers carry this passage:

> Remember man as you pass by
> As you are now so once was I
> And as I am so must you be
> Prepare for death and follow me.

On the 1794 grave of James Leeson is one of the most notable tombstones in the churchyard. Leeson, who left behind only scant records of his life, did leave something for future generations to ponder. Engraved with Masonic symbols, an hourglass, and flames rising from an open vessel is a cryptogram etched along the top edge of the tombstone. The grave can be seen at the northernmost edge of the graveyard, the last grave next to the tall, steeple-shaped Revolutionary War monument, the second row back from the Broadway fence. The Leeson cryptogram reads as follows:

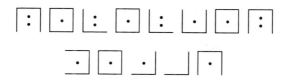

The message, inscribed in oddly shaped cubes and dots, can be deciphered by using the following method: Make a tic-tac-toe design, placing a dot in the middle of each of the nine squares that the design creates. Each of the squares, beginning with the top row of squares and going left to right, represent the first ten letters of the alphabet (*j* and *i* are represented by the same square). Thus, *E* is represented by a four-sided square (the middle of the tic-tac-toe board) with a dot in the center. Referring to the cryptogram, you can see that the message contains four *e*'s in the two-word cryptogram. For the next nine letters create another tic-tac-toe diagram and place two dots in each square. For the final seven letters of the alphabet create a third tic-tac-toe diagram, but place no dots. The solution is available to all those who seek to decode this rather gruesome message. (For everyone else, the solution will be revealed at the end of our tour.)

A few rows away, on the south side of the middle graveyard plot, is a headstone marked "Comedian." This is the final resting place of Adam Allyn, a colonial comedian attached to the American Company, one of the nation's first repertory companies of actors. Allyn died just before he was to have gone on stage for a performance of the then-classic *The Recruiting Officer*. The show went on, but Allyn did not. At least two Trinity Churchyard visitors say they have heard laughter as they passed his grave.

Although she's not been reported as a ghost, the story of Charlotte Temple—who is buried near the cemetery's entrance—certainly is a haunting one. Temple was a young girl who became the tragic subject of America's first romance novel, *The History of Charlotte Temple Founded on Truth*, by Sarah Haswell Rawson, published in 1801 in Hartford. The novel told the true tale of Charlotte, an English schoolgirl—and a granddaughter of the earl of Derby—who fell in love with a British officer, who stowed her away on his ship when he came to America to fight in the Revolutionary War. Charlotte ended up pregnant, and the military man dumped her, leaving her to fend for herself in a strange, chaotic city in the midst of war. She died a few years later in the wretchedness of a squalid New York slum. The two-volume story became one of the nation's earliest best-sellers.

Another graveyard personality is that of Catherine, also known as Lady Cornbury, wife of royal cross-dresser Lord Cornbury. Lady Cornbury is supposedly one of those poltergeists who enjoy pulling pranks. When Catherine was alive, she was something of an unwanted guest. When visiting homes, if she saw something she liked, she would later send a servant around to borrow the item and the owner would likely never see it again. Oddball thefts such as disappearances of unimportant items at the back of the church, even today, are said to be the work of Lady Cornbury.

Lieutenant Augustus C. Ludlow, the second in command to Captain James Lawrence—naval hero of the War of 1812 whose famous last words were "Don't give up the ship!"—also has a spirit who wanders the grounds, say ghost watchers. While Lawrence seems to be resting peacefully in his tomb next to the church's southern wall (visible from Broadway and notable for its anchor motif and cannons pointing into the ground, a sign of peace), Ludlow's spirit is not so comfortable. Perhaps it's because he shares his tomb with Captain and Mrs. Lawrence. Whatever, Ludlow's spirit has been reported strolling the graveyard, even once introducing himself to a visitor as Lieutenant Ludlow.

One final Trinity ghost worth mentioning is that of Thomas Addis Emmet, who roams the church grounds looking for his gravesite. Perhaps a sympathetic passerby will lead him to his actual resting place, at St. Mark's Church in the East Village.

The large steeplelike churchyard monument at the northernmost edge of the churchyard near the Broadway fence, which stands next to the Leeson cryptogram mentioned earlier, is a memorial to American prisoners of war from the Revolution. Ravaged by diseases and malnutrition aboard derelict British ships docked in America and in abandoned factories such as the old Sugar House on Liberty Street, more soldiers died in these prison camps than in battle. The graveyard contains the graves of several fallen soldiers, but the real reason for erecting the monument may be that it served as a perfect foil to a 1852 City Hall plan to extend Pine Street (which begins directly across Broadway) to the Hudson River. What politician could tear down a monument to fallen soldiers?

On the opposite side of the street at the intersection of Pine and Broadway, at 100 Broadway, is the **American Surety Building**, constructed in 1896. It was on this site that the first official presidential inaugural ball was held the evening after George Washington took the oath of office.

Across Pine Street, at 120 Broadway, is the building that forever changed America's urban landscape. Built in 1915, the **Equitable Building** was erected in a way that took full advantage of the building site. The one-acre plot has been totally covered with an edifice that is, basically, thirty acres stacked one upon the other. Take a moment and ponder the enormity of this structure. Separated only narrow streets from its neighbors, the Equitable Building appalled New Yorkers for the way it cheated them of sky and light. Within one year of its completion, the city passed the nation's first zoning law restricting building size, largely by calling for mandatory setbacks and limiting building volume to twelve times the site area. This brick whale is well built, though. The block-long, barrel-vaulted lobby exits to four streets and is a gilt and marble showcase.

Cedar Street borders the Equitable building to the north. Cedar, like Pine Street, recalls that this area used to be groves and forests two hundred years ago. Originally called Little Queen Street, antiroyal sentiments caused it to be renamed in 1794.

Equitable's next door neighbor at 140 Broadway is

the **Marine Midland Bank**. Notable for its plaza featuring the orange *en point* cube sculpture by Isamu Noguchi, this matte black skyscraper shows how a plaza can provide air and light without setbacks. Across the street is a small park—accessible, but uninviting—created to allow its benefactor, 1 Liberty Plaza to the north, to build a more massive building. About half a block into the park on the Liberty Street side, toward the Hudson River, is a Seward H. Johnson (of the Johnson & Johnson fortune) sculpture from the 1970s. Seated on a park bench, rummaging through his belongings, is a slightly harried business-man—rendered life-size in bronze—going through his briefcase. Talk about old New York! Even though the statue is less than two decades old, already the business accoutrements in the case seem like retro artifacts: A crushed pack of filterless cigarettes, a personal tape re-corder the size of the Manhattan phone book, and a pocket calculator that would hardly fit in a pocket. The steely fellow is, however, probably the only New Yorker who will never forget his umbrella, since it's welded be-side him.

The park, along with the Marine Midland plaza, also permits a breather from the otherwise claustrophobic streetscape of Broadway. This is a good skyscraper view-ing spot. Those twin beauties toward the river are, of course, the towers of the World Trade Center. The "papier-mâché" trees, the giant sculpture by Jean Dubuf-fet visible when you look east on Cedar, are at the base of the Chase Manhattan Bank near Nassau Street. The bank was a David Rockefeller project that created the first plaza-in-exchange-for-height skyscraper in New York. The Marine Midland Bank and 1 Liberty Plaza followed.

Walking north, across the street from 1 Liberty Plaza at 160 Broadway, is a McDonald's that offers much more than burgers and fries. This town-house restaurant makes a great place to take a break. McDonald's has made this one of their flagship restaurants, featuring a doorman, a grand piano played throughout the day, and an electronic

ticker tape displayed above the order counter—an indication of their clientele. Espresso and cappuccino are
served and waiters insist on cleaning up after you, instead
of letting you throw away your own trash. Restrooms are
downstairs. Upstairs is a gift shop.

Proceed up Broadway to the north side of 1 Liberty
Plaza. The street here has two names: Maiden Lane,
named for the young girls who came here to do their
laundry, on the right (east) and Cortlandt Street, named
for a Dutch farm family that once lived here, on the left.

Back in the early 1800s, before street lighting came
to Manhattan, Cortlandt Street was the home of the
Screeching Woman, better known as the Ghost of Maiden
Lane. Almost eight feet tall with a long, flowing mantle,
the ghost made a habit of freezing the blood of night
strollers by suddenly appearing on the street, screaming
and ranting. One night, the Screeching Woman made the
mistake of trying to spook an army captain who happened to be hiding a stout hickory club beneath his cloak.
As the specter tried to overtake him, the captain dealt out
a few chops with his truncheon and the ghost hit the
deck. It turned out that the feared apparition was nothing
more than a little man with a white cloth draped over a
tall wooden frame.

On the next block north, you come to **John Street**
on the east side of Broadway. John Street was once home
to the John Street Theatre, a colonial-era show palace that
entertained George Washington and, later, British occupation troops. The theater, destroyed long ago, stood
about half a block from Broadway on the north side of
the street. Unfortunately, the plaque commemorating the
site has been stolen (plaques are valuable because the
bronze can be melted down), but the four bolts that once
held it in place are still there.

John Street is also reportedly the home of what may
be New York's nicest ghost. Office workers leaving the
Financial District late at night say they have seen a heavy-
set, elderly black woman who makes clucking sounds

as if calling a dog or cat. It is the ghost of Chloe. When a yellow fever epidemic struck in 1822—one of the worst of the series of breakouts that killed hundreds of New Yorkers over a thirty-year period—John Street was the center of this horrible scourge (the city had already quarantined the area around Trinity Church, considered a mosquito breeding ground). Everyone who could fled the John Street area for the more salubrious climes of Greenwich Village. Everyone, that is, except Chloe.

Chloe could not bring herself to leave behind her pets to take care of themselves, nor could she abandon the dogs, cats, goats, and birds that the other residents of John Street had skipped out on. So she stayed behind, risking death to tend to the animals that likely would have died without her care. When the epidemic ended and John Street residents returned, they found Chloe in her small home surrounded by all the pets they had abandoned. Some ghost watchers take a certain comfort in knowing that Chloe is still on John Street.

One block north of John Street, at 222 Broadway between Fulton and Ann streets, is a 1960s skyscraper that stands on the site where P. T. Barnum showcased the most fascinating attractions of his circus. Famous midget Tom Thumb lived here with his miniature wife, Lavinia Warren, the two regularly displaying themselves for paying gawkers. Barnum was an early master of getting a big crowd in and getting them out. It was for this freak emporium that he created the "This Way to the Egress" sign that has come to epitomize make-a-buck hucksterism. Incorrectly deducing "egress" to mean yet another freak attraction, patrons would follow the signs, eventually ending up outside the showhall, needing to pay another entrance fee to continue their visit.

After becoming Barnum's showhouse, the site served as the headquarters of the New York *Herald*, one of the city's early newspapers. It was from here that Stanley left on his expedition to find Dr. Livingston, a project sponsored by the *Herald*.

Across the street at 195 Broadway is the old national headquarters of AT&T. The building has an architectural reputation as a classic masterpiece. Built in 1912, the entrance on Broadway features bronze panels representing the elements of earth, wind, air, and fire by the same artist—Paul Manship—who created the statue of Prometheus at Rockefeller Center. This building reputedly has more columns than any other structure in the world—note the rows at ground level and a few stories above street level. Enter the lobby for more columns and a serene space off busy Broadway. (Check out the lobby's mailbox, carved from marble and based on the design of a Roman altar.) If you need it, there's a handy pedestrian guide at street level on the Broadway facade of the building.

Now cross Fulton Street to **St. Paul's Chapel**. This is the only building in New York City that has survived fully intact since before the Revolutionary War. Completed in 1766, the brownstone chapel was built to serve Trinity Church's country parishioners who lived "way uptown," five blocks north of today's Trinity Church. When independence fever began to heat up, services were suspended over parishioner objections to official prayers being said for the hated King George III. The chapel was built facing the Hudson River—which used to flow next to the churchyard, prior to landfill—and its design echoes its rural calling.

Unlike much of the rest of lower New York, including Trinity Church itself, St. Paul's survived the great fire of 1776. It was here that George Washington and the *entire* Congress came to worship after the first presidential inauguration. For two years, while New York was the nation's first capital, Washington regularly worshiped at St. Paul's. His pew has been preserved inside the chapel, beneath an oil painting that represents the first rendering of the presidential seal.

Much of the altar was designed by Washington, D.C., architect Pierre L'Enfant, including the pulpit. Note how

Graveyard behind St. Paul's chapel

the top of the pulpit includes a featherlike crown. It's significant because it's one of the few crowns from the colonial era that still survives. All the others—like those on the fence surrounding Bowling Green—were destroyed by angry patriots.

The churchyard outside holds the graves of several early Americans. Among them is George Frederick Cooke, buried almost in the middle of the graveyard to the west of the church. Like legions of struggling actors who would follow, Cooke was the first important stage star who came to New York to be discovered. Arriving in 1810 from England, Cooke was well respected, but his acting was hampered by alcoholism, which killed his career and, eventually, him. As the poor actor slowly edged toward death, the ailing Cooke asked his doctor if he might be able to make a bargain to pay his medical bills. The doctor and actor worked out a trade. Cooke proposed that after his death, the doctor would be allowed to use his body parts for the advancement of science.

The doctor, keen on seeing that his fee be paid one way or the other, took the desperate actor up on his offer. Soon after Cooke's death, his head, finger, and a few other parts were removed, and the rest of the body was interred in St. Paul's Churchyard. Cooke's head made the scientific circuit, but really was most popular as a prop in several stage versions of *Hamlet,* thus continuing a stage presence the actor had so earnestly sought while living. Later, the skull returned to its scientific career, heading to where it is today, resting in a glass case in the Jefferson Medical College in Philadelphia.

According to ghost watchers, the poor actor doesn't seem to have ever gotten over the loss. Sightings of his ghost have been reported several times (often on Halloween), roaming headless through the graveyard, searching for the rest of himself. By the way, a few rows back from Cooke's grave is the final resting spot of George Eacker, the man who killed Alexander Hamilton's son, Philip, in a duel.

Detail of the Woolworth Building

But enough levity. It's time to leave the graveyard and continue our tour. Before you go, however, look directly north from Cooke's grave and notice the medium-sized building at 20 Vesey Street, the **old** *New York Post* **building**. The statues that adorn the facade were carved by Gutzon Borglum, creator of Mount Rushmore.

Returning now to Broadway, on the northwest corner of Vesey Street and Broadway you will see the old site of the Astor House, a hotel that catered to the elite visitors of antebellum New York. It was also a favorite spot of Confederate spies who used it as a headquarters for sabotage and espionage during the Civil War. The spies started several fires in the hotel, but all were quickly extinguished. P. T. Barnum's emporium across the street at 222 Broadway wasn't so lucky. The rebels started a fire there that destroyed it. The hotel was torn down in 1913 and replaced with the present neo-Federal confection.

Now, walk one block north to the 1913 **Woolworth Building**, 233 Broadway. Known as the "Cathedral of

Commerce," this is one of the world's most famous sky-scrapers. In a soaring Gothic design that was altered several times during construction to ensure that the building would be the world's tallest, Cass Gilbert created a monument to the five-and-dime empire of F. W. Woolworth. The lobby, a small mosaic treasure, features caricatures of the architect (holding a model of the building) and Woolworth (counting out nickels).

Across the street, you see **City Hall Park**, beginning where Broadway is met at an acute angle by Park Row, a street lined with nineteenth-century buildings. Park Row, which begins at Broadway and extends to the modern white skyscraper of Pace University near the entrance to the Brooklyn Bridge, used to be the center of New York's publishing world. **Number 15 Park Row**, notable for its "twin tower" design and visible from the southern tip of the park, was the tallest building in the world when it was built in 1899.

The bookend for Park Row, the awkward white tower of **Pace University**, was the site where Jacob Leisler and son-in-law Jacob Milborne were hanged on orders of New York's Royal Governor Sloughter (pronounced "slaughter"). During a lapse of British power in the late 1600s, the two Jacobs attempted to seize control of the colony, or so it was said before they were brought to the hanging tree that once grew here. Years later, the two were exonerated.

Cross Broadway to City Hall Park, marked at its toe by the circular fountain at Park Row. The park, a splendid spot for relaxing, overflows in historic significance. Walk north to **City Hall**, completed in 1811 from a design by John McComb. This once was the City Common, where George Washington insisted that he personally read the newly printed Declaration of Independence on July 9, 1776, the moment that marked New York's entry into the Revolutionary War. The Common was defined by Broadway to the west and, on the east, the main route to Boston (today's Centre Street). Lincoln, after his assassination, was laid out here to lie in state, allowing thousands of New Yorkers to file past his coffin. When dignitaries and heroes complete their ticker-tape parades up Broadway, it is on these steps that mayors traditionally bestow the keys of the city to the honored guests, such as Nelson Mandela in 1990.

When this building was constructed, it was meant to be the city hall forever, and so far it's worked out that way. The mayor's office is here, as is the city legislature. Access is restricted, but for those who want to see the interior, the guards at the entrance are fairly sympathetic. The upstairs rooms are loaded with political portraits by John Trumbull and Samuel F. B. Morse and furniture from the original Federal Hall.

Outside City Hall, proceed to the eastern side of the building, to the right as you face the main entrance. Walk about halfway up the eastern face and look to your right. Here stands a small, sloping bronze monument that memorializes American soldiers starved to death by the British during the War of Independence in the gruesome Provost Prison, which stood here during the revolution.

Walking now past the rear of City Hall, you see the infamous **Tweed Court House** (officially known as the **Old New York County Court House**) to your right. Built during the corrupt era of "Boss" Tweed, the court house cost $14 million when it was built in 1878, but only about four million of that went for construction—the rest ended up in the pockets of the greedy politicos who came to symbolize the worst of American payola.

Continuing through City Hall Park toward Broadway, you come upon a relatively quiet stretch of park benches and grassy lawns. The walk is coming to an end, and on a most somber note.

Beneath you are the graves of hundreds, perhaps thousands, of poor African Americans who were buried here in the eighteenth and nineteenth centuries. The **Negro Burial Ground**, unrecognized even today, is now at least in peace. It was not always so.

On February 15, 1788, the New York *Daily Advertiser* received a letter, signed pseudonymously by "Humano," begging the medical students of a nearby hospital to quit digging up the freshly buried dead of the burial ground. The letter touched a nerve, reading in part: "It is said that few blacks are buried, whose bodies are permitted to remain in the grave. Swine have been seen devouring the entrails and flesh of women, that human flesh has been taken up along the docks, sewed into bags and that this horrid practice is pursued to make a merchandize of human bones."

The fact was that in the late 1700s, medical students were expected to provide their own cadavers in much the same way that today's students must pay for their own books. The kids (most medical students began as fifteen-year-olds) who had to fulfill this requirement might try the cemeteries at Trinity or St. Paul's, but the tall fences made grave robbing difficult. The potters' fields and Negro burial grounds were much easier pickings.

Soon after the letter to the newspaper appeared, a young boy and friends were playing outside the hospital (which was two blocks north on Broadway). A ladder, which had been left by a repair crew, was leaning against the building and the boy climbed it out of curiosity. What he saw turned out to be a grim collection of body parts and cadavers fresh from experimental surgery. When the boy was noticed by a doctor, the doctor (in a fit of thoroughly insensitive humor) picked up a random disembodied arm and waved it at the boy, taunting him with, "This is your mother's arm."

Unfortunately for the doctor, it just so happened that the boy's mom *had* recently died. Running down Broadway to where his father was working on a construction crew, the boy told his story. Ever since the letter from "Humano" had appeared, the public had been primed to believe the worst. With his comrades in tow, the construction worker went to his wife's grave and unearthed her coffin, which—ouch!—was empty.

A riot ensued. The construction workers marched to

the hospital, gathering a wildly angry crowd along the way, and stormed it. They rampaged through Columbia College (the hospital's sponsor) and trampled past the university's defender, Alexander Hamilton. They besieged the City Common, knocking John Jay to the ground with a brick. For their own protection, the doctors were placed in the city jail, which the citizens attempted to tear down. Three days of rioting finally ended with five New Yorkers dead and the city's militia shamed by the power of an angry mob.

Eventually, the state legislature passed the "Bone Bill," as it was known. The law allowed doctors to have the bodies of indigents for the practice of anatomy and eliminated the need for grave robbing.

As you have now finished your walk and are sitting on the quiet benches of City Hall Park, perhaps this is an appropriate time to reveal the solution to the Leeson cryptogram of Trinity Churchyard:

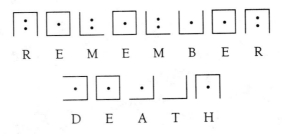

R E M E M B E R

D E A T H

Felix Cuervo is a retired federal worker and president of the Native New Yorkers Historical Association, an organization he founded over thirty years ago, dedicated to marking significant historical sites in the city with plaques. His latest effort is to place a plaque honoring Marilyn Monroe at the Summit Hotel on Lexington Avenue, the place were the actress's skirt was inflated as she stood over a breezy subway grate in *The Seven Year Itch*. A tour guide for more than three decades, Cuervo was born in Brooklyn and raised in Manhattan's Hell's Kitchen. Robert P. Mangieri assisted with this tour.

Walk · 2

MMMMMMMMMMMMMMMMMMMMMMMMMM

The Lower East Side

NEW YORK'S
IMMIGRANT FRONTIER

JAMES P. SHENTON AND

EDWARD T. O'DONNELL

Pell Street, Chinatown

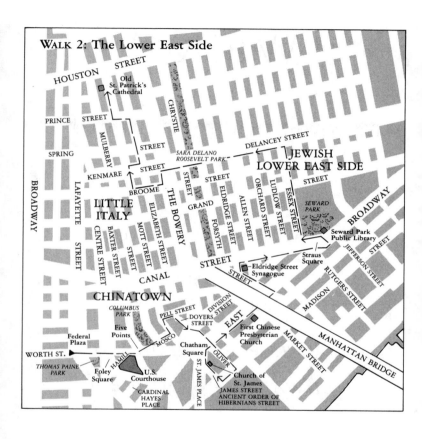

WALK 2: The Lower East Side

HOUSTON STREET

Old St. Patrick's Cathedral

PRINCE STREET

SPRING STREET

BROADWAY

LAFAYETTE STREET

MULBERRY STREET

KENMARE STREET

BROOME STREET

LITTLE ITALY

ELIZABETH STREET

MOTT STREET

CENTRE STREET

BAXTER STREET

THE BOWERY

CHRYSTIE STREET

SARA DELANO ROOSEVELT PARK

DELANCEY STREET

STREET

GRAND

FORSYTH STREET

ELDRIDGE STREET

ALLEN STREET

ORCHARD STREET

LUDLOW STREET

ESSEX STREET

STREET

JEWISH LOWER EAST SIDE

SEWARD PARK

Seward Park Public Library

BROADWAY

JEFFERSON STREET

CANAL STREET

Eldridge Synagogue

Straus Square

CHINATOWN

COLUMBUS PARK

Five Points

PELL STREET

DOYERS STREET

MOSCO

DIVISION STREET

EAST

STREET

First Chinese Presbyterian Church

MADISON STREET

RUTGERS STREET

MARKET STREET

MANHATTAN BRIDGE

Federal Plaza

WORTH ST.

THOMAS PAINE PARK

Foley Square

HAMILL

U.S. Courthouse

CARDINAL HAYES PLACE

Chatham Square

ST. JAMES PLACE

OLIVER

Church of St. James

JAMES STREET

ANCIENT ORDER OF HIBERNIANS STREET

Starting Point: Foley Square, one block east of Broadway
Walk Length: About 3 hours
Subway Stop: Brooklyn Bridge (4, 5, or 6 train); exit at Chambers Street and walk three blocks north

The Lower East Side, though comprising only a few square miles, is an area of immense historical richness and importance. Ever since the founding of the Dutch colony New Amsterdam in 1624, the region has been home to New York City's newest arrivals. Thus, the predominant theme of the Lower East Side is *immigration,* or put more precisely, immigrations—of different ethnic groups arriving at different times. Each group worked to establish its own secure community to protect it from the strangeness and dangers of a chaotic urban society. Life here was not easy. Immigrants fought native-born Americans, they fought other immigrant groups, and they fought among themselves. Yet they also built churches, formed clubs, established newspapers, opened restaurants, and organized businesses—all of which bore the special characteristics of each immigrant group's culture.

As you travel through this remarkable area, another theme becomes obvious, that of recycling. So many of the Lower East Side's buildings, streets, businesses, neighborhoods, and institutions have experienced over and over a process of decline and rebirth. The energy behind this process is the same today as it was a century ago: the sweat and dreams of immigrants seeking to better their lives in a new country.

The Lower East Side has always been a place of diversity. Its architecture ranges from late colonial to neoclassical to modern. Socially, the Lower East Side has been home to some of the richest and poorest citizens of the city, living only a short distance from each other. People of diverse faiths and creeds have lived and worshiped here. Economically, the working class made their living here by sewing garments, preparing food, constructing buildings, hawking wares from pushcarts, performing on stage, and lest we forget, stealing.

Perhaps the most inviting source of diversity is the food, which alone is worth a trip to the Lower East Side. Here, in the space of just a few square miles, one can sample authentic cuisines from all over the world. And the best part is that it costs so little!

The Lower East Side has long been an ethnic mosaic, with some groups dominating the picture at different times. Today, the dominant group is the Chinese. Yet upon closer examination one can see the Dutch, English, Irish, African, German, Italian, Polish, Romanian, Russian, Latino, Jewish, and other groups' contributions and realize that they too played a part in the area's development. More important, one can also see where these distinct groups come together to form a unique, distinctly American, cultural blend.

So as you walk the legendary streets of the Lower East Side, keep these things in mind. Remember also that what you see may not be there the next time you look. At the very least, it will be different. As you walk, you will travel back one, two, even three centuries to a different world, where people came from all over the globe to start fresh in a new nation. Too often we tend to think of the pioneers as the men and women who sought their fortunes in the American West. But as your walk will reveal, the people who traveled to America as immigrants and settled in areas like New York's Lower East Side faced equally formidable dangers and displayed an equal amount of courage. They too were pioneers.

We begin our walk at **Foley Square**, one block east of Broadway at the corner of Lafayette and Worth streets. The corner on which you stand is part of **Federal Plaza**. As you look out over the square with the park in the middle, keep in mind that this current configuration is an early-twentieth-century creation. Prior to 1900 the area was quite different.

In the late colonial era, a body of water known as Collect Pond covered this area. Fed by underground natural springs, the Collect, or Fresh Water Pond as some called it, provided much of the city's water supply. In the eighteenth century, the city's wealthy residents frequented Collect Pond to enjoy the cool fresh air and swimming in the summer and ice-skating in the winter. Some built small villas along the pond's shore and enterprising businessmen opened shops offering a variety of things to eat and drink.

As the city spread northward and grew in population, stockmen began to use Collect Pond as a watering hole for the livestock being brought in to feed the city. Slaughterhouses, stockyards, and tanneries soon replaced the quaint tea shops. Needless to say, it was not long before the wealthy chose to take the breezes in more hospitable places like Greenwich Village!

By 1800 all that remained of the once idyllic Collect Pond was a fetid swamp. When a depression hit in 1808, the city fathers decided to drain the pond and cover it with earth as a public works project to provide idle workmen with employment. Though gone forever, the waters of Collect Pond continue to reassert themselves. In fact, all the buildings before you are equipped with pumps operating 24 hours a day to relieve flooding from the springs that once fed the pond. On any rainy day, the water cascades down the hills looking for the pond, only to find the municipal sewer system.

During the nineteenth century, as the wealthy moved away and the poor moved in, this area became known as Five Points, the most notorious slum in the United States. The name came from the intersection of three main streets, which created five corners or "points."

The Irish made up the principle residents of Five Points before 1870. Though present in New York from the very beginning (Irishman Thomas Dongan served as the colony's seventh governor from 1683 to 1688), the Irish did not begin to arrive in significant numbers until after the Great Famine struck Ireland in 1845. By 1860 the number of Irish-born people in New York City numbered 200,000, a figure that does not include the tens of thousands of second-generation, American-born Irish who also lived here.

Though some of these immigrants, particularly the Protestant Irish of Ulster, came as skilled laborers in search of greater economic opportunity, the majority arrived as impoverished, preindustrial farmers who lacked any useful skills. As they crowded into Five Points, the men took what heavy manual labor jobs they could find while the women worked as domestics. Statistics from the 1850s reveal the extent of their plight. Although the Irish comprised a little over half of New York's foreign-born population in 1855, they made up 85 percent of the foreign-born patients admitted to Bellevue, the city's public hospital. Over two thirds of the foreign-born patients admitted to the lunatic asylum in the 1850s came from Ireland. Of 2,000 prostitutes held at the prison hospital on Blackwell's Island, 706 came from Ireland. In 1858, the Irish made up three out of every four immigrant prisoners held in the city jails. Life in the New World was difficult, indeed.

In the few square miles that made up the Five Points area, approximately 25,000 to 30,000 Irish immigrants lived in squalid, packed warrens. Housing was so scarce and the poor so desperate that many thousands lived in tenement cellars, amid the rats and disease and with no light or fresh air. Some lacked enough money to rent even a cellar, but many shrewd landlords and subletters rented beds around the clock at 25 cents for each of three eight-hour shifts. In dangerous Five Points, shelter for one third of a day beat no shelter at all.

Cholera swept through New York City many times in the nineteenth century, the worst outbreaks being in 1832, 1842, and 1849. As one might·expect, the vast majority of the dead came from the Five Points region. To some New Yorkers, horrified by the depravity and filth of Five Points, cholera seemed to be the answer to their prayers. One Protestant minister thundered during the epidemic in 1832:

> *Drunkards and filthy, wicked people of all descriptions,* are swept away *in heaps,* as if the Holy God could no longer bear their wickedness, just as we sweep away a mass of filth when it has become so corrupt that we cannot bear it. . . . The cholera is a rod in the hand of God.

Such extremes of crime, disease, and poverty produced the city's first gangs—the Plug Uglies, the Dead Rabbits, and the Shirt Tails to name just a few. They roamed the narrow streets, setting upon unsuspecting victims and fighting with rival gangs. Because of these dangerous conditions, it is not surprising that the New York City police force observed an unwritten policy of never entering the area in armed squads numbering less than ten.

As early as the 1840s, Five Points had acquired a reputation that went far beyond New York City. In 1842 the famed English writer Charles Dickens visited the slum on a tour of America and wrote:

Poverty and wretchedness are rife. The coarse and bloated faces at the door have counterparts at home and all the wide world over. Debauchery has made the very houses prematurely old. See how the rotten beams are tumbling down, and how the patched and broken windows seem to scowl dimly, like eyes that have been hurt in drunken frays.

By 1860 the slum's notoriety was such that when Abraham Lincoln came to New York for the first time, he asked to see two things: Henry Ward Beecher's Plymouth Church (see Walk 6, page 279) and Five Points.

We see evidence of the harsh and dangerous environment of Five Points as we look to the north up **Lafayette Street**. City officials widened the street and extended it to the Five Points area after the Civil War. The decision followed the infamous New York City Draft Riots of 1863. Thousands of laborers, mostly Irish, went on a four-day rampage in protest over the draft. Their rage stemmed from three facts. First, the Irish could not afford the $300 fee that allowed the wealthy to avoid the draft. Second, as Democrats they opposed the Republican Party's war. And third, they feared labor competition with blacks should they be freed.

Seething with resentment, they rioted for four days, looting the homes and businesses of the wealthy, attacking policemen, and lynching free blacks. A panicked President Lincoln sent 30,000 Union soldiers from the fields of Gettysburg to quell the unrest. When it ended, 119 people, mostly rioters, lay dead and millions of dollars' worth of property was missing or burned. Since much of the rioting took place in the relatively inaccessible Five Points region, city authorities chose to add the short extension to Lafayette so as to provide, in the event of another civil disturbance, easy access for troops and, more importantly, artillery.

By the late nineteenth century, when Italians and Jews began to replace the Irish and Germans, city officials decided that Five Points had to go. Many reformers had tried since the 1830s, but property owners successfully resisted all attempts. By the 1880s, however, the housing stock had so deteriorated that the city began to condemn large numbers of tenements, buy the property, and raze the buildings. In their place they constructed the government buildings that stand before us. Hence, Foley Square represents a classic case of early urban renewal or slum clearance.

These magnificent buildings represent the headquarters for almost every conceivable branch of government in New York City. **The Jacob K. Javits Federal Building**, named for the longtime U.S. senator from New York and easily the least attractive of these buildings, towers over the plaza behind you. As you turn around again to face the park, on your right in the distance is the **Municipal Building**, the main headquarters of the city government. Completed in 1914, this grand civic structure is where New Yorkers go for all their licenses. Every year over 7,000 couples not only stand in line for marriage licenses, but also to get married in the chapel across the hall—an average of one wedding every twenty minutes!

To its left stands the **United States Court House**. Built between 1933 and 1936, its large tower looms over the square. The last building designed by the noted American architect Cass Gilbert, Jr., it also represents one of the last neoclassical-style office buildings erected in New York. Persons charged with violating federal law stand trial here. Noteworthy defendants in recent years have included John Mitchell for moonlighting as a plumber while serving in Nixon's cabinet, hotel magnate Leona Helmsley for spending a couple of million on plastic surgery instead of paying her taxes, junk bond king Michael Milken for making more money in one year than the GNP of many third-world countries, and dictatorette Imelda Marcos for conspiring to corner the international market in ladies' dress shoes.

Continuing left you see the **New York State Supreme**

Court Building, the second-highest court in New York State. Its impressive size and beautiful Corinthian portico once dominated Foley Square and, given the region's infamous history, was probably designed to evoke respect for the law among the masses (note the inscription above the entrance). Considering the fact that the city built it after Five Points no longer existed, such messages of law and order seem a bit late.

Cross Lafayette Street and walk along Worth. To your right is **Thomas Paine Park**, named for the influential political radical whose 1776 pamphlet *Common Sense* contributed much to fomenting the American Revolution. Legend has it that he read parts of another famous revolutionary writing, *The Crisis*, at one of the nearby cafés around Collect Pond. Next to Alexander Hamilton, he is probably the one figure from the revolution most clearly associated with New York City.

Cross Centre Street, Hamill Place, and Cardinal Hayes Place and stop at the next corner. You are now standing at the place where Orange (now Baxter), Anthony (now Worth), and Cross (now Mosco) streets came together to form Five Points. Ironically, the open area at the intersection's center used to be called Paradise Square, a name reflecting the area's past beauty. By the 1840s people used the term Five Points to describe not just the intersection, but the surrounding area as well.

Looking south down **Baxter Street**, you see the site where a large, three-story building called the Old Brewery once stood. Built in 1792, in the waning years of Collect Pond, it produced Coulter's Beer, well known throughout the northeast at the time. When it began to crumble, its owner sold it in 1837, and it soon began a second life as a tenement house for Irish immigrants and free blacks. Legend has it that by the 1840s, upward of five hundred people lived there at any one time in horribly overcrowded rooms. Some contemporary accounts alleged that murders took place there at the rate of one per day!

U.S. Courthouse

After fifteen years of notoriety, the Old Brewery began its third and final life. In a decision pregnant with symbolism, the Ladies Home Missionary Society of the Methodist Episcopal Church purchased the brewery in 1852 and established the Five Points Mission, a paternalistic charity established to alleviate the slum's horrible conditions by elevating the morality of the poor who lived there. Though they immediately tore down the structure, the name Old Brewery stuck to the point that when the society published a book on their work, they titled it *The Old Brewery*.

The large building occupying the southeast corner of Baxter and Worth stands on the site of what used to be called Cow Bay, a notorious subsection of Five Points. Cow Bay, named for an inlet of the old Collect Pond, was a collection of decrepit tenement houses that lined a narrow dead-end street no longer in existence (Little Water). Some buildings, bearing names such as Gates of Hell and Brickbat Mansion, possessed underground tunnels that allowed the lawless to evade the police.

Directly to the north down Baxter we see the **Criminal Courts Building and Tombs Prison.** The original Tombs Prison was built in 1838 and received its name because its Egyptian architectural style reminded people of the pharaohs' tombs. Designed to house two hundred inmates, it often held over five hundred at a time. As with everything else at Five Points, conditions and food were dismal inside the prison, yet a certain informality relieved its gloomy atmosphere. Prison officials permitted family members or friends to come and go as they pleased. Many brought in food and blankets to supplement the meager provisions offered inside.

The stories surrounding the Tombs are legion. One of the most famous involved all the elements that make up a good cheap novel: murder, lies, love, and suicide. It all began in 1841 when an author named John Colt got into an argument with his printer Samuel Adams over unpaid bills. In the heat of the tussle, Colt killed Adams. Quickly he wrapped the body, packed it in a crate, and put it aboard a ship bound for New Orleans. Unfortunately for Colt, the ship failed to sail on time and the captain ordered the reeking box opened. When the police arrested Colt he confessed and a jury convicted him to hang in November 1842.

Colt's lone request was that he be allowed to marry his mistress, Caroline Henshaw, before meeting his maker. The warden agreed, and at 11:30 A.M. on the day of the scheduled execution, Colt married Henshaw in his cell, accompanied by his brother and a minister. As part of the arrangement, the warden granted the couple a one-hour "honeymoon" alone in the cell. At the appointed hour they parted, with tears in their eyes. But when the guard returned later that afternoon to fetch Colt to the gallows, he found him dead by his own hand, a knife protruding from his chest. Some, when they heard the news, surmised that Colt was simply not the marrying type, but most agreed he simply lacked the grit to face the gallows.

Hangings, such as the one Colt successfully escaped, were forms of popular entertainment. Throughout the nineteenth century, people gathered outside the prison on hanging days to witness the grisly affairs. Many brought their lunch or bought it from vendors who sold their wares as though they were at a fair. Pickpockets had a field day, darting through the crowds and snatching purses from those too absorbed in the spectacle of execution.

The location of the Tombs reveals an important fact about urban life—law enforcement is never placed at a distance. City officials built the Tombs here because of the area's tremendous crime rate.

These features of Five Points, simultaneously colorful and horrible, represent the infamous side of the slum, which became part of the legend. Most of it, however, was a nameless, faceless parade of human misery and tragedy. It is a sobering reminder to those who argue that the New York City of yesteryear was so much less violent than today.

Cross the intersection of Baxter and Worth streets to

the northeast corner, the edge of **Columbus Park**. Formerly named Mulberry Park, it stands as a monument to the work of reformers like Jacob Riis who clamored for the city to relieve unhealthy slum conditions here by providing open spaces for children to play sports and games under adult supervision instead of taking their amusements in the area's vice-ridden back alleys. Construction crews destroyed dozens of tenements between 1892 and 1894 to make way for the park, which the city renamed Columbus Park in 1911 in recognition of the neighborhood's dominant Italian presence. Today, the hopes of Riis and others are still being realized. In the warmer months of the year, the park is alive with youngsters playing basketball and elderly men and women enjoying the sun.

Enter the park through the gate in the wrought iron fence and walk ahead to **Mulberry Street**. There, examine the names of the various restaurants and businesses that line it—many are Italian, such as **Giambone's** at no. 42 and **Antica Roma** at no. 40. Other establishments bear Chinese names. Examine closely the restaurant at **32 Mulberry**. Note that just above its new sign in both Chinese and English you can still see the vague outline of the original Italian name, Moneta's. This is an excellent example of the predominant theme of the Lower East Side: the forming and reforming of ethnic villages over the generations. As recently as the 1970s Mulberry Street used to be exclusively Italian. Now it is almost completely Chinese.

As we gaze to our left down Mulberry Street we see the infamous **Mulberry Bend** where the road curves sharply to the right. Before the construction of Columbus Park, crumbling tenements with names like Bandits' Roost, Thieves' Alley, and Ragpickers' Row lined both sides of this narrow street. Conditions here rivaled those in Cow Bay, with murder, assault, and debauchery punctuating daily life. In 1890 Jacob Riis wrote, in his famous book *How the Other Half Lives*, of the horrific conditions here:

Where Mulberry Street crooks like an elbow within hail of the depravity of the Five Points, is "The Bend," foul core of New York's slums. . . . Around "the Bend" cluster the bulk of the tenements that are stamped as altogether bad, even by the optimists in the Health Department. . . . In the scores of back alleys, of stable lanes, and hidden byways, of which the rent collector alone can keep track, [the poor] share such shelter as the ramshackle structures afford with every kind of abomination rifled from the dumps and ash barrels of the city. . . . There is scarce a lot that has not two, three, or four tenements upon it, swarming with unwholesome crowds.

Now you can see why Riis made such a big deal about getting a park built here!

By now you may have noticed a number of Chinese funeral homes. Like the other establishments along Columbus Park, they used to be owned by Italians. If you happen to be in the area on the day of a funeral for a prominent member of the Chinese community, you will see one of the most telling examples of the blend of history on the Lower East Side. Remarkably, the funeral procession is often led by an Italian band staffed by men averaging seventy-five years of age. The Chinese adopted this practice generations ago when their traditional method of raising a clatter—firecrackers—was made illegal. The tradition has continued ever since, even as the Italians have moved away. As one stands there and watches the band stop in front of the home of the deceased and play "When the Saints Go Marching In," one is aware of a great deal not just about the Lower East Side, but about America and the curious ways in which newcomers assimilate into a nation of immigrants.

Next to 30 Mulberry Street is **Mosco Street**, named for a notable local politician from the Italian community. Head up Mosco to the corner of **Mott Street.** There on the left you immediately confront the **Church of the**

Transfiguration. This Catholic Church has an extraordinary history that typifies the Lower East Side. Built in 1801 as the English Lutheran First Church of Zion, it remained so until the 1850s when the growing numbers of poor and foreign-born people coming to the neighborhood convinced the congregation to move to a new location. Fr. John McClellen, pastor of the Church of the Transfiguration on Chambers Street, purchased the site in 1853 and moved his flock of Irish immigrants here.

Transfiguration and other Catholic parishes provided a key source of strength and unity to the Irish and German immigrant communities, offering spiritual strength to those overwhelmed by life's trials and establishing numerous charitable and fraternal organizations to alleviate the conditions of poverty and misery. Such work played a significant role in aiding them to eventually escape the horrible conditions of Five Points. Later, the church would accomplish the same for Italian and Latino immigrants.

By the 1880s, Italian Catholics began arriving in increasing numbers and used Transfiguration's basement chapel for services in their native language. At the turn of the century most of the Irish had left, and Fr. Ernest Coppo arrived in 1902 as the first Italian pastor, moving the Italians out of the basement and into the main place of worship. You can see clear evidence of this fact on the face of the church where a plaque commemorates the dead during World War I. Italians make up the majority of the two dozen names, broken only by an occasional Donohue or Durkin, names that seem strangely out of place. Today, after changing from English to Irish to Italian, Transfiguration is a Chinese Catholic church run by the Maryknoll order.

Transfiguration counts among its alumni the religious figures Cardinal Patrick Hayes, the third cardinal of New York, and Mother Cabrini, the first American (naturalized) saint. Other notables include the entertainers Enrico Caruso and Jimmy Durante. Two current prestigious members of

Transfiguration are Fr. Ignatius Kung, the bishop-in-exile from Shanghai, and Fr. Dominic Tang, S.J., the archbishop-in-exile of Canton. Imprisoned in the 1960s during the Cultural Revolution, they remained in jail for twenty years until being released with the understanding that they leave China. Kung, like most Chinese immigrants, chose to come to New York. Tang went to Hong Kong, but annually visits Transfiguration. In May 1991, Pope John Paul II elevated Bishop Kung to cardinal. When either man says Mass, the church is packed to overflowing.

As the ethnic makeup of Transfiguration indicates, we are now in **Chinatown.** Immigrants from China have been living in New York since the 1840s and 1850s when approximately 150 Chinese sailors resided here. Many more came in the 1870s as anti-Chinese racism on the west coast drove many east in search of jobs. By the 1880s between 8,000 and 10,000 Chinese lived throughout the city, though a core community existed right where you stand, centered around Mott, Pell, and Bayard streets. The Chinese worked principally in the hand-laundry and restaurant industries, both of which required little capital, skill, or knowledge of English.

Up to the end of World War II, the Chinese community was overwhelmingly male. Most immigrants came to America not as settlers but as transient fortune seekers, hoping to work for ten or twenty years in America and return to China as wealthy men. The Chinese Exclusion Act of 1882 prevented virtually any Chinese women from entering the U.S., and by 1910 Chinese men here outnumbered Chinese women by an astounding forty to one. By 1940 this had diminished to nine to one. The U.S. repealed the exclusion act in 1943 (China was an ally in the war) and passed other laws that allowed for more women to migrate.

Since that time, Chinatown's "bachelor society" has given way to a more normal social arrangement. The influx of women also provided the basis of the resurgence of the city's garment industry—cheap labor, about which we will hear more later. Today, Chinatown is the largest Chinese settlement in the United States. Nearly 150,000 Chinese and Chinese Americans live here, making the total Chinese population for all of New York City 400,000, with an average age of eighteen. The ratio of male to female is about even. All this has made China-town arguably the most dynamic area of the city.

Chinatown is busy, noisy, and crowded and will grow only more so as you venture farther into it. Examine the Chinese-owned businesses: Like most neighborhoods every conceivable need and service is provided—household goods, gifts, groceries, clothing, and especially restau-rants. By all means go into these stores and examine the wares. Some offer cheap, tourist-oriented goods, but those places are fairly easy to recognize.

One of Chinatown's most celebrated residents at the turn of the century was George Washington "Chuck" Connors. He grew up in the area as a streetwise tough who managed to learn enough Chinese to form friend-ships with many local residents. Known as the Bowery Philosopher and the Mayor of Chinatown, he held court in a pub called the Old Tree House where he drank for free and entertained customers and the press.

In the 1890s, Connors became what the Chinese called a "lobbygow," or tour guide. New Yorkers and tourists at the time were fascinated by the Chinese, mostly because of the sensational "Horrors of Chinatown" sto-ries of life here that appeared regularly in the two-penny press. Connors carefully included a little of everything in each tour—prostitutes, murderers, crooked policemen—even to the point of arranging for a middle-aged Chinese couple to pretend their run-down home was an opium den so he could parade his horrified guests through it. Alas, these "lobbygow" authors must confess, no opium dens lie ahead on this tour.

Unfortunately for the residents of Chinatown, the vice and violence described by Connors in his tours has once again returned. Between 1930 and 1965, when the U.S.

government sharply curtailed immigration and Five Points existed only as a memory, Chinatown became the safest police precinct in New York City. Today, Chinatown boasts the city's fastest-rising crime rate. This trend is a remarkable replay of events a century ago.

Just ahead on Mott, at the point where it bends to the right and intersects with **Pell Street**, you can see a tall white building on the left with a pagoda on the roof. The building is owned by one of the many family or clan associations that dominate the life of Chinatown. They were initially formed in the late nineteenth century by wealthy Chinese merchants to protect immigrants in their new and often hostile surroundings by providing loans, burial money, job referrals, and legal services. They soon

acquired much power in the community and banded together in an umbrella organization known as the Chinese
Consolidated Benevolent Association. Many considered it
the unofficial government of Chinatown.

Those Chinese who did not belong to a strong family
or village network formed secret societies called "tongs"
to rival the powerful associations. These gangs also soon
acquired immense local power, fracturing Chinatown into
clearly defined domains within which they operated lucrative opium dens, prostitution rings, and gambling
rackets while extorting protection money from local businessmen. "Tong wars" of extraordinary violence between
rival gangs erupted frequently over contested turf or disputes between rival leaders. In 1909 alone, the police
estimated that over 350 people died in tong violence in
Chinatown. These tongs endure today and account for
much of Chinatown's resurgent crime rate, terrorizing local residents and spreading the deleterious effects of crime
and drugs throughout the community.

But enough of such negative talk. Let's continue our
exploration of Chinatown's vibrant and unique character.
Make a right onto Pell Street and to your right at no. 25
is **Pell's Dinty**, a wonderful place to get authentic and
inexpensive Chinese food. What an odd name for a Chinese restaurant! Neither Dinty nor Pell are Chinese names:
an Irish saloon named Dinty's predated the current restaurant and Pell is the name of a prominent eighteenth-
century butcher for whom the street is named. The
current owners decided to keep the name (and save the
expense of a new sign!).

A good indication of the quality of the food here is
the fact that representatives of the Chinese and Tai-
wanese governments take their clients there for dinner. If
you're hungry, this would be a good place to stop. The
restaurant features a remarkably inexpensive menu of
Cantonese food, with entrées ranging from only $3.50 to
$5.00.

Pell Street reveals an interesting fact about the Chinese community—it is religiously diverse. In addition to the Roman Catholic Church of the Transfiguration around the corner, just after Pell's Dinty at no. 21 is the **Chinese Christian Center of the First Chinese Baptist Church.** Down the street on the left at no. 16 is the **Buddhist Temple**, made obvious by its Asian-style roof. Later you will pass the First Chinese Presbyterian Church.

Make a right onto **Doyers Street** and walk until you encounter two classic establishments that have been here for years. One is a rice shop named **Bow Luck** (no. 17) and the other a tea parlor named **Nom Wah** (nos. 11–13). Like Pell's Dinty, one can find great food here for only a few dollars.

Moving ahead a few steps to the place where Doyers bends to the left you can see more evidence of the emerging diversity of Chinatown. On the right there is the **Vietnam Restaurant**, a product of increasing immigration to New York City from that nation. Interestingly, most people are unaware that a substantial proportion of the "boat people" who fled Vietnam were Chinese who had moved there earlier and formed a thriving middle class. Next door we find the **Southeast Asia Seafood Pavilion**, featuring Malaysian cuisine. This is Singapore street food, which again is Chinese cuisine adapted to Malaysia by overseas Chinese who then came to America.

These relatively new establishments, in contrast to Bow Luck, are evidence of a shift taking place in Chinese immigration patterns. The original Chinese immigrants came overwhelmingly from the province of Kwangtung, or Canton. Today, as one moves around Chinatown one can find restaurants featuring food from many provinces of China such as Szechwan and Hunan, not to mention other Southeast Asian nations. This emerging complexity is reflected in the fact that New York City has seven daily Chinese newspapers of numerous dialects and editorial positions, ranging from calls to restore the Manchu dynasty to supporters of the Gang of Four.

In the nineteenth century, a score of seedy saloons

lined Doyers Street. Gambling, fighting, dancing, and, of course, cheap booze made them favorite spots for locals and sailors alike. Some hired singing males and scantily clad females as waiters and waitresses to attract more customers. Two of the most popular singing waiters were young men named Asa Yoelson at Callahan's and Israel Baline at Saulter's. As soon as they managed to escape the low life of the slum, they changed their names to Al Jolson and Irving Berlin.

The place where you stand once bore the name "bloody angle," after the tong wars fought there between 1880 and 1926 by the On Leong Tong and Hip Sing Tong for control of local gambling and opium markets. Armed with knives, clubs, and guns, the combatants waged fights so violent and ruthless that witnesses often reported rivers of blood running down the street into the sewer grates.

As you come to the end of Doyers Street you arrive at the beginning of **the Bowery**. The name comes from the Dutch word for farm, "bouwerie." This reminds us that before the English took possession of New York City in 1664, Dutch settlers lived here in a city they called New Amsterdam.

Twenty years ago the Bowery marked the place where Chinatown ended and the Jewish Lower East Side began. Since that time, however, Chinatown has grown and expanded across the border to form the "new Chinatown." Across the way to the left stands a large modern brick building named **Confucius Plaza**, which exclusively houses residents of Chinese ancestry. A monument to Confucius sits in front of the looming structure. Anyone doubting the movement of the Chinese in this direction need only look directly across the street from where you stand. There is the **Manhattan Savings Bank**, built to resemble a Buddhist temple. Later, on East Broadway, you will see telephone booths with mini pagoda roofs.

Cross the Bowery to the Manhattan Savings Bank and walk south past it. Ahead of us lies the center of **Chatham**

Vendor on Mott Street

Square, named for William Pitt the Elder, the prime minister of Britain, who bore the title Earl of Chatham. Chatham Square is a pedestrian's nightmare—ten streets feed into it—so be careful as you continue south and cross to its center island. Walk up to the tall Asian-style monument that commemorates the "Americans of Chinese ancestry who lost their lives in defense of freedom and democracy" in World War II. This monument reflects a common theme in the immigrant experience: the desire among immigrants to demonstrate patriotism and devotion to their adopted country. Wartime military service is often the most impressive manner in which immigrants have done this. One remarkable, but little chronicled, aspect of American military history is the significant contribution made by immigrants. Often such sacrifice came after much soul searching. In World War I, for example, German and Italian Americans fought against their ancestral homelands, while Irish people swallowed their pride and fought on the side of Great Britain, the historic oppressor of Ireland.

Due east from where you stand (the twin towers of the World Trade Center are to the south) lies Oliver Street. Carefully cross over to the corner of Oliver Street and St. James Place. A few paces down Oliver, and you come across a large and decaying Greek Revival–style church on the left, the **Mariners' Temple Baptist Church**, built in 1843. Its founders established the church in the hope that it would preserve the morals of seamen living in the city. Such an effort was a candid admission about the reality of New York City in the mid-nineteenth century. It is estimated that in a city of 500,000 people in 1850, there were 10,000 prostitutes, or one for every fifty persons. This figure becomes slightly more believable when one considers the fact that at any one time there were anywhere from 50,000 to 100,000 male sailors in the city who never showed up in the census figures. Given this situation, the success of the Mariners' Temple in terms of curbing the wanton behavior of sailors was limited at best.

Since that time the church, like practically everything else in the Lower East Side, has changed dramatically. While still a Baptist church, it currently serves a predominantly black congregation and features a woman minister. If you happen to be here on a Sunday you will hear some of the most inspirational gospel singing and fiery preaching the city has to offer.

Continue on Oliver to **no. 25**, the childhood home of Alfred E. Smith, the onetime governor of New York State and Democratic presidential candidate in 1928. Smith rose to prominence in the 1910s as a member of the powerful Democratic machine, Tammany Hall. Tammany, long associated in the nineteenth century with the Irish and corruption, changed under the leadership of men like Al Smith who, having grown up in abject poverty and witnessed firsthand the plight of honest working people, saw the need to institute reforms in government and business. Smith's terms as governor stands as one of the most progressive in the state's history, with the passage of numerous landmark labor, safety, and health laws.

Notice the row of buildings on either side of the Smith birthplace. They date back to the 1820s when prosperous merchants lived in this neighborhood, near to the waterfront and their businesses. By the time Smith's family moved in (in the late 1870s) the merchants were long gone, and five, six, and seven families crowded into these once single-family dwellings.

At the end of Oliver make a right onto **Madison**. The buildings across the street make up the **Alfred E. Smith Houses**, a public housing project. Make a right onto James Street and walk until you come to the **Church of St. James** on the right, established by Irish immigrants in 1837. Note its similarity in style (Greek revival) and materials (Connecticut brownstone) to the Mariners' Temple. They were designed by the same architect.

Today, St. James's serves a predominantly Latino community. You can see evidence of this on the left side of the building where a plaque commemorates Fr. Felix Varela, founder of the parish in 1827. To this day Fr. Varela remains one of Cuba's most celebrated national heroes, because before coming to New York City he was an early and passionate supporter of Cuban independence. Note that the plaque's inscription is in both Spanish and English.

A second plaque, on the left side of the church, commemorates the founding of the Irish benevolent society, the Ancient Order of Hibernians, in 1836. The AOH provided charitable services, such as job referrals, legal services, and small cash handouts, to Irish immigrants. It also rallied the Irish on many occasions to protect their churches and homes from nativist mobs.

St. James Parochial School occupies the block across the street from the church on the corner of St. James Place and James Street. As the inscription over the front door indicates, its great claim to fame is that Al Smith received his entire formal education here. He left St. James School somewhere between the sixth and eighth grades, leading many to compare him to Abraham Lincoln, whose formal education stopped after the fourth grade. For Smith, his log cabin was a run-down and overcrowded tenement.

Take a right onto St. James Place and walk north 150 feet until you come to a small cemetery on the right. This is the **First Cemetery of the Spanish and Portuguese Synagogue, Shearith Israel** ("Remnant of Israel"), established in 1654. The oldest piece of property in continuous use in all of Manhattan, it reflects a little-known fact about the city—Jews have lived here from the very outset, long before they came in great numbers in the late nineteenth century.

The Congregation Shearith Israel is the oldest Jewish congregation in America, dating back to the same year. It began with a secret New Year's service held somewhere in Chatham Square by recently arrived Spanish and Portuguese Jews, descendants of those expelled from Spain in 1492. Their forefathers first settled in the colony of Brazil, but fled again when the Portuguese took over that colony in 1654. Twenty-three refugees escaped by ship, only to be captured by pirates and stranded in the West Indies. A friendly French captain rescued the group and took them to the Dutch colony of New Amsterdam, where they formed the city's original Jewish settlement. Some of the original founders are buried here in the graveyard before you.

Continue north to Chatham Square and head for **East Broadway.** As you look up East Broadway, you see the southern border of the former German neighborhood called **Kleindeutschland,** or Little Germany. Germans constituted the largest European immigrant group in both the U.S. and New York City. In 1840 only 24,000 Germans lived here; by 1900 over 785,000 did so.

The Germans who settled Kleindeutschland grouped themselves according to what part of Germany they came from: Westphalia, the Rhineland, the Saar, the Palatinate, etc. All wanted to retain their separate provincial identity. This reflected the reality of Germany before 1870, when it was not yet a unified nation. Germans also settled according to their religious faiths and Kleindeutschland featured enclaves of German Catholics, Lutherans, and Jews clustered around their respective churches and synagogues.

Kleindeutschland remained a tight-knit neighborhood past the turn of the century until the fateful day of June 15, 1904. On that day, St. Mark's Lutheran Church sponsored an outing up the Hudson River. Over 1,500 Germans, mostly women and children as it took place during the week, boarded the excursion liner *General Slocum* for the trip. Thirty minutes into the journey, while still in view of Manhattan, the ship caught fire. Rotted life preservers, insufficient lifeboats, and an incompetent captain and crew resulted in over 1,200 deaths—by far the worst disaster in New York City history. Nearly every family in Kleindeutschland lost at least one relative, and many a man returned home to find he had lost his entire family. Kleindeutschland never recovered and by the outbreak of World War I most Germans had moved away.

Kleindeutschland was not exclusively German. Indeed, it was within Kleindeutschland that the Jews who migrated to America in the late nineteenth century made their home. The bulk of these Jews came not from Germany, but from Eastern Europe: Hungary, Romania, Galicia, and Russia (which at that time included Poland). They came to escape the rising anti-Semitic persecution and violence of these places. In Russia, for instance, the law confined Jews to a region known as the Pale of Settlement (Eastern Poland, Lithuania, Byelorussia, and the Ukraine). Here, as in Galicia, Romania, and Hungary, they suffered under laws that restricted their ability to transact business, receive an education, own property, or freely practice their religion. The effect of these disabilities worsened sharply after 1850 as Eastern Europe began to industrialize and many Jews chose to leave and seek a better life in America. Between 1880 and 1910, however, what had begun as a trickle turned into a torrent as murderous anti-Jewish riots, or pogroms, repeatedly swept the cities of Eastern Europe, forcing millions to flee.

Of those that came to New York City, about 325,000 had settled here on the Lower East Side by 1914. Like the Irish, Germans, and Chinese, the Jews who settled here did not do so as Jews, but as Jews of a particular ethnic origin. You now stand on the southwestern border of the Russian Jewish settlement. Romanian and Levantine Jews settled directly north of here, Galician Jews just east of there, and Hungarian Jews north of them. Many synagogues, like the Catholic churches nearby, organized along these ethnic lines.

One of the principal explanations for Chinatown's boom in recent years lies across Chatham Square to the west at the corner of Worth Street and Park Row. The rather ugly black brick and mirror structure housing Chemical Bank is called the **Macao Building**. This financial institution serves as the repository for "flight capital" from the Portuguese colony of Macao. Businessmen there fear they will lose everything when the thriving trading center reverts back to the Communist government of China in 1998. Other banks in the area handle the flight capital from Hong Kong, the neighboring British colony, which returns to Chinese rule in 1997. This injection of capital into New York City explains in part why the Lower East Side in general, and Chinatown in particular, is experiencing a boom in manufacturing and real estate development.

As we approach the beginning of East Broadway, notice the top of the building at no. 9 bearing the sign of the seemingly incomprehensible **Cuban Chinese Benevolent Association**. A remarkable story surrounds this organization. After the Communist takeover of China in 1949, many Chinese fled the country. A small group made their way to Cuba, then a thriving center for tourism and gambling. For ten years they lived there until 1959, when a second Communist takeover—this time by Fidel Castro—forced them to flee to the U.S. In many areas of the city one can now find restaurants boasting Chino-Latino food—a wonderful combination of Cuban and Chinese cuisines.

Note the building directly above the Manhattan Savings Bank with the prominent water tower. The upper floors house modern-day sweatshops. Venture ahead along East Broadway. At the northeast corner of Catherine Street and East Broadway is the **Wing Hee Mansion** (nos. 17–23), another of these intensive manufacturing operations. Incredible as it may sound, it is now possible to produce clothing cheaper in this area than in Southeast Asia.

This reflects a number of recent trends. The combination of the massive influx of flight capital mentioned before and the large pool of cheap female immigrant labor has led to an emerging garment industry. These industries operate for the most part beyond the reach of normal business regulations governing safety, hours, and minimum wages. Workers often toil twelve, even fourteen hours a day in stifling heat and dangerous conditions for as little as two dollars an hour. Almost none of them are willing to report their bosses to the proper authorities—to do so would cost them their jobs. If you look at the top floor windows of these buildings you might see the faces of little children peering out, biding their time while their mothers work the sewing machines.

A century ago this same area constituted the heart of the Jewish garment industry. Here poor Jewish and Italian women labored in similar conditions producing clothes for the national market. These terrible conditions, highlighted by the horror of the 1911 Triangle Shirtwaist factory fire in which 146 women perished in a sweatshop blaze, gave rise to one of the most important unions in this century—the International Ladies' Garment Workers Union (ILGWU).

The Jewish garment industry petered out after World War II due to increased competition from manufacturers in the American South and in foreign countries. Today the garment industry is back. Only time will tell if its exploited workers will form a union to fight for better wages and conditions, or if another Triangle Fire must happen before city officials address the problem.

Now cross Catherine and continue down the length of East Broadway. One can hardly fail to notice the hustle and bustle of this avenue, as street vendors, fresh fish markets, and restaurants compete for the business of the many passersby. This area of the new Chinatown, like that of Mott Street in the old, pulsates with activity and hard work.

Andrew Carnegie donated the **Chatham Square Library** at 33 East Broadway in 1903. It contains the largest collection of Chinese-language titles in America. Next to the library at no. 35 is the **Nice Restaurant.** For those interested in trying the Chinese delicacy dim sum—a variety of steamed dumplings, usually filled with pork or shrimp and served with tea—this is the place to stop. The restaurant features excellent food and a rather fancy interior, and its prices are higher than more homey places like Pell's Dinty.

For anyone curious about Asian religion, the **Buddhist Temple** at 48 East Broadway welcomes visitors to come in and look around. If you have time, it is well worth a visit.

On the southwest corner of Market Street and East Broadway you see the **Sheils Building**, a former clothing factory, now a series of sweatshops. Cross Market Street and look down two buildings to the right past the Sheils. There you see the **First Chinese Presbyterian Church** mentioned earlier. Originally built in 1817 by the Rutgers family (of Rutgers University fame), it took on the name **The Sea and Land Church** in 1866 when, like the Mariners' Temple, it devoted itself to the needs of wayward seamen.

Cross East Broadway, pass under the Manhattan Bridge, and make a left at Forsyth Street. Walk along the bridge side of the street to Division Street and cross the intersection to the odd triangle-shaped building directly ahead, then on to the Eldridge Street past this building, keeping it on your right. Thirty years ago this part of Eldridge Street was solidly Jewish; fifteen years ago it was Latino. Today, as one can easily detect, it is Chinese. Halfway down the block on the right stands the **Eldridge Street Synagogue**, built in 1886 by Polish Jews. This was the first synagogue built by East European Jews in America and stood as one of the community's major synagogues until the 1930s, when it closed due to dwindling membership.

The exterior design of the building is quite interesting, mixing Moorish, Gothic, and Romanesque styles. Many visitors to this site at first think the building is a converted Christian church because of its form and, in particular, its large rose window usually associated with a Roman Catholic cathedral. But it has never been anything other than a synagogue. Its design reflects both the degree to which the congregation had assimilated American culture and the desire to blend unobtrusively into a predominantly Christian society. Commentator Bill Moyers, the featured speaker on the occasion of the 100th Anniversary Ball for the synagogue, spoke of the symbolism of the facade:

> The configuration of twos, for the tablets of the ten commandments; the three points of the central pediments for the three fathers of Israel, Abraham, Isaac, and Jacob; the four doors for the four daughters, Sarah, Rebecca, Leah, and Rachel; the cluster of five small windows for the five books of Moses; and the twelve roundels of that magnificent rose window, for the twelve tribes of Israel.

The synagogue's interior includes an immense sanctuary and separate women's balconies in an orthodox

Moorish/Sephardic style. Many famous people worshiped here, including entertainer Al Jolson, composer Ira
Gershwin, artist Ben Shahn, actors Edward G. Robinson
and Eddie Cantor, and scientists Dr. Jonas Salk and Linus
Pauling. The synagogue, designated a National Historic
and New York City Landmark, is in the process of being
restored by the Eldridge Street Synagogue Project. Those
wishing to view the interior of the building should call
(212) 219-0888 to make an appointment.

Continue along Eldridge to the corner of **Canal Street**
and turn right. Follow Canal to **Allen Street**, which, like
East Broadway (and Delancey as you will see shortly),
was one of the main thoroughfares of the Jewish Lower
East Side. Allen Street in the late nineteenth and early
twentieth centuries was much narrower than it is today
and the Second Avenue Elevated roared overhead. Dark,
dirty, and noisy, it also acquired a sordid reputation for
being a red-light district.

Crossing Allen and continuing along Canal, your eyes
meet a large building on the right. This is the former
Jarmulowsky Bank, established by Sender Jarmulowsky,
a Jewish immigrant who arrived in the early 1870s. In
an era of small and informal banks, Jarmulowsky's appealed to the Jewish immigrants who felt more secure
placing their hard-earned dollars in a bank owned by a
Jew and staffed by people who spoke Yiddish. Soon his
became one of the most successful immigrant banks in
New York, leading Jarmulowsky to construct this edifice,
which was completed in 1912, the same year he died.
Taken over by his sons, the bank failed in 1914 with the
outbreak of World War I as thousands of immigrant de-
positors staged a "run," demanding gold and silver for
their deposits, which they intended to send to their distressed relatives in Europe. The Jarmulowskys barely escaped over the rooftops as an angry mob gathered outside
their homes. Today, as the signs above the sidewalk indicate, the entire building houses sweatshops.

Continue east down Canal Street until you reach Ludlow Street. Here we find one of the more ingenious businesses on the Lower East Side. Facing Canal Street at no. 41 is the **Hong Kong Funeral Home.** Around the corner at 5 Ludlow is the **Morace Macagna Funeral Home.** Although distinct in location and name, they are in reality the same enterprise operating out of an L-shaped building! One caters to Italian funerals, the other to Chinese.

Back in the nineteenth century, this unique building used to house the Independent Kletzker Brotherly Aid Association, established in 1829. Like dozens of Jewish benevolent societies then and the many family associations in Chinatown now, this one catered to a specific group of Jewish immigrants: East Europeans.

Continuing to the end of Canal Street, you reach **Straus Square**, named for the businessman and philanthropist Nathan Straus, a co-owner of the famous R. H. Macy department store. Straus emerged as a leader of the Jewish community in the early twentieth century and donated large sums of money to philanthropic causes on the Lower East Side. He is most famous for establishing facilities to distribute purified baby milk on the Lower East Side and in poor neighborhoods throughout the country, saving countless lives as a result.

Head to the right to the corner of East Broadway and Rutgers Street to the **Wing Shing** restaurant. Until the mid-1980s this was the Garden Cafeteria, a 24-hour coffee shop and diner frequented by some of this century's most renowned revolutionaries. Bukharin, Trotsky, and Castro all came there to eat cheap food and plot the overthrow of their home governments.

Walk past the Wing Shing and immediately you will see, looming up in front of you, the old ***Daily Forward* building**, built in 1912. The *Forward*, founded by Abraham Cahan in 1897, was the leading Yiddish newspaper during the heyday of the Jewish Lower East Side, and featured a strong socialist and labor editorial stance. By the 1920s it had a circulation of over 200,000—one of the largest in the country for a newspaper in any language. Note the Yiddish word *Forverts* adorning the top of the building.

The *Forward* vacated the building in 1972. Today, the Unification Church uses the lower floors as a church and a Bible factory. Quotes from Christian scripture adorn the building in both Chinese and English writing. Until recently, the upper floors housed sweatshops. For Abraham Cahan, a secularist, socialist, and champion of labor, the fate of his once magnificent building is truly ironic.

Just beyond the *Forward* is the **E. B'way Bakery**, the only surviving Jewish bakery on the street. If you'd like to try some delicious Russian black bread or classic Jewish pastries, this is the place to stop.

Pass the bakery to Jefferson Street. The large, light brown brick edifice on the opposite corner is the **Educational Alliance**, built in 1891 with funds provided by "uptown" German Jews embarrassed by their awkward and unsophisticated immigrant counterparts. The first Jewish settlement housed in the area, its founders hoped it would facilitate the Americanization of newly arrived immigrants by providing classes in English, civics, and hygiene. Today, the Alliance is alive and well, providing training and services to the surrounding Latino, black, and Jewish community.

Directly across to the north side of East Broadway stands the **Seward Park Branch** of the New York Public Library. Built in 1910 with money donated by Andrew Carnegie, it was probably the most heavily used library in all New York City until World War II. Unable to study in their loud and overcrowded tenements, immigrants both young and old came to the library, which stayed open from 6:00 A.M. until 1:00 A.M.

Cross East Broadway to **Seward Park**, built in 1901 and named for William H. Seward, governor of New York in the 1840s and secretary of state in Lincoln's cabinet. During the great cloakmakers strike of 1912, 60,000 striking workers used the park and Straus Square in front of the *Daily Forward* as their rallying point.

Keeping the park on our right, walk west to **Essex Street**. Cross Essex to the west and continue northward. As the store signs indicate, we are entering an area that has managed to retain its Jewish character. At no. 11 we see the **Bezalel Jewish Art Gallery**, owned by an elderly Hungarian-Jewish couple who survived the Holocaust. Visitors are welcome to enter and view the works on display.

Note the other stores selling religious goods. Jews from the neighborhood and throughout the city looking for prayer shawls and skull caps come to **Zelig Blumenthal's** religious article shop (no. 13). A few doors down we find **Weinfeld's Skull Cap Mfg.** (no. 19). More than one hundred years old, it is the oldest such factory in the neighborhood. The proprietor, Mr. Weinfeld, is the great-grandson of the founder. He is currently training his son to carry on the business when he retires.

At Hester Street, on the north side at no. 51, is the **Kadouri Import Corporation**, a marvelous place for obtaining dried fruit, nuts, and spices. Next door is a fabulous bakery, **Gertel's**, where one can get some of the best Jewish bread and pastry in New York. All the food is kosher and delicious. Don't hold back!

Continue north along Essex Street. On the left-hand side is one of the last pickle shops on the Lower East Side. The famous **Guss's Pickles**, featured in the movie *Crossing Delancey*, offers a wide variety of pickles and pickled vegetables. Years ago there were dozens of such shops in the area featuring wooden barrels and far cheaper prices. Today, people came from all over on Sundays and stand in lines of twenty people or more to buy Guss's famous fare.

Head back to Essex and turn left, continuing on to Grand Street. At the intersection of these two streets on the northwest corner sits the **Seward Park Public High School**, the most racially and ethnically integrated school in New York. Actor Walter Matthau attended high school here.

Originally the Essex Market Court House and Ludlow

Street Jail occupied this site. The warden who ran the jail allowed prisoners to bribe their way into better accommodations: The most celebrated resident at the jail, "Boss" William Tweed of the Tammany Hall political machine, lived in a two-room cell complete with window boxes of flowers and a piano. Unfortunately for Tweed, even these comforts were not enough and he died there in 1878 while serving a sentence for embezzlement of public funds.

Farther north along Essex, about halfway between Grand and Broome streets, you come upon a plaque mounted high on the wall to your right surrounding a recreation area. This was the former site of Sinsheimer's Cafe and it was here, as the plaque indicates, that the **B'nai B'rith** was founded on October 13, 1843. The German Jews who established the protective association did so in reaction to the rising anti-immigrant sentiment in the city. One year later, New York elected James W. Harper (of later publishing fame) mayor on a staunchly nativist platform, pledging among other things to increase the period of naturalization for immigrants from five to twenty-one years. Since the nativist wrath was focused primarily on Irish Catholics, one might ask why a small community of Jews would found the B'nai B'rith. The answer is clear: they feared they might be next.

On the northwest corner of Broome and Essex is the **Isner Bros. Clothing Outlet**, at 75 Essex. Originally the Good Samaritan Dispensary, it served as one of the busiest hospitals in the city in the late nineteenth and early twentieth centuries. Directly opposite the hospital to the north is the beginning of the **Essex Street Retail Market**. The city built it in the 1930s to accommodate vendors after Mayor Fiorello La Guardia decided to ban pushcart peddlers from the city streets. The market runs for three blocks and is still in operation today, though as a mere shadow of its former glory. Interestingly, Mayor Ed Koch also battled to restrict street vendors during his administration in the 1980s.

Recross Essex Street and head west down Broome toward the establishment named **Wolsk's**. You are now approaching one of the finest chocolate shops in the city, offering chocolate and other candy at wholesale prices.

Continue west on Broome another block to **Orchard Street** and make a right. At the turn of the century, Orchard was one of the city's busiest streets, teeming with pushcarts full of household goods and food products. Close your eyes and imagine the loud noises that daily filled the air—merchants hawking their wares, shoppers haggling over prices, pushcart men arguing over who was first at a key selling location. And imagine the smells, from the good—bread, soup, and cooked meats—to the not-so-good—rotting vegetables and horse manure.

Today Orchard Street is still a place of bargains, but a far more pristine setting. Crammed with mostly wholesale shops and outlets, you can buy anything here at cut-rate prices. On weekends the street above Delancey is closed to traffic, and merchants and peddlers—sometimes friendly and sometimes haughty, but distinctly Lower East Side—display their wares for wandering bargain hunters to peruse.

At 97 Orchard Street on the left is the **Lower East Side Tenement Museum.** Built in 1863, the tenement was used to house thousands of immigrants from over twenty-five different nations. The museum was chartered in 1988 and the restoration of the tenement to its original turn-of-the-century condition is ongoing. When completed, the museum intends to offer a "living history" experience with actors and actresses portraying some of the many immigrants who occupied the building. Currently the museum offers a wide variety of programs and exhibits and is well worth a short visit. You may wish to call ahead before arriving. The number is (212) 431-0233.

At the end of Orchard you come to **Delancey Street**, made famous by the aforementioned movie *Crossing Delancey*. The street got its name from the Delanceys, a very wealthy family that owned most of the area as a farm at the time of the American Revolution. Unfortunately for the Delanceys, they backed the wrong horse and like most other Tories had all their property confiscated by the Americans. Only the name has endured.

Proceed west on Delancey to Allen Street. At the southeast corner of these streets stands a large building adorned with tall Doric columns in front. This was once the site of the **Hebrew Publishing Company**, and during the first half of this century it was the largest Hebrew- and Yiddish-language press in the world.

Farther west on Delancey at Forsyth Street is a large mural on the right, championing the cause of Puerto Rican independence, indicating another Latino enclave in the Lower East Side. Further evidence of this can be seen on the southeast corner of Forsyth and Delancey, where a rather garish-looking maroon-and-beige building stands. Originally a Baptist church, it later became one of the most important Jewish synagogues of the Lower East Side. The synagogue owned and rented the row of stores on the street level along Delancey to provide income to the synagogue; a skillful combination of God and Mammon. Today the building is occupied by a **Seventh-Day Adventist church** servicing a predominantly Dominican congregation.

As you continue along Delancey you come to the **Sara Delano Roosevelt Park**, which runs for seven blocks between Forsyth and Chrystie streets. Named for FDR's mother, the park was built in 1936 on the former site of dozens of run-down tenement houses. In the park to the south you can see the old public bathhouses, erected in an effort to improve the sanitary conditions of the neighborhood.

Moving on from here, walk ahead along Delancey to the Bowery. In the nineteenth century, New Yorkers who wanted a fast-paced nightlife headed for the Bowery, one of the city's most famous night-club districts. Bars, theaters, and dance halls lined the avenue, and at night the place buzzed with activity. The Bowery served as the poor man's Broadway, offering cheap theater, cheap booze, cheap eats, and cheap sex. Rivals of the Five Points gangs roamed the sidewalks looking for fights and/or young women. The most famous of these were the Bowery Boys, whose confident swagger and flashy style of dress made them easy to spot. The Bowery brought together the many ethnic groups of the Lower East Side who nightly poured in from their surrounding neighborhoods. It also gave unprecedented freedom to the young women who frequented the dance halls and bars after work. After World War I the Bowery began a decline that continued until only a few years ago.

At the Bowery, walk one block south and take a right again onto Broome Street and walk another block west to **Elizabeth Street.** On the northeast corner of Broome and Elizabeth at no. 354, we see a very solid redbrick building with a granite foundation. Constructed in the early twentieth century as the **Knickerbocker Ice House**, it provided ice for individuals and businesses in the era before refrigeration. Perhaps the most interesting fact about the building is that the term "iced" (i.e., murdered) was coined here. Very often mobsters brought their victims here and kept them on ice until safe disposal of the body could be arranged. Today, like many other magnificent structures in the Lower East Side, it has been transformed into condominiums. One of their strongest selling points is that many of the units are separated by walls eight feet thick!

Gaze up at the northwest corner on Elizabeth and notice an excellent example of "dumbbell tenement." The name comes from the fact that, viewed from the top, this type of tenement, with indentations in the middle, resembles the shape of a dumbbell. This design, which became the dominant form of tenement after 1879, came about as a result of a law passed in that same year requiring all new tenements to have ventilation and light in every room. The indentations created a small airshaft between adjacent dumbbell tenements. Though an improvement over earlier designs, the dumbbell law proved to be a failure. First, it did not apply to existing buildings; and second, residents used the airshafts to dispose of trash and the contents of chamber pots. Indeed, the dumbbell may have created worse health conditions for the people it was intended to protect.

A short distance ahead on the other side of Broome stands an old church named the **Holy Trinity Ukrainian Orthodox Cathedral.** If you look closely at its facing above the door you can see the vague outline of the church's name, Church of San Salvatore. Strange as it may seem, this was never an Italian Roman Catholic church. Rather, it was built by the Episcopal diocese of New York at the turn of the century to attract Italian Catholic converts by offering Italian priests and Italian-language Mass. Many Italian Catholics, resenting their status as a basement congregation within Irish parishes like Transfiguration, broke with tradition and joined Protestant churches.

As San Salvatore indicates, you are now entering the outskirts of **Little Italy.** Italians began arriving in New York City in small numbers in the 1870s and by 1880 they numbered almost 20,000. Just twenty years later 220,000 Italians lived in New York and by 1910 the numbers had risen to 545,000. The vast majority of those arriving after 1880 came from southern Italy, which lagged far behind the north in levels of education and industrialization. Mostly poor farmers fleeing earthquakes, droughts, high taxes, and overpopulation, these Italians took the place of the Irish as the city's broad-shouldered labor force. They built many of the tenement houses nearby, as well as roads, buildings, and subways throughout the city.

Italians, however, differed from other immigrants in one respect: many, perhaps a majority, migrated with no intent of settling permanently in America. As a result, nearly two thirds of the Italians arriving before 1910 were men. A majority of these "birds of passage" took advantage of the faster transatlantic voyage made possible by powerful ocean liners and traveled back and forth between Italy and America. Like the Irish and the Jews, they sent millions of dollars to their families in Italy. Further evidence of their lack of roots in America is revealed in the fact that only 15,000 of the 545,000 Italians living in New York in 1910 were registered voters.

Nonetheless, many of those who vowed to return never did. They remained to establish a series of thriving ethnic enclaves, or Little Italys, in the city. The Little Italy where we stand today is but a mere shadow of its former self. In the late nineteenth and early twentieth centuries it pulsated with people, noises, smells, and sights, much like Chinatown does today. Only a sentimental remnant of the old Italian enclave remains. Note how different it is from Chinatown—quiet, clean, and still. Its main businesses are food and tourism. Within a generation, it is unlikely that Little Italy will withstand the pressure of the expanding Chinatown.

Now journey ahead, stopping in front of 378 Broome, the **Church of the Holy Crucifix**. This church, constructed in 1926, provides a fine example of the typical Italian immigrant's view of his or her stay in America. Because many fully intended to return to Italy, they did not see the need to build an ornate and expensive monument. Moreover, in Italy the government gave financial support to the Church and Italians who came to America lacked a strong tradition of making regular donations to their parishes. Made of simple brick and mortar construction, Holy Crucifix more than fulfilled the needs of the area. Compare it to the elaborate style of the former Church of San Salvatore—that church was built by wealthy Episcopalians, *not* Italian immigrants. Today the church has adapted to its new environment and features masses in Italian, English, and Chinese every Sunday.

Across the street at **no. 375** stands a restored tenement, originally built around 1885. Notice the bust peering out of the cornice at the top. One rumor claims that the figure is Moses and was placed there by the Jewish builder to glower over the Catholic church. To back up this claim, they note the terra-cotta stars of David that adorn the facing. But this cannot be true, given the dates of construction and the fact that turn-of-the-century architects often used stars of David as decoration with no Jewish connection. Other, more credible, sources say that the figure could be the Italian hero Garibaldi or the Roman god Neptune, but it is just as likely that he is no one in particular.

Ahead at the corner of Mulberry and Broome is **Caffe Roma**, one of the finest places in Little Italy to get sinfully delicious Italian pastry and cappuccino.

Take a right at Mott Street and walk up to Kenmare Street. Make another right and walk to Elizabeth Street, where just in from the northeast corner at **166 Elizabeth** stands a tenement with walls adorned by sculptures of Roman goddesses. This tenement probably reflects the work of the skilled Italian stonecutters who lived and worked on the Lower East Side.

Farther on at the northeast corner of Elizabeth and Spring streets is a large warehouse. Unoccupied and in disrepair, it is waiting for something to happen. It is likely that it will be bought in the near future, perhaps by Chinese entrepreneurs, and converted into condominiums.

As you cross Spring Street and continue along Elizabeth, evidence of Chinese penetration into this area is clear, especially in the form of signs in Chinese characters above new businesses. Halfway down the block, you come upon the **Elizabeth Street Garden**, an outdoor gallery featuring statues, fountains, and ornaments for sale. These items, authentic eighteenth- and nineteenth-century sculptures, are not cheap and clearly are aimed at the upscale market of young professionals needing to decorate their recently purchased condos nearby or their weekend homes on Long Island. The office across the street welcomes inquiries.

Sculpture garden on Elizabeth Street

Another example of change in this neighborhood is directly across the street from the garden. **The Connecticut Muffin Co**. is a modern bakery that provides muffins to hundreds of restaurants across the city. Walking north up the street to the left is the aged, but still functioning, **La Rosa and Son Bread Co.**, which bakes traditional Italian breads for local consumption.

One tradition that still lives on in Little Italy occurs every September two blocks over on Mulberry Street: the annual San Gennaro festival. Held in honor of San Gennaro, the patron saint of Naples, it brings thousands of New Yorkers into Little Italy for bright lights, food, entertainment, and more food. Cars are forbidden on Mulberry from Columbus Park to Spring Street and lights and tinsel are draped overhead to decorate the thoroughfare. The smells of Italian sausages, pizza, and fried dough fill the air as do the cries of the vendors selling them.

At the corner of Prince and Elizabeth there is a tea room bakery called **La Poeme**. It is the only Corsican restaurant in New York City and features wonderful fare.

Turn west on Prince Street and walk one block to Mott. As you walk notice the rectangular cobblestones used to pave the road. New Yorkers used to call them "Belgian stones," because they came from Belgian ships that used them for ballast in the eighteenth and early nineteenth centuries. When the ships arrived to take on their cargo, they dumped the stones at the head of Manhattan, and the city government then used them as paving stones. During the 1850s they became known as "Irish confetti" due to the frequent riotous behavior of Irish immigrants in their clashes with the police or other immigrant groups.

Make a right onto Mott Street and walk until you approach the **14th Ward Industrial School of the Children's Aid Society**. Constructed from funds donated by fur and real estate magnate John Jacob Astor III, the building stands as a fine example of Victorian Gothic-style architecture and was completed in 1889. The society, founded in 1853 by missionary Charles Loring Brace, was the first organization in America dedicated to aiding indigent children. The school instructed young Italian immigrant children in the "three R's" as well as mechanical arts to make them productive workers. The building now houses cooperative apartments.

Across the street is **Old St. Patrick's Cathedral** and cemetery. Built between 1809 and 1815 by Irish Catholics, it served as the diocese's main cathedral until the completion of the new St. Patrick's on Fifth Avenue in 1879. The plain facade and lack of ornamentation obscure the fact that, before it was rebuilt in 1868 following a disastrous fire, St. Patrick's represented one of the earliest attempts at Gothic architecture in America. Halfway between the top of the central columns and the apex of the facade there used to be a large window, and above that rose a tower topped with a spire. After the fire, the diocese chose a simple restoration, due to a lack of funds.

The wall surrounding the cathedral recalls the era of violent anti-Catholic nativism. On more than one occasion, Archbishop Hughes rallied armed Irish Catholics to circle the cathedral grounds to protect it from nativist mobs that threatened to burn it down. Below your feet are catacombs—tunnels where parishioners were buried in the walls to protect their remains from grave robbers and acts of vandalism. Once or twice a year a priest leads a group on a tour through the tunnels.

Pierre Toussaint, the black layman and former slave who in the early nineteenth century established a wide reputation in the city for his works of charity, was buried in the adjacent cemetery. Currently considering him for sainthood, the Church had Toussaint's remains exhumed and sent to Rome to undergo the ancient beatification ritual of inspection. If his bones pass muster, Toussaint will be the American Catholic Church's first black saint, adding to St. Patrick's list of "first" American saints: Elizabeth Seton, the first American-born saint, founded the cathedral's school, the oldest Catholic school in the city. John

Noyman, the first American male saint, was ordained a priest there.

We are now at the end of our tour. If you haven't gotten your fill from the dim sum, bialys, chocolates, black bread, and other ethnic fare along the way, perhaps now is a good time to stop at one of the many "Original Ray's," near the corner of Mott and Prince, for a delicious slice of authentic New York pizza. Whatever the effects of centuries of immigration on New York, it certainly will never leave you hungry.

James P. Shenton has served as professor of history at Columbia University since 1951, teaching Civil War, Reconstruction, Segregation and Racism, Peace in the American Tradition, and the History of New York. He has led seminars on America for the National Endowment for the Humanities and has conducted walking tours for twenty-five years. He is currently developing a history of food in New York, from 1892 to the present, with the New York Public Library.

Edward T. O'Donnell is a graduate student of Professor Shenton's American history courses at Columbia University. He is currently working on his dissertation based on politics and the labor movement in New York City during the 1880s. He conducts a wide variety of tours of Manhattan through his company Big Onion Walking Tours, (212)439-1090.

Old St. Patrick's Cathedral

Walk · 3

Historic
Greenwich Village

TERRY MILLER

The Washington Square Arch

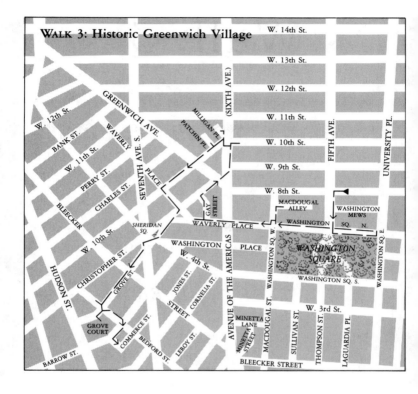

WALK 3: Historic Greenwich Village

W. 14th St.

W. 13th St.

W. 12th St.

W. 11th St.

W. 10th St.

W. 9th St.

W. 8th St.

GREENWICH AVE.

W. 12th St.

BANK ST.

WAVERLY ST.

W. 11th St.

PERRY ST.

CHARLES ST.

BLEECKER

W. 10th St.

SEVENTH AVE. S.

PLACE

MILLIGAN PL.

PATCHIN PL.

(SIXTH AVE.)

FIFTH AVE.

UNIVERSITY PL.

GAY STREET

SHERIDAN SQ.

WAVERLY PLACE

MACDOUGAL ALLEY

WASHINGTON

WASHINGTON MEWS

WASHINGTON SQ. N.

HUDSON ST.

CHRISTOPHER ST.

WASHINGTON

W. 4th St.

GROVE ST.

JONES ST.

CORNELIA ST.

STREET

GROVE COURT

COMMERCE ST.

BEDFORD ST.

LEROY ST.

PLACE

AVENUE OF THE AMERICAS

WASHINGTON SQ. W.

MACDOUGAL ST.

SULLIVAN ST.

THOMPSON ST.

LAGUARDIA PL.

WASHINGTON SQUARE

WASHINGTON SQ. S.

WASHINGTON SQ. E.

W. 3rd St.

MINETTA LANE

MINETTA STREET

BARROW ST.

BLEECKER STREET

Starting Point: Fifth Avenue at Eighth Street
Walk Length: 2¹/₂ to 3 hours
Subway Stop: Eighth Street (N or R trains); Astor Place (6 train); West Fourth Street (A, B, C, D, E, or F train, use Eighth Street exits)

Unlike many of New York's world-famous attractions, Greenwich Village doesn't try to impress or overwhelm. It doesn't have to.

The pleasures of Greenwich Village are intimate, and the pace is leisurely. There's a special feeling you can sense here, an exhilarating reverie fostered by the connections between Greenwich Village and its artists, writers, and actors.

Greenwich Village is part of American mythology, but it is hardly a place lost in the past. The Village is very much alive today—a community of residents aware of their neighborhood's heritage and of the visitors who make this their spiritual home. While walking through historic Greenwich Village, don't lose touch with the Village of the present, or you'll miss half the fun. Of course, you may spot behavior or a manner of dress that seems odd (or even outlandish!). Keep in mind that it represents a personal statement or an honest expression of someone's feelings, and not an affront. Should the occasion warrant, a warm smile of goodwill goes a long way.

Greenwich Village seems isolated from the rest of Manhattan—and actually once was. A natural marsh originally separated New Amsterdam from the fertile land two miles north. What became Greenwich Village began as farmland, the chief crop being tobacco. The land passed from the Indians to the Dutch and later to the British. Large estates were built as wealthy landowners expanded their holdings, but few of these estates remained intact after the landowners' deaths. Over two centuries, the process of assembling and dividing property worked in concert with the local topography to produce the broad outlines of the present street grid of Greenwich Village.

In 1804 the marsh to the south was drained by a canal (built on what is now Canal Street). This made it easier for New Yorkers to travel north to the Village of Greenwich, and just in time! Since the 1790s, a series of yellow fever epidemics prompted New Yorkers to abandon the city in summer, taking refuge in Greenwich Village. In time, improved sanitary conditions in the city reduced the threat of the disease, but by then Greenwich Village was well on its way to settlement. Estates that had been cut into farms were further divided and subdivided into street blocks and property lots. By the close of the 1820s, Greenwich Village had assumed its present layout. Many of the structures that were built along these unpaved Village streets are still standing today.

The decades following the 1820s have left their mark on Village streets, leaving them far from uniform. There are the six-story tenements of the 1890s, the carriage houses of the 1910s, the stylish apartment towers of the 1920s, and their unstylish counterparts from the 1960s. Any Village block may offer a jumble of such styles and periods and yet, by some alchemy, it usually retains a sense of architectural harmony. Physically, Greenwich

Village exhibits both diversity and individuality, qualities that engender an attitude toward life known as the "Village Mentality."

This walk is designed to take in familiar Village spots (for example, Washington Square) and to feature as well some enclaves off the beaten path. Any two and one-half hour Village walk inevitably leaves large sections unexplored. You may choose to wander beyond our twenty-block route, or to return to any of the restaurants you may spot along the way.

One word of caution: public restrooms in this residential area are few (actually, just about nonexistent). There are no major hotels in Greenwich Village and even the public library here provides no public facilities. However, the Village is laced with cafés, restaurants, and bars. You may be able to prevail upon a cashier or bartender or, better still, you may elect to pause in the walk for a break. This may add to the tour time, but it's another way to enjoy the ambience of Greenwich Village.

We will begin our walk by approaching Washington Square from the north, starting at Fifth Avenue and Eighth Street. Fifth Avenue buses stop at this corner, but the nearest subway stops are a short distance away. From the West Fourth Street station on the A, B, C, D, E, or F lines, use the Eighth Street exits and walk east (with the flow of car traffic) along Eighth Street to Fifth Avenue. If you prefer, you may take the N or R train to the Eighth Street station and walk west along Eighth Street to Fifth Avenue. Both of these options involve the same amount of walking, while the Astor Place station on the no. 6 line is one block east of the N/R Eighth Street station.

A more direct approach is on a downtown Fifth Avenue bus (#2, 3, or 5 only)—be sure to have a token for the fare or the exact fare in coins. The bus will turn onto Eighth Street from Fifth Avenue, and as you step from the bus, turn right. A few steps will bring you to Fifth Avenue and a view of Washington Square Arch.

As you walk toward the arch you follow the path of Minetta Brook, one of several streams that once drained Manhattan Island. In the 1820s, Minetta Brook was channeled underground to permit development of this area. The brook served as a property line for several estates and farms in the earliest years of Greenwich Village, and some Village property lines reflect the course of the brook to this day.

Some Villagers believe Minetta Brook is still part of the present man-made underground drainage system. You can decide for yourself by crossing Fifth Avenue and looking through the lobby window of **no. 2**. Between the lobby entrance and the bank on the corner, the management of this 1950 apartment building has set up a tall tube that encloses a spray of water. Depending on your susceptibility to legend, this is—or isn't—Minetta Brook on tap.

Return across Fifth Avenue (carefully!—you are midblock) for a glimpse of **Washington Mews**. Your view may be restricted by a closed gate, since the mews is privately owned, both the houses and the alley itself.

This cobblestone alley, built in 1831, provided Washington Square's elegant houses with access to their private stables or carriage houses. With the rise of the automobile at the beginning of this century, these unheated one- and two-story structures fell into disuse. Many were rented to artists who were willing to endure cold and any lingering equine scent, simply because the rent was cheap.

The original stables were built only on the north side of the mews, on your left. Those across the alley stand where private gardens once grew—one garden for each of the thirteen houses fronting the square. Of these structures, **nos. 11 and 15** replaced their gardens with additional stables as early as the 1840s or 1850s. The uniform row of buildings on your right, nearest to you—**nos. 1–10**—appeared as recently as 1939. Fortunately, they maintain the intimate scale of the rest of the mews. Several original stables on your left bear the mark of rebuilding over the years, but **nos. 54–62** retain much of their original 1831 appearance.

The scent of horses is long gone from Washington Mews, and so is the cheap rent. Most interiors here have been renovated more than once, and several are now quite dazzling. You may notice that the address numbers of the north side (nos. 42–62) aren't in keeping with those on the south (nos. 1–16). In the late nineteenth century, those on the north adopted the address numbers of the houses they backed on Eighth Street (then known as Clinton Place), which had a numbering sequence all its own. The structures on your right generally reflect the numbers of the Washington Square Row houses standing behind them.

A few steps south of the mews is a small, Greek-style portico. This serves as the entrance to **7–13 Washington Square North**, which is a 1939 apartment building hidden behind the facades of former row houses. Glance up and you will see the separate wings of the back of the building, rather than the continuous back wall of seven houses. If all had gone as planned, this reconstruction was to have claimed the row house facades as well, but Village protests edged the property owner into this less drastic solution.

Continue to the corner. **Washington Square** is now spread out before you, its nine and one-half acres dominated by the famous arch. The square was once a marshy lowland fed by Minetta Brook on its way to the Hudson River. By 1797, the marsh was in use by the city of New York as a potter's field and a final resting place for yellow fever victims. Other burials were those of condemned criminals, hung by the neck until death on the sturdy lower branches of the "Hanging Elm" (this famous tree is still growing here in the square—as we will soon see). There are, by some estimates, as many as 22,000 people buried for one reason or another beneath the present Washington Square.

Hangings here were stopped in 1819 and all burials were discontinued in 1826. The area was becoming residential, leading the city to landscape the marsh and open it in 1828 as the Washington Military Parade Ground. The first in a succession of fountains was installed in 1851, by which time the parade ground had evolved into a park. Washington Square has been redesigned several times since then, and today reflects the landscaping design of a 1970 renovation.

The most famous symbol of Greenwich Village is **Washington Memorial Arch**, but the present arch is not the original. Today's arch is the marble successor to a temporary wooden arch built for the 1889 centennial of George Washington's inauguration. Both versions of the arch were designed by celebrated architect Stanford White—a native Villager who was born on nearby Tenth Street.

The wooden arch stood north of the present arch, spanning Fifth Avenue more or less where the present apartment portico is located. The arch was illuminated with hundreds of small incandescent bulbs and proved to be the hit of the centennial festivities. Within days there was talk of a permanent arch, and over the next year that talk turned into reality. Ground was broken in May 1890 for the present arch, which was completed two years later. Its site within the square was chosen so as to prevent any interference with Fifth Avenue traffic. Ironically, Fifth Avenue traffic was soon interfering with the arch. Traffic was run south into the square through the arch, and Fifth Avenue buses used the square to turn around in for the trip back uptown. Old photos and a few movies preserve views of Washington Square as it looked before bus traffic was banned there in 1963.

But the damage had already been done. Traffic pollution is often cited as having caused the decay of the two statues of George Washington that grace the north

Entrance to Washington Mews

"Washington in Peace," north face of the arch

face of the arch. *Washington in War*, standing on the pier on your left as you face the arch, is a 1916 work by Hermon A. MacNeil. On the west pier is *Washington in Peace*, sculpted in 1918 by A. Stirling Calder. Cross Washington Square North for a closer look and you will see that both works are in serious disrepair, particularly about the face. However, Calder's signature is still clearly legible on the base of his creation, near Washington's left foot. Studies are now under way to determine whether the statues can be saved; if not, they may go into storage and be replaced on the arch with replicas.

Inspect the carved decoration of the arch, in which the letter *W* is a motif. Also, notice the marble American eagle set atop the keystone of both the north and south faces of the arch. Few people are aware that, behind the eagle, the massive span of the archway is hollow—permitting it to stand on former marshland. An empty chamber is hidden within the arch, which can be reached by way of a stairwell inside the west pier. A miniature Alice-in-Wonderland door there opens to the stairs that lead to the hidden chamber and then up to the roof of the arch. These 110 steps are unlit and very precarious, and so the door is always kept securely locked.

The security system was far less secure in 1917, when the roof of the arch was made the setting of the declaration of Village independence. At that time, most New Yorkers were joining the nation in edging the United States into World War I. The Villagers, however, preferred the isolationism that had been, until then, the policy espoused by President Wilson. One of these antiwar Villagers was a sharp-witted art student named Gertrude Drick, up from Texas to study with painter John Sloan. Drick managed to get into the arch one night, bringing Sloan, his friend and fellow artist Marcel Duchamp, and three friends who were actors at the nearby Provincetown Playhouse theater company. Once on the roof of the arch, the six revolutionaries fired cap guns and proclaimed the Village to be the Independent Republic of Washington Square, free of all ties to uptown. After they had all gotten suitably drunk, they left. The balloons they had tied to the arch roof were all that could be seen the next morning to hint that anything at all had happened. The Drick Rebellion was primarily a prank, but it's also a vivid illustration of Greenwich Village iconoclasm. So far as is known, this declaration of Village independence has never been rescinded.

Another 1890 work by Stanford White provides the ideal counterpart for his arch. **Judson Memorial Church** stands on Washington Square South, across the square from the arch. Judson was founded to foster community support of recent immigrants, but, since the 1950s, the church has become better known as a bastion of the arts. Plays and dance events have often filled its main hall, and art shows have graced its walls. Judson's activism is displayed in the glass case mounted outside, next to the main entrance. Pedestrians have seen statements and quotations here in support of abortion rights and gay rights, and in opposition to sexism, racism, and the Vietnam War.

Adjacent **Judson Hall** and its accompanying ten-story tower were once owned by the church, but they are now part of New York University. Individual landmark status has been conferred on both the church and the hall, and neither can legally be altered without permission from New York City's Landmarks Preservation Commission. The same is true of the two thousand structures within the Greenwich Village Historic District, established in 1969 and including every building and street mentioned in our walk.

As you face Fifth Avenue, the original Washington Square Row runs to your right for one block. The row can be seen from here, beside the arch, but you may enjoy a closer look. Stroll along the park sidewalk, then, at the end of the block, cross Washington Square North and walk back to Fifth Avenue along the row.

These thirteen houses, **1–13 Washington Square North**, have been cited by the Landmarks Commission as "the most important and imposing block front of early nineteenth century town houses in the city." This graceful row was planned as one unit and built jointly by John Johnston, John Morrison, and James Boorman—who were also the original residents of nos. 7, 9, and 13, respectively.

As we have seen, each house in this row held property that extended back across Washington Mews. Together, these property lots were part of a larger property, the farm of Robert Richard Randall. This farm ran north as far as the present Tenth Street, and more or less between Fifth and Fourth avenues. Randall died in 1801, leaving a will stating that his farm was to be used to provide shelter for aged and destitute sailors. Randall's trustees had other ideas. They sensed an imminent rise in local property values, a belief that was verified in 1807 when Broadway was extended north across the new Canal Street to the edge of the Randall farm. The trustees decided the farm could provide the requisite shelter without actually being the location of it. Accordingly, the estate began leasing the use of the land (rather than selling it off), and the proceeds went into creating the Sailor's Snug Harbor, built on Staten Island in 1831. The estate still owns the former farmland, and now owns the Washington Square Row houses as well. The estate elected to rebuild nos. 7–13 as one apartment house, and, in a 1949 agreement, it chose to lease nos. 1–6 to New York University, through the year 2002.

Washington Square Row was home to many of the city's elite through the nineteenth century, including its three joint builders. Numbers 1, 10, 12 were each home to a mayor of New York; the neighbors were merchant-princes, financiers, and statesmen. Number 2 was the last home of America's first fully-trained architect, Richard Morris Hunt, who died here in 1895. Numbers 7 and 11 were owned by descendants of their original owners until 1935. Number 6 was the last house in the row that was home to a resident owner; it was also the only one, as of 1950 when the owner died, that has kept the original 1831 interior intact. The house has undergone little change since the 1949 agreement that made it part of New York University. Today it is NYU's Graduate School of Arts & Sciences.

One of New York's leading cultural institutions, the Metropolitan Museum of Art, has its origins in the row. John Taylor Johnston, the son of John Johnston (one of the builders of the row), was married in his father's home at no. 7, and in 1856 built himself a house around the corner on Fifth Avenue—now the site of the corner bank. He assembled a personal art collection on the second floor of his stable on Eighth Street, behind his house. The collection was to become one of New York City's finest, and as the city then had no public art museum, Johnston opened his stable to the public on Thursday afternoons. From these humble beginnings grew the world-renowned Metropolitan Museum of Art, organized in 1870 with John Taylor Johnston as its first president and his art collection as the first holdings of the museum.

Washington Square Row retains a uniformity of style while still allowing for individuality. Number 1 has a columned side porch on University Place; stone lions grace the entrance of no. 6; nos. 7–13 are wider than their neighbors to the east (since eight houses were planned and only seven were built); and no. 13 lacks a front stoop, which was removed in 1872 when the house was joined to no. 12.

Most noticeable are the alterations of no. 3, which was rebuilt in 1884 into artists' studios. These studios served as the homes and workplaces of Rockwell Kent, Ernest Lawson, Walter Pach, William Glackens, and Edward Hopper—who died here in 1966.

Walk across Fifth Avenue and continue along Washington Square North. The modern row houses on your right seem to mimic the modest scale of their more elegant neighbors. Actually, these houses are a wing of 2 Fifth Avenue. As planned in 1950, the apartment tower was to abut the square rudely. Protesting Villagers again interceded, and these low-level houses were the compromise. In the building process, several stylish old row houses were lost.

A few steps farther along, the entrance to an underground garage marks the **site of 19 Washington Square North**; the actual house was demolished in 1950. In the 1840s, no. 19 was the home of Henry James's grandmother, Elizabeth Walsh. The house was built for her in 1836 and remained her home until her death ten years later. Young Henry was still a child at the time; he was born in 1843 across the park on Washington Place East.

Town houses along Washington Square North

Henry lived with his parents on nearby Fourteenth Street and had many occasions to stroll through the square and gaze at the door to no. 19. Years later, in England, Henry James returned to the house in his imagination, and used it as the setting of his novel, *Washington Square*. This 1881 tale established the writer's reputation and gave American readers their first awareness of Washington Square.

Just beyond the site of no. 19 stands . . . no. 19! This apparent contradiction is explained by the fact that the houses on this stretch of Washington Square North were renumbered in the late nineteenth century.

20 Washington Square North is both the widest original house on the square and the oldest. Begun in 1828, it was the first house constructed on the north side of the square, within a few weeks of the square's formal opening. When completed the following year, its splendid isolation enhanced its grandeur—it was already pretty grand, as its thirty-seven-foot width provided considerable frontage on the square. Number 20 became even wider in 1880 when an extension was built that increased its frontage to fifty feet. The line running from basement to roofline, between the last two windows on your left, marks the point at which the added section begins.

Continue to the corner, noting the Greek Revival houses at **21–26 Washington Square North**. They offer gentle variations on the style established with the 1831 row we have just seen. Before continuing across MacDougal Street, turn right at the corner for a half-block detour to MacDougal Alley.

Like Washington Mews, **MacDougal Alley** was built as an access route to stables and carriage houses. Unlike the mews, both sides of the alley were originally lined with stables; those on the south side served houses on Washington Square North and those across the alley served Clinton Place (Eighth Street). Another difference: the alley has always been entered only from MacDougal Street, while the mews is accessible from either end. MacDougal Alley's address numbers are a bit more confusing than those of the mews. As you look through the gate into the alley, the addresses on your right begin logically enough as nos. 6, 8, 10, and 12 (nos. 2 and 4 were demolished for the neighboring apartment building). However, no. 12 is followed by nos. 22, 21, 20, and 19. Numbers on your left begin with no. 1 and run as odd numbers through no. 15, followed by nos. 15½, 17½, and, in a final burst of eccentricity, 17½ (also known as no. 19 and as no. 19½!).

MacDougal Alley has numerous connections with the cultural community. **12 MacDougal Alley** was the studio used at different times by painters Ernest Lawson and Guy Pène du Bois, and by sculptor Jo Davidson—the house was known as no. 23 at the time. The studio next to the alley entrance, above **no. 1**, was home to Edwin

Arlington Robinson, who here worked on one of the poems that won him the 1928 Pulitzer Prize, "Tristram."

The most important connection between the alley and the arts was the residency of Gertrude Vanderbilt Whitney. A great-granddaughter of Cornelius Vanderbilt, Gertrude was thirty when she separated from her husband and decided to try her hand at sculpting. By 1907, she was installed in the studio she created from an old stable, **17½ MacDougal Alley** (the multinumbered one, known in 1907 as no. 19). Her neighbors here were fellow artists with shaky finances, people Gertrude decided to support by buying their works. By 1929, Gertrude Vanderbilt Whitney owned some six hundred pieces by such new American masters as John Sloan, Jo Davidson, Robert Henri, and William Glackens. She decided these works should be accessible to art lovers, and approached the Metropolitan Museum of Art to negotiate an arrangement. The Met had little interest in these works and declined the offer, which annoyed Gertrude. She decided to make her collection the nucleus of a new museum, one that recognized the value of American artists. The result was the Whitney Museum, now located on the Upper East Side. The Whitney opened in three row houses on Eighth Street directly behind Gertrude's MacDougal Alley studio. The original 1932 Whitney building was the home of the museum for twenty-two years, until a larger space was needed for the expanded collection. The first home of the Whitney still stands at **8 West Eighth Street**, one door away from the site of the stable where the Metropolitan Museum of Art started in 1870.

Now retrace your steps back to Washington Square. At the corner, Waverly Place extends to your right, but before turning that corner take a moment to look diagonally across the street intersection toward the square. This is the best spot to view the **Hanging Elm**.

This giant English elm is well over three hundred years old—probably the oldest living tree on Manhattan Island. At seventy feet high, it towers over other trees in

133

the square. Notice the horizontal branches that give this elm its unique place in Village history. They were ideal for use by the neighborhood hangman, Daniel Megie, from 1797 through 1819.

Megie lived in a two-story wooden shack that stood where today's Washington Square South intersects Thompson Street. Megie didn't have far to go to get to work—the Hanging Elm was nearby, as was an old German cemetery opened circa 1800 where Washington Square Arch now stands. Even closer to home for Megie were the trenches on the south side of the square, where bodies were buried in yellow sheets, indicating the disease that claimed each victim.

Megie began using the Hanging Elm to execute convicts the year the state opened a new prison nearby. It stood on the Hudson River at the foot of the Skinner Road (soon renamed Christopher Street). Convicts sentenced to die were brought up from the waterfront prison along Christopher Street, then along a now vanished dirt road leading directly from Christopher Street to the Elm. As mentioned, executions here ceased in 1819, and there were no burials after 1826.

Incidentally, the state prison was closed in 1828, the same year Washington Square was created from a burial site. During its thirty years of use, the prison developed something of a reputation among the criminal class of the city. The phrase—and we still use it today—"being sent up the river" refers to this waterfront prison two miles north of the city.

Leave the corner, continuing along the extension of Washington Square North, **Waverly Place**. This was once known as Sixth Street, but its residents voted to change the name in 1833 to honor Sir Walter Scott, the recently deceased novelist. His 1814 *Waverley* provided the source of the new street name, but the spelling became garbled in the transition, and Waverly Place lacks a letter to this day.

This one short block offers architectural diversity and

Chess players in Washington Square Park

numerous ties to the arts. **111 Waverly Place** may look familiar to you, as its facade was seen as the home of the young marrieds in the 1967 film *Barefoot in the Park*— although the interiors for the film were shot on a studio set. Across the street is **no. 108**, the former home of Philip Moeller, cofounder of the Theatre Guild and a prominent stage and film director. The top floor was also briefly home to Miriam Hopkins, before she moved on to Hollywood and film stardom. Earlier, in the late nineteenth century, this was the home of Richard Harding Davis, a gentlemanly news correspondent who covered the Spanish-American War (and also wrote popular romance novels).

Number 108 is the first of a row of four identical 1826 houses that were each rebuilt, creating an almost giddy variety. The granite blocks that give no. 108 the look of a miniature castle were set in place in a 1906 reconstruction. Beyond it, **no. 110** retains a semblance of its original Federal design, though its two and one-half floors have been augmented to four. **Number 112** was rebuilt around 1960 with the present brickface. Its dullness is overshadowed by the adjacent **no. 114**, with its flamboyant salmon-pink facade and sweeping 1920 roofline.

The Coach House at no. 110 has long been a stylish Village restaurant, but no. 112 has the row's greatest history. In 1911, it became the home and studio of Everett Shinn, a painter of the Ashcan school and one of the artists known collectively as "The Eight." Shinn not only worked on numerous paintings here, but also used no. 112 to demonstrate his considerable love of the theater. He rebuilt a backyard shed into a theater that, as he put it, "seated fifty-five uncomfortably." There he staged plays for friends, and in short order the Village elite were clamoring to see the Waverly Place Players and their spoofs of nineteenth-century melodramas. Shinn wrote scripts with such overwrought titles as *Hazel Weston; or, More Sinned Against Than Usual* and *Lucy Moore; or, The Prune-Hater's Daughter*. These performances became such popular Village events that they were eventually reviewed by *The New York Times*.

A house at **116 Waverly Place** was once part of this 1826 row. In 1845 it became the residence of Anne Charlotte Lynch, an English teacher with poetic aspirations. The weekly gatherings that she instituted in her parlor have often been called America's first literary salon.

Among those who shared in the conversation and sherry were novelist Herman Melville, newspaper editor William Cullen Bryant, feminist and critic Margaret Fuller, journalist and novelist Bayard Taylor, and satirist Fitz-Greene Halleck. Another occasional guest was Edgar Allan Poe, who entertained one gathering with a first reading of his newest poem, "The Raven." The site is now occupied by The Cecelia, an 1891 house of apartments—or "French flats," as they were then called.

This block was certainly familiar to Poe in 1845, since he had lived on Waverly Place just across Sixth Avenue eight years earlier. His house still stands, but before crossing Sixth Avenue to see it, take a moment to look at **St. Joseph's Church** on Sixth Avenue to your left. Built in 1834, it is the oldest surviving Roman Catholic church in Manhattan. In the opposite direction on Sixth Avenue is the splendid 1876 Jefferson Market Courthouse. We will be taking a closer look at it shortly.

Now cross Sixth Avenue and continue west on Waverly Place. On your left is **no. 138**, built in 1895 as a rectory for St. Joseph's; it is now a private residence. It's a rare survivor of an architectural style known as Venetian Gothic, which enjoyed a brief vogue at that time.

Poe's residence in 1837 stands at **137 Waverly Place**. It had previously been the home of John Trumbull, an early American painter best known for his 1794 tableau, *The Signing of the Declaration of Independence*. Just next door is **no. 139**, which was home in 1917 to poet Edna St. Vincent Millay. Although she came to New York intending to be an actress, the Maine-born poet was destined to come to Greenwich Village: she was named after St. Vincent's Hospital not far from here on Seventh Avenue, after the hospital saved the life of her mother's brother. Incidentally, both of these houses were built in 1829, but the fading paint of no. 139 makes it look older.

Continue west on Waverly Place and you will come to an enticing alley named Gay Street. Before entering it, continue another half-block along Waverly to see the well-preserved Greek Revival row dating from 1839, on your left. The last house on this row, **no. 158**, was the home of Judy Holliday when she starred on Broadway in 1948 in *Born Yesterday*.

Notice the street sign in front of no. 158. No, you're *not* seeing things. You *are* at **the corner of Waverly Place and Waverly Place**. Originally, Waverly Place continued only another few feet to Christopher Street, where it dead-ended. Another street began where you are standing, and it ran to your right across Christopher another five blocks to Bank Street. This was called Factory Street, named for a well-known factor that stood nearby in the early nineteenth century. Its removal prompted a name change, and in 1853 this became an extension of Waverly Place.

Wedged between the split sections of Waverly Place is the 1831 **Northern Dispensary**, so named because it was then the northernmost medical facility in New York City. This triangular building provided care for those Villagers who couldn't afford a visiting doctor. The third floor is an 1854 addition, and you can see where the new bricks begin in the line that is visible just above the second-floor windows. After 158 years of service, the Dispensary closed in 1989. It's to undergo an interior renovation and reopen as an AIDS hospice.

Now retrace your steps and enter **Gay Street**. Except for nearby Weehawken Street, Gay Street is the city's shortest. The name is of uncertain origin, but the street itself began as another stable alley. The first houses that replaced stables in 1827 are still standing, on your left. The stables across the alley began to be replaced in the 1840s by the Greek Revivals, on your right. However, the stigma of the stables lingered, and Gay Street became and remained for decades a one-block ghetto of impoverished black families.

The fortunes of Gay Street began to change in the

Gay Street

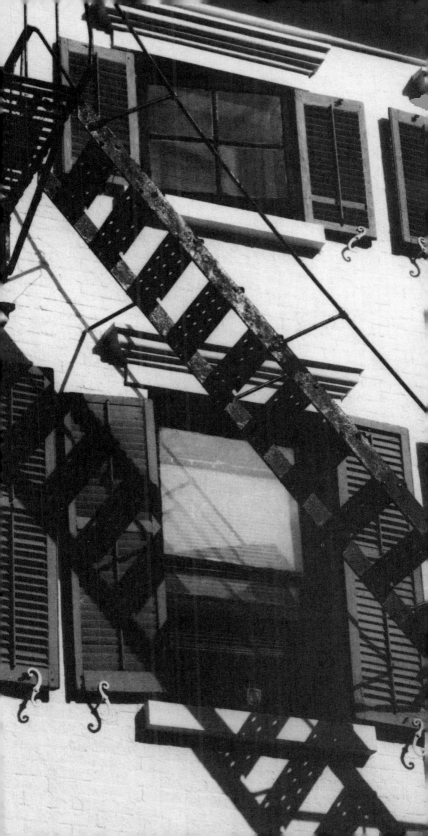

1920s. A literary connection drew recognition to Gay Street in the mid-1930s, when the low-rent basement apartment of **no. 14** was rented by two sisters from Ohio. The result was a Village myth of amazing durability. Eileen McKenney sought a career on the stage, and her sister, Ruth, hoped for success as a writer. Ruth wrote up their Village adventures in essays that were published by *The New Yorker*. She then whipped them into her 1938 novel, *My Sister Eileen*, which later was adapted into a stage comedy, two Hollywood films, and a Broadway musical.

Number 14 has changed little since the McKenney sisters lived here. In fact, nos. 12 and 14 have changed little since they were built. Numbers 16 and 18 also date from 1827, but their half-floor dormers have been removed to permit the addition of the third and fourth floors. Numbers 12 and 14 retain their dormers, though paired single-window dormers are more typical of the period than these three-window dormers.

Proceed through Gay Street to **Christopher Street**. To your left, a cluster of squat Federal houses will catch your eye. Federal style was prevalent in the 1820s and was gradually succeeded in the 1830s by Greek Revival. There were few architects in America then, and most private homes were simply the work of master craftsmen and their apprentices. Carpenters and masons repeated with minor alterations the work they did on their previous job. Not until the 1850s did an American receive the formal schooling in architecture offered by the École des Beaux-Arts in Paris, and he came to the Village for his first commission—as we will see.

The Federals here on Christopher Street all date from 1827 to 1828. Those on the odd side of the street, facing you, are five survivors of a row of ten. The row was built as an investment by Samuel Whittemore, who owned the nearby factory for which Factory Street was named. The third and fourth floors were later additions; as originally built, they must have looked rather like the miniatures facing them across the street. Notice the sunrise pattern worked into the triple-window dormers of **nos. 18 and 20**.

Incidentally, **Rumbul's** at 20 Christopher Street is an excellent candidate for a refreshment stop if a break is needed. Its coffees and cakes are a treat, as is the fireplace in the back room that is lit on most winter afternoons. This cozy eatery evokes the tearooms so popular in the Village during the 1910s, though Rumbul's is about twice their size—it seats about twenty-five.

Continue on Christopher Street, walking against the flow of car traffic. Notice the apartment tower on your left, **no. 1**. When built in 1931 it consumed the sites of several structures, including Luke O'Connor's saloon, one of the first Village bars to acquire a literary aura. The initial connection was John Masefield, who was later to be named Poet Laureate of Britain, but who in 1896 was a runaway sailor hired to sweep O'Connor's floors and empty the spittoons. In later years, O'Connor proudly hung a portrait of Masefield over his bar.

O'Connor's saloon figures in numerous books on the Village of this period, but seldom under his name. The place was better known at the time as the Working Girls' Home, a nickname conferred by Village writer Mary Heaton Vorse when she noticed three prostitutes stumble in one afternoon. In addition to the stuffed elk heads and tall Chinese vases, O'Connor kept a collection of bad checks. A tribute to his own soft-heartedness, the pile grew in time to be over a foot tall. Several of these checks were undoubtedly written by Eugene O'Neill, who spent most of 1916 in Village dives and flophouses inspecting the bottoms of whiskey glasses. By one account, O'Neill met a blond girl at the Working Girls' Home who worked in a cigarette factory. Conversation revealed that she'd been long separated from her sea captain father, but that a reunion was soon to occur at O'Connor's. Evidently O'Neill was witness to this event, and several years later used it to help turn an unworkable play script called

Chris Christopherson into his 1921 Pulitzer Prize winner, *Anna Christie*.

Continue on Christopher Street to the corner. Cross Greenwich Avenue and, with the help of the traffic island, continue across Sixth Avenue. Here at the corner of Sixth Avenue and Ninth Street is an excellent view of **Jefferson Market Courthouse**. Completed in 1876, it was soon named the fifth of America's ten most beautiful buildings in a poll of American architects. Its name recalls the farmers' market that opened on this site in 1833. Villagers had been lobbying for a market closer than the one on the Hudson River, just south of the old state prison. A few years after the prison closed, the city purchased this irregular plot and began the construction of new market stalls. Hoping to get the most for its money, the city also elected to build public assembly rooms over the market stalls to meet the civic needs of the growing Village community. The whole affair was named to honor the recently deceased Thomas Jefferson. At the northern end of the property, the city built a fire watchtower—one of many that guarded private property during the age of the volunteer fire brigade. Once the Municipal Fire Department was established in 1866, these towers were no longer needed. In 1870 the city chose to close Jefferson Market and rebuild the site as a courthouse complex.

Designed by Calvert Vaux (codesigner of Central Park) and Frederick Clarke Withers, the complex originally had its own adjoining jail. Though the courthouse remained, the jail was replaced in 1929 by the Women's House of Detention, which was in turn demolished in 1971. Unable to find a suitable use for the land, the city turned the jail site over to the Village for use as a garden. Villagers have operated and maintained this garden since 1972.

The Jefferson Market Courthouse has had many moments in the spotlight. It was here in 1907 that the world's first session of night court was held, and here also, a year earlier, that Harry K. Thaw was tried and convicted for assassinating architect Stanford White, who was scandalously involved with Thaw's wife, Evelyn Nesbitt. The most curious event to occur here was undoubtedly the 1896 encounter between the New York City Police Department and writer Stephen Crane. His *Red Badge of Courage*, written in part in a boardinghouse on Washington Square South, had been published in the spring of 1896 and brought Crane his first great success. As his reputation crested that autumn, Crane chose to turn his writer's eye to focus on the denizens of New York's underworld. He accidentally witnessed the arrest of a streetwalker on trumped-up charges, and decided to defend the woman in court. As the incident grew more tangled, Crane went so far as to falsely claim to be the husband of a second streetwalker, who was threatened with arrest. Through it all, Crane felt his friendship with Police Commissioner Teddy Roosevelt would allow Crane to issue with impunity his charges of false arrest. However, the future president turned a deaf ear to the corrupt proceedings, and Crane emerged from the trial with a somewhat sullied reputation, but with ample material for his writing.

Court sessions here ended in 1945, and the abandoned courthouse went into a fifteen-year decline. In 1959 the city was ready to accept a bid for the building, which would result in its being torn down and an apartment building erected in its place. Villagers rallied to save the old courthouse—despite the absence at that time of any city landmarks preservation law. The campaign was a success, and in 1962 the city authorized an interior renovation to turn the old courthouse into a branch library. The Jefferson Market Courthouse Library, a branch of the New York Public Library, opened in 1967. It is a living testament to the power of community activism and a stunning example of adaptive reuse. As you pass its front door in a few moments, check the schedule posted there to find out if the library is open (budget cuts have forced some weekday closings). The numerous stained-

The Jefferson Market Courthouse Library

glass windows and the curved stairs to the second floor reward a brief detour.

The most prominent feature of the old courthouse is its 150-foot clocktower. The tower occupies the site of the original fire watchtower. The present tower is visible across much of the West Village, a fact that proved useful in saving the building. Villagers who opposed demolition guessed that they could gather public support by restarting the great clock atop the tower. Their guess proved correct.

Notice the opening in the tower, a columned space just below the clock face. If you are in the right position, you can see the silhouette of the last firebell used in the previous tower. It was cast in 1863 and is nearly eight feet tall. Village legend claims that this walled-up bell can't be rung because doing so would shatter the tower. Actually, the bell has been rung on a few occasions—

when Dewey returned victorious from Manila in 1899, and when the building was saved in the 1960s.

Leave the corner of Ninth Street and walk one block up Sixth Avenue to Tenth. You will pass 424 Sixth Avenue, home of **Balducci's**. This paradise for gastronomes offers an amazing array of fresh-baked breads, pastries, fruits and vegetables you've never heard of, cheeses, prepared gourmet foods, and its own select meat and fish markets. It takes a lot of self-restraint to pass Balducci's without entering, as the constant crowd inside the store attests.

Turn right on West Tenth Street and walk a few steps to **no. 45.** This 1959 apartment building occupies the site of the historic Tenth Street Studio building, which stood here for 101 years. Built in 1856, it provided America's leading artists with a combined workspace and residence, designed expressly for their needs. Eight interconnected studios on each of the three floors encircled a sunny central attrium. These well-lit studios were initially used by painters of the staid Hudson River School. In time, struggling artists of all disciplines discovered Greenwich Village to be the workplace of their famous counterparts. Nearby attics and stables became makeshift studios for younger artists who were willing to endure physical discomfort just to be here. If one building could be credited for forging the link between artists and the Village, it would be the Tenth Street Studio.

Artists who lived here over the years include Winslow Homer, Eastman Johnson, William Merritt Chase, and Augustus Saint-Gaudens. A. Stirling Calder also lived here with his son, the future artist and inventor of the mobile, Alexander Calder. And life at the Studio must have appealed to John La Farge, for he lived here for over fifty years, virtually his entire artistic life.

The designer of the Studio, and also a tenant, was Richard Morris Hunt, the first American architect to be schooled at the École des Beaux-Arts in Paris. The Studio was his first commission after his return, and his innovative design fostered a communal life for artists that, until then, was unknown among respectable New Yorkers. A dozen years later Hunt reworked the plan and came up with his design for the Stuyvesant, generally cited today as America's first refined apartment building. It's somewhat fitting that an apartment building replaced the Tenth Street Studio here; it's just unfortunate that the replacement is so uninspired and dull.

Just across Tenth Street is **no. 58**, a sedate row house that has its own artistic connections. Under its front stoop you can see the former entrance to a passageway that once led underneath the house to a back house inside the block. In the 1880s **58¹/₂ West Tenth Street** was the headquarters of the Tile Club, a legendary gentlemen's club for artists. Among its members were most of the residents of the Tenth Street Studio, along with a Tenth Street neighbor, sculptor Daniel Chester French—best known today for the massive *Lincoln* he created for the Lincoln Memorial in Washington, D.C. The front house has been reworked a number of times since its construction in 1836. The elaborate lead-glass window of the parlor floor was installed under the direction of Stanford White. He could hardly have imagined that the courthouse around the corner would one day hold the trial of his murderer. Fortunately this window was spared when fire swept the upper floors of the house in 1989. Number 58 is now used as offices for New York University.

Return to the corner, then cross Sixth Avenue to the front of the old courthouse; now turn right, cross Tenth Street, and walk up Sixth Avenue one-half block to **Milligan Place**. Careful, or you'll miss it! A gate no wider than an average door is the entrance to this unique "street without a street," situated between 451 and 453 Sixth Avenue. The four houses you see beyond the gate date from 1852 and were named after local landowner Samuel Milligan, whose manor house they replaced. Milligan Place figures in the history of the Provincetown Players, the experimental Village theater troupe that performed from 1916 through 1929 at their own playhouse on MacDougal

Street, south of Washington Square. The troupe's cofounder, George Cram Cook, lived here in Milligan Place, along with his wife, playwright Susan Glaspell (winner of the 1931 Pulitzer Prize for her play *Alison's House*). Among the many Provincetowners to pass through these gates into Milligan Place were Eugene O'Neill, Edna St. Vincent Millay (during her acting phase), and John Howard Lawson, a playwright who was later blacklisted from movies and a member of the Hollywood Ten of the late 1940s.

Milligan Place is one of those Village streets famous for seeming to run at the wrong angle. In fact, it is Sixth Avenue that is about forty-five degrees out of kilter with the street grid of Greenwich Village, as neighboring Patchin Place shows.

Retrace your steps back along Sixth Avenue, then turn right onto Tenth Street. Large gates halfway down the block mark the entrance to **Patchin Place**. It conforms with the angle of Milligan Place and cuts off from Tenth Street at a proper right angle. This land was given by Milligan in 1848 to his surveyor, Aaron Patchin, on the occasion of his marriage to Milligan's daughter. This secluded, dead-end enclave consists of ten simple houses built by Patchin in that year. They face each other across the alley in two irregular rows of six and four houses. **4 Patchin Place**, on your right, was the home of poet e. e. cummings for forty years. Writer Djuna Barnes was his neighbor for much of this time, living in splendid isolation at **no. 5** until her death in 1982 at the age of ninety. Patchin Place was also for years the legal address of journalist and activist John Reed, though much of the time he was elsewhere, covering such events as the 1917 Russian Revolution. His vivid account of that turbulent affair was published as *Ten Days That Shook the World* in 1919, a year before his death. But Reed's lease here continued for some time after his death. His widow, Louise Bryant, wanted to insure the safety of Reed's notes for the book and continued to pay rent on the unoccupied apartment for years.

Continue along Tenth Street, across Greenwich Avenue and toward the next corner. Midway on this block is an 1839 row house that deserves note. **139 West Tenth Street** won literary and artistic fame as the home of Regnaneschi's. The 1898 opening of this family restaurant, in what had been a private home, drew a loyal band of creative Villagers who were to make the Italian food served here famous. Poet Edwin Arlington Robinson made it his hangout, and John Sloan made it the subject of his 1912 painting, *Regnaneschi's Saturday Night*, now in the collection of the Art Institute of Chicago. The restaurant passed out of family ownership in the 1940s and through several changes of name. One night in 1954, playwright-to-be Edward Albee stopped in for a beer and discovered, written on a mirror with a bar of soap, the graffiti he later appropriated as a play title: *Who's Afraid of Virginia Woolf?* The present name of the restaurant, The Ninth Circle, was adopted in the early 1960s, though by the close of that decade it ceased to be a restaurant and became the gay bar it remains today.

At the end of this block is the corner of Tenth Street and Waverly Place (the former Factory Street section), and here for over a century is **Julius'**, the oldest bar operating in the West Village. The first floor of this 1826 wood-frame house became a general store in 1840, and the store became a bar in 1864. Julius' was a speakeasy during the 1920s, and it was then that the bar acquired its back door entrance at 159 West Tenth Street—the address the bar now uses. By the late 1940s, Julius' had found new popularity as a neighborhood bar offering live jazz performances. Some twenty years later Julius' became a gay bar with a casual atmosphere, making Julius' today a spot known throughout the country.

Be sure to notice the Tenth Street side of Julius', which bears clear signs of the building's reconstruction from a two and one-half story Federal to a somewhat taller house. You might also glance to your left to the blank wall marking the **site of 165 West Tenth Street**. Today this is the backside of a restaurant fronting Seventh Avenue South, but until 1929 a house stood here. It was home from 1914 through 1919 to Theodore Dreiser, and here he wrote his most controversial novel. *The "Genius"* was a fictional version of Dreiser's own life, masked with details of a painter's life (borrowed from his friend Everett Shinn). When published late in 1915, *The "Genius"* was branded as obscene by the Society for the Suppression of Vice, then withdrawn by its timid publisher. Dreiser's long-standing battle against censorship found a focus, but it took him until 1923 to get his book cleared and back in bookstores. By then he was living elsewhere in the Village, writing the novel that he had conceived while still living here on Tenth Street: *An American Tragedy.*

Speaking of books, across Tenth Street from Julius' is the Three Lives Bookshop (its name was borrowed from Gertrude Stein). It operates from the storefront of **154 West Tenth Street**, another wood-frame house dating from the 1820s. Three Lives & Company specializes in literature and unusual art books, and its wood-paneled interior and private-library ambience recall the famous bookstores of the Village of the past.

From Tenth Street, walk along Waverly Place past Three Lives for one short block. Standing here, at the corner of Waverly Place and Christopher Street, you are looking at the third face of the triangular Northern Dispensary. The side fronts the block that is common to both Christopher and Grove streets. These two streets diverge to your right, forming Christopher Park between them. As a result, not only does the Dispensary have one side (this side) on two streets, it also has two sides on one street (the forked Waverly Place, seen earlier).

Cross Christopher Street, walking over to the Dispensary, then turn right. Cross Waverly Place and continue along Grove Street, along the side of Christopher Park. This little triangle of greenery was laid out in 1837 and is often confused with Sheridan Square, another triangle just around the corner. Little wonder, since Christopher

Park contains a 1936 statue of General Philip Sheridan, the Civil War officer for whom the square was named.

As you reach the corner, glance into Sheridan Square, to your left. Though the name is loosely applied to this entire tangled intersection, technically only this one triangle is Sheridan Square.

Sheridan Square is the Times Square of Greenwich Village. There's a faster pace here, as well as a crowded cluster of restaurants, night clubs, and theaters. Off-Broadway began here in the 1950s in a theater on Sheridan Square, now lost to a 1960 apartment building (the one whose ground floor is the large supermarket). There was also an earlier heyday of "little theater" here in the 1920s, and several productions were quite historic. Look to your right beyond Christopher Park and you will see a two-story, yellow-and-black brick building fronting Seventh Avenue South. From 1917 through 1930, this was the site of the **Greenwich Village Theater**, a Broadway-style theater seating less than four hundred. Here, in 1919, the first edition of the *Greenwich Village Follies* breathed new life into the musical revue by replacing lavish display with intelligence and intimacy. After six sold-out weeks, the production moved to Broadway—an event without precedent—and there it spawned a series that continued through the decade, and changed Broadway's approach toward the revue. (Incidentally, it was in one of the uptown editions that dancer Martha Graham got her much-deserved first break as a performer). The Greenwich Village Theater was taken over in 1924 by the Provincetown Players to use in conjunction with their smaller theater on MacDougal Street. Among the plays they presented here were the world premieres of two major works by Eugene O'Neill: *The Great God Brown* and *Desire Under the Elms*.

Cross the intersection to the traffic island with the subway entrance and newsstand. At the newsstand, glance down Seventh Avenue South and you'll see two current Off-Broadway theaters. On your left is the **Circle**

Repertory Theater, in which the Circle Repertory Company has staged the premieres of its playwright-in-residence Lanford Wilson (including his 1980 Pulitzer Prize winner, *Talley's Folly*). As you can see, this theater still sports the "garage" mosaic attesting to its former life; with so many theaters being replaced by garages, it's refreshing to see evidence of the reverse. Across Seventh Avenue South and a bit farther down is the marquee of the **Actors Playhouse**, a theater best remembered as the Off-Broadway home of Harvey Fierstein's *Torch Song Trilogy*. These two theaters have offered on their stages early performances by such "unknowns" as James Earl Jones, Colleen Dewhurst, Lily Tomlin, Matthew Broderick, Robert Duvall, George Segal, Lainie Kazan, Larry Hagman, Estelle Getty, F. Murray Abraham, Rue McClanahan, and Jon Voight.

Prior to World War I, the Sheridan Square area was considerably more cloistered than it is now, since Seventh Avenue South didn't exist then. Originally, Seventh Avenue extended south no farther than Eleventh Street. During the war years, the city authorized the creation of Seventh Avenue South to facilitate the construction of a subway line under Greenwich Village. Eleven blocks of the Village were bisected, and all structures in the path of the subway/avenue route were demolished. Because the route was at odds with the angle of Village streets, some buildings protruded only slightly and were sheared back rather than destroyed. To this day, numerous buildings along Seventh Avenue South bear the scars of what Villagers still call "The Cut." Some lost only a sliver. For example, if you look up the avenue to your right, you'll see one such scar on the Tenth Street house now home to John Clancy's Seafood Restaurant. Others lost a larger segment, as did **70 Grove Street**, next door to Circle Rep. The surgery here was drastic; wide picture windows overlooking the avenue indicate the new wall that was added. The triangular section that was removed permitted construction of the sidewalk.

Cross Seventh Avenue South to **Village Cigars**, an informal local landmark since it opened here in 1922. The building itself has changed little over the years; however, a sidewalk mosaic in front recalls a historic dispute; it's all that's left of a building claimed by The Cut. Here, extending back across the present avenue, once stood a five-story residence named The Voorhis. It was condemned by the city due to the subway and avenue construction, and only this tiny plot remained unneeded and under the control of the owner, the Estate of David Hess of Philadelphia. The city invited the estate to donate this useless land for incorporation into the sidewalk. The request must have angered the estate trustees, for they refused to surrender any land they didn't have to, and instead installed this defiant mosaic statement of private ownership. It remained on the tax roll for years as the smallest piece of real estate in New York. Village Cigars bought the property in 1938 for a thousand dollars, and the mosaic has been part of the Village Cigars property ever since.

Walking with the flow of car traffic, take a few steps along Seventh Avenue South and turn right onto Grove Street. Just off the avenue are three popular Village nightspots in old row houses. For over thirty years the ground floor of 59 Grove Street has been **Marie's Crisis**. The club's name evokes two strands of local history separated by one century. "Marie" recalls Romany Marie, a local celebrity who affected gypsy garb and operated a series of tearooms and restaurants from the 1910s through the 1940s. "Crisis" is a reference to Thomas Paine, whose pamphlets *The Crisis* and *Common Sense* were crucial in encouraging the revolutionary break from England, and who died in 1809 in a house on or near this site. The present 59 Grove dates from 1839.

Until 1990, **55 Grove Street** was the home of The Duplex—which moved in that year across Sheridan Square to new, though equally cramped, quarters. In the early 1960s, the original Duplex hosted performances by such "unknowns" as Barbra Streisand and Woody Allen. Another early stand-up comic here was Joan Rivers, who recalled in her autobiography the tiny Duplex stage and the nearby toilet for patrons, which flushed away many of her punch lines. Tomorrow's stars may well be performing here on Grove Street (and on nearby Sheridan Square) tonight, so you might want to look over posters outside the clubs here. Who knows?

Walk farther along Grove Street, crossing Bleecker Street. A few steps beyond the corner is **45 Grove Street**, on your right. It was built in 1830 for Samuel Whittemore as his own residence, only a few years after he constructed the small houses we've already seen on Christopher Street. As you can see, Whittemore had a far grander idea of his own home, which is why 45 Grove Street is about twice the width of a typical row house. Of all the manor houses built when Greenwich Village was still chiefly estates and farms, this was the last to be built and the only one that survives. It presided over adjoining gardens and had its own cistern, stables, and even a greenhouse. After Whittemore's death in 1835, his surviving relatives divided his property into lots, producing by the 1850s most of the neighboring structures still standing here today. The old Whittemore manor house was raised from two floors to five in 1871, and its interior was later divided into separate apartments. As an apartment house, it became home in the 1920s to Hart Crane, who here began writing his poetic portrait of America, *The Bridge*.

Whittemore's old house may seem familiar to you—if so, it's probably because it was featured in *Reds*, the 1981 film about John Reed. 45 Grove Street was used as Eugene O'Neill's house (which it never was), to set up a scene about a love affair between O'Neill (played by Jack Nicholson) and Louise Bryant (Diane Keaton), who was Reed's wife (Warren Beatty played Reed). Incidentally, the affair actually did occur and was O'Neill's inspiration for his 1927 play, *Strange Interlude*.

Facing 45 Grove is **The Pink Tea Cup**, a unique restaurant that has been a Village fixture for decades. Southern cooking is the specialty of the house, and it's served up in an amusing setting of suitable bric-a-brac. The Pink Tea Cup originally operated around the corner on Bleecker Street, and made the move to 42 Grove without losing any of its charm.

The rest of Grove Street is resolutely residential, the image of Greenwich Village as we imagine it to be. The well-preserved houses on your left are transitional Greek Revivals of 1851–52, showing signs of the Italianate detail that became fashionable a few years later. The houses on your right are more varied in age and style. The last of them is the gem of the block. **17 Grove Street** is the largest and best-preserved wood-frame house in the Village. It has been standing here at the corner of Bedford Street since 1822. The original owner was a local sash-maker whose work is undoubtedly on display in some of the old houses nearby. Much of his work was done in a workshop built behind his home. If you turn right at the corner, onto Bedford Street, you will see that it's still there, today a miniature residence all to itself.

Towering behind the two-story workshop is one of New York's most bizarre buildings. Officially this is **102 Bedford Street**, but since its completion in 1925 it has been better known among Villagers as "Twin Peaks." The double gable roof and pseudochalet appearance of this five-floor apartment house are the work of Clifford Reed Daily. He fancied himself an architect, and a chance meeting with financier Otto Kahn gave Daily his chance to prove it. Kahn was a willing benefactor to deserving, needy artists, so he was ready to back Daily's plan for a Village residence fanciful enough to inspire creativity in others. But Daily's eccentricities got the better of him and Kahn soon realized that he was being fleeced. Kahn reclaimed the building and dismissed Daily, who died within a year. Twin Peaks has survived as Daily's monument to creativity, but not in quite the way he had intended.

Return to the intersection of Bedford and Grove, and cross diagonally to take in the last block of Grove Street. Mid-block, Grove Street shifts forty-five degrees to the right, and here on your left is the entrance to **Grove Court**. The alley between nos. 10 and 12 Grove Street leads deep inside the block to a row of back houses dating from 1854. When built they were intended for local laborers, since respectable families then would never have considered living in an alley. The seclusion makes these houses seem to be exclusive and desirable today. And they have been, at least once, inspiring. Grove Court was adopted by O. Henry as the setting for his 1902 tale, *The Last Leaf.*

Walk a few steps farther along Grove Street for a view of **St. Luke-in-the-Fields**. This 1822 chapel was built by Trinity Church in Lower Manhattan, and stands on the northernmost section of a tract along the Hudson given to Trinity by a royal decree in 1705. When St. Luke's opened its doors the warden was Clement Clarke Moore, who filled the spare time of his first Christmas here by composing a holiday poem for his children. Published the following year, its opening lines are now familiar to almost everyone: " 'Twas the night before Christmas . . ."

St. Luke's was built by James N. Wells, a master carpenter who also designed the first few houses of Grove Street in harmony with his chapel. With a bit of imagination, it's easy to see Hudson Street as a dirt road, with horses and carriages drawing up to the church entrance. St. Luke-in-the-Fields is the third-oldest church in Manhattan, although a 1981 fire gutted its interior. The present chapel interior was completed and dedicated in 1985.

Retrace your steps on Grove Street to turn right onto Bedford Street. Near the end of this block, on your left, an unmarked door conceals the most famous secret in Greenwich Village. 86 Bedford Street is the entrance to **Chumley's**, a restaurant unlike anything anywhere. Chumley's began as a speakeasy in 1928, and its interior has hardly changed over the past six decades. The door at 86 Bedford still does not bear the restaurant's name. The great oak tables inside are still a relaxing place to share a burger or a brew with some friends. After seeing so many Hollywood incarnations of speakeasies, it's interesting to see exactly what the real thing looked like.

But Chumley's was a special place even when it opened. Owner Lee Chumley encouraged authors who were regulars to bring him dust jackets of their latest books. Chumley mounted them on the walls of the restaurant—and they are still there. The restaurant remained a literary hangout after Chumley's death in 1935, and another tier of dust jackets was added in the 1950s. A third set was installed in 1988 as part of Chumley's sixtieth-anniversary celebration. A list of the writers who have made Chumley's their clubhouse could easily fill this page, and it would include John Steinbeck, Ernest Hemingway, Eugene O'Neill, Theodore Dreiser, Edna Ferber, e. e. cummings, William Faulkner, John Cheever, Simone de Beauvoir, J. D. Salinger, Dylan Thomas, Jack Kerouac, Allen Ginsberg, and Edmund Wilson. Don't miss the hidden entrance inside Pamela Court, around the corner at **58 Barrow Street**.

Return to the corner of Bedford and Barrow streets, and cross this intersection diagonally to the corner opposite Chumley's. Now continue west along Barrow Street one-half block to the point where Barrow twists to the right. The twist marks the intersection with Commerce Street, a secluded corner that is the most picturesque enclave of Greenwich Village. Its most prominent feature is the pair of twin houses, **39 and 41 Commerce Street**. Legend has it that these houses were built for sisters who never spoke to each other. The fact that they were truly built in 1831 by a milkman from Englewood, New Jersey, may dispel the legend—but not the romance. Facing them across narrow Commerce Street is the **Blue Mill**, a homey restaurant that has prospered here on the ground floor of 50 Commerce since 1941. One of the upper floors of this commercial structure was for years the home and studio of noted photographer Berenice Abbott, who made frequent use of the Village as her subject. Around the bend of Commerce Street is the **Cherry Lane Theater**, at no. 38. Opened in 1924 in a former brewery, the playhouse is said to have gained the participation of Edna St. Vincent Millay (who lived around the corner then, at **75½ Bedford Street**—at 9½ feet, the narrowest house in New York). Though many stars of stage and screen have appeared at the Cherry Lane, the biggest name connected with the theater never did. One of the apartments upstairs above the theater served in the late 1920s as bachelor digs for four fellows, including John Orry (later, Hollywood costume designer Orry-Kelly) and Archie Leach (better known as Cary Grant).

Crowded into the crook of Commerce Street are three delightful houses that evoke a sense of historic Greenwich Village—right down to the gas streetlamp that burns in front of **no. 48**. This cozy corner marks the end of our tour.

Terry Miller is the author of *Greenwich Village and How It Got That Way*, the first comprehensive history of Greenwich Village. He has also written another work of history, *It Happened in New York*, and the 1984 novel *Standing By*. He has conducted walking tours of Greenwich Village for the 92nd Street Y and for the Museum of the City of New York, and has served the Museum as the Research Consultant for its 1990 exhibit, "Within Bohemia's Borders: Greenwich Village 1830–1930."

Walk · 4

Midtown Manhattan

THE CITY'S
HIGH-CHARGED CORE

BARRY LEWIS

St. Patrick's Cathedral, Fifth Avenue

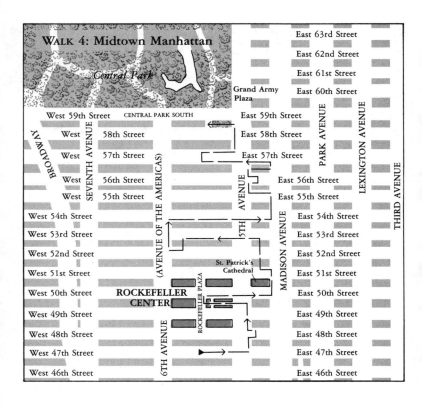

WALK 4: Midtown Manhattan

Central Park

Grand Army Plaza

West 59th Street   CENTRAL PARK SOUTH   East 59th Street
West 58th Street   East 58th Street
West 57th Street   East 57th Street
West 56th Street   East 56th Street
West 55th Street   East 55th Street
West 54th Street   East 54th Street
West 53rd Street   East 53rd Street
West 52nd Street   East 52nd Street
West 51st Street   East 51st Street
West 50th Street   East 50th Street
West 49th Street   East 49th Street
West 48th Street   East 48th Street
West 47th Street   East 47th Street
West 46th Street   East 46th Street

BROADWAY
SEVENTH AVENUE
(AVENUE OF THE AMERICAS)
5TH AVENUE
MADISON AVENUE
PARK AVENUE
LEXINGTON AVENUE
THIRD AVENUE
6TH AVENUE
ROCKEFELLER PLAZA

ROCKEFELLER
CENTER

St. Patrick's
Cathedral

Starting Point: West 47th Street, between Fifth Avenue and the Avenue of the Americas (Sixth Avenue)
Walk Length: About 2½ hours
Subway Stop: Rockefeller Center (B, D, F, or Q trains); using 47th Street exit at Sixth Avenue, walk one-half block east

Midtown, the heart of Manhattan, lies between Third and Eighth avenues, 34th and 59th streets. Within that area you can find fashion, entertainment, shopping, and business districts that are known throughout the world: Times Square and its Broadway theaters, Herald Square and its grand department stores, 57th Street with its collection of art galleries, and Fifth Avenue with its luxury shops.

Jammed into Midtown is a concentration of office skyscrapers containing over 225 million square feet of office space, more office space than the entire cities of Houston and Denver combined. To fill these skyscrapers, every weekday 750,000 people—a population the size of San Francisco—move in and out of Midtown New York. Add to that the millions of visitors who pass through Midtown's streets, including two million foreigners per year, some of whom stay in Midtown's 90,000 hotel rooms. Last, but not least, are Midtown's 100,000 residents who tolerate this tumult so they can live in the "center of the universe."

At the nucleus of it all—at the core of the core—is Fifth Avenue from 47th to 59th streets, the subject of our tour.

After the Civil War, when this area was first developed, the city's center was much farther downtown, beginning at the Battery and extending to 23rd Street. Business was conducted in the Wall Street area, wholesalers and garment workers were jammed together near Canal Street, and the shopping and entertainment district lay between 14th and 23rd streets. Where we're standing was the northernmost fringes of the city, with scattered woods and marshes dotted with shanties lying farther north. In 1860 this area was largely rural, with a few private houses and institutional buildings marking the landscape. The only major construction was the new St. Patrick's Cathedral at Fifth Avenue and 50th Street, started in 1858.

Why was St. Pat's placed so far "out of town"? Because everyone knew that the area's grasslands would soon be devoured by the rapidly expanding city. By 1877, when the cathedral was completed, the area was filling up with mansions on Fifth Avenue and haut bourgeois town houses on the side streets. New York's phenomenal growth spared no one. Manhattan Island's population was 800,000 when the Civil War began; by 1900 an extra million people had crowded onto the island. Even the very rich and powerful could not stop this urban crush that constantly devoured itself to build bigger and supposedly better.

By the turn of the century, commerce was invading the neighborhood. This was all part of a continuing northward expansion that typified Manhattan development, with commerce following in the path of residential construction. This pattern had been established since the arrival of the British in New York, who took it upon themselves to expand beyond the northern wall built by the Dutch. New Yorkers of the mid-nineteenth century were so sure of the inevitability of this continued northward expansion that it was predicted that by 1910 Midtown Manhattan would be located at 125th Street. It was for this reason that Columbia University and the Cathedral of St. John the Divine were sited above 110th Street on the Upper West Side. But, it appears—at least for now—this area of Manhattan is destined to remain Midtown.

As commerce moved into Midtown, mansions that had been built to stand forever were being demolished. In Europe, chateaux and palaces stayed intact for centuries. In America they became "mobile homes" for the rich. Today, only a smattering of town houses survive.

As Fifth Avenue was becoming a commercial boulevard, a new Theater District was emerging to the west around Times Square. Grand Central Terminal, at 42nd Street and Park Avenue, was becoming a major hub for both commuters and long-distance travelers. In the center was Fifth Avenue, and by World War I its name was synonymous with luxury retailing where price is never discussed.

About the same time, New York's business center moved northward, leaving behind the banks, brokers, and insurers of Downtown and Wall Street. The first Midtown office district was exuberantly decked in the modernistic Art Deco style—exemplified by streamlined design and a combination of classical and modern materials, such as aluminum and granite. The Daily News Building at Third Avenue and 42nd Street and, later, the Chrysler Building at Lexington and 42nd and the Empire State Building at Fifth Avenue and 34th Street in 1931 are good examples. Many Midtown buildings sprang up around Grand Central Terminal in the 1920s; by the 1930s, the huge Rockefeller Center complex pulled the district northward.

During the "glass box" era—which embraced clean lines, walls of glass, and a form that followed function—

after World War II, Park Avenue above Grand Central Terminal became a prestigious corporate address while the Midtown skyscraper district pushed outward, engulfing Third to Sixth avenues.

A new crop of skyscrapers was built in the Fifth Avenue district beginning in the late 1970s, reflecting New York's strengthening as an international business center. Low-rise, serendipitous row-house blocks on side streets, such as 47th through 55th streets, were demolished for new towers. Madison Avenue in the 50s was rebuilt at a blockbuster scale and several huge skyscrapers went up on Fifth itself, including Olympic Tower at 51st Street and Trump Tower at 56th Street, both of which featured spectacular galleries at the street level and plush offices and luxury apartments above.

Midtown in the 1980s became denser, richer, and more internationally chic, reflecting its pivotal role in a denser, richer, more internationally chic Manhattan. Although the 1990s have brought harsh realities to bear on New York, this is still a world capital city—and Midtown, the subject of our tour, proves it.

We begin our walk in the kind of specialized district that makes New York so fascinating. On West 47th Street between Fifth and Sixth avenues lies New York's **Diamond District**, where over 85 percent of America's wholesale gem transactions are made. Formerly located at the Bowery and Canal Street, in the Jewish Lower East Side where most of the diamond merchants lived, the district began to move uptown in the early twentieth century, following an elite clientele taking up residence farther north. By the 1980s, offices of the dealers were spilling over to West 46th and 48th streets and onto both Fifth and Sixth avenues.

West 47th Street buildings are crammed with wholesale diamond dealers from the street level to the roof line—thousands of dealers on this block alone. Most are

strictly wholesalers, but those on the street level also deal in retail. You may notice that all the diamond shops are very small, but what you may not realize is that virtually without exception there is only one way in and one way out to discourage back-door escapes by potential thieves.

Diamond merchants in the United States, indeed throughout the world, form a very small club, with dealers closely related to each other, often literally. This is a business that depends on word of mouth and the goodwill of customers (you will rarely see an advertisement placed by one of these dealers). You will see that many dealers are Hasidic Jews who dress themselves in long coats and large black hats and sport dark beards and side curls, a fashion left over from when this ultra-orthodox and mystical sect of Judaism was founded in eighteenth-century Poland.

The "government of 47th Street," the **Diamond Dealers Club**, 580 Fifth Avenue, is located on the northwest corner of 47th and Fifth. The club moved here in 1985 and its members are still trying to get over the shock: "So fancy-shmancy," to quote one dealer's reaction on opening day. This facility handles the dealers' important

165

functions, trades are consummated here, disputes settled in "court," and "laws" promulgated for the "street."

Although you might miss it amid the clutter of all the diamond dealers, toward the Sixth Avenue end of this highly concentrated block sits one of New York's most venerable bookstores: **Gotham Book Mart**, 41 West 47th Street. The store has stood here since 1920, long before the Diamond District surrounded it. Its stock of over half a million vintage magazines and books and its upstairs gallery draw pilgrims from all over the world, due to its history as a salon for well-known writers, such as Ezra Pound. The store's logo, "Wise Men Fish Here," is proudly displayed over the entrance.

Proceeding east to Fifth Avenue, you may notice that it looks and feels more like a European boulevard than any other street in Manhattan. Although it's the same width as Manhattan's other avenues—one hundred feet from building line to building line—Fifth looks different for two basic reasons. The city, after much urging from the merchants' Fifth Avenue Association, kept the sidewalks wide for more elegant promenading. Second, Fifth has a solid street wall: not projecting and receding storefronts, but contiguous buildings with brick and stone facades that hold a visual alignment up the avenue as far as the eye can see. Most American city streets look more like Las Vegas than Paris, but not New York's Fifth Avenue.

Cross Fifth Avenue now and turn right at 48th Street. On the north side of the street, at 5 East 48th Street, is the **Church of Sweden**, originally the International Bible Society, designed in 1921 by Hardie Philip.

To serve as a "home away from home" for the city's 3,000 Swedish citizens and its many Swedish visitors, the Church of Sweden bought this Gothic/Deco jewel in 1978 for $570,000, just before Manhattan's real estate market soared. Four years later the church sold the building's "air rights" to the aquamarine skyscraper next door for $1 million. The people back home in Sweden couldn't understand it—a city where builders buy air for a million bucks!

Air rights refer to the potential development rights of a particular site. If, for instance, the site has a five-story building, but could be developed under the zoning laws to create a twenty-story building, those fifteen unbuilt stories constitute that site's air rights. These rights can be sold to the developer of an adjacent plot so he can put up a bigger building than would normally be allowed for that location. Once sold, those air rights are permanently forfeited. If the five-story building is ever demolished, it can only be replaced by another building no more than five stories tall. Selling air rights has been one way that historic buildings such as churches have managed to survive the pressure to sell their valuable property.

You are actually looking at the backside of the skyscraper that bought the Church of Sweden's air rights, **Tower 49**, 10 East 49th Street, designed in 1982–1984 by Skidmore, Owings & Merrill. This sixteen-sided glass tower, providing the executive cadre eight corner offices per floor, has been outfitted for a Buck Rogers future. Constructed with a fiber-optic network, tenants plug in computers and other electronic equipment as if they were plugging in their toasters. The internal network allows for satellite communications systems and long-distance data transfer as well as running the building's own in-house services: heat, air-conditioning, fire prevention, and elevators. This is one of the so-called "smart" buildings.

Just as buildings that had steam elevators had to update or be left behind at the turn of the century, the new breed of smart buildings threaten to make older office buildings obsolete if their systems are not updated. Virtually every midtown high rise constructed within the last ten years qualifies as a smart building and virtually every building constructed before then will likely have to update or be relegated to "old-fashioned" status.

Return now to Fifth Avenue, staying on the east side of the avenue. Just north of 48th Street, at no. 597, you

The Church of Sweden on East 48th Street

come upon **Brentano's** bookstore, originally Scribner's bookstore, built from a design by Ernest Flagg in 1913. Charles Scribner's Sons, the venerable publisher of American greats like F. Scott Fitzgerald and Ernest Hemingway, created for its Fifth Avenue home a building whose Art Nouveau storefront is attention-getting, yet functional. This is a mellow bookstore where the bibliophile is welcome and browsing is considered an accepted pastime.

Across the avenue, just south of 49th Street, you see a striking Art Deco building, **608 Fifth Avenue**, originally the Goelet Building, built between 1930 and 1932. The Goelets, an old New York family who made their fortune in real estate, were known as people who created buildings of quality and distinction. A good example is an 1885 McKim, Mead & White building located on the southwest corner of Broadway and 20th Street, one of New York's earliest skyscrapers. For 608 Fifth, the Goelet mansion made way for this blue-ribbon structure contrasting green marble, white marble, and aluminum. Its street presence is reinforced with a slim, aluminum-leafed lobby that snakes to the building's incredible elevators. Adorned with unicorns and nudes crafted from what was then hi-tech aluminum, the elevator doors are matched by stunning designs in marble and granite on the floor and with more aluminum work on the ceiling. This is probably one of the most tightly compact pieces of Art Deco beauty in the city and definitely worth a visit.

Leaving the lobby, continue north to 49th Street and cross Fifth Avenue to **Saks Fifth Avenue**, 611 Fifth Avenue. Saks opened here in 1924, when the area was still considered "way uptown." It had originally been located at Herald Square, at Broadway and 34th Street, in the Herald Square building (now clad in a dark glass facade); but as the rich moved up Fifth Avenue, the merchants decided to follow the silk-stocking crowd, as they were known. Nowadays, the clientele is a mix of the well-to-do businessmen and women who work in the area—slightly more urbane than the Bloomingdale's crowd and a little less fancy than those who shop at Bergdorf Goodman. It's a niche that allows Saks to continue to be one of Fifth Avenue's busiest clothing department stores. The store's elegant Christmas windows are a popular part of Fifth Avenue's legendary holiday ambience.

This building of restrained elegance, like Brentano's, reinforces the avenue's European feel. The architects took a three-story Italian Renaissance palazzo and deftly stretched it on a steel frame to make an eleven-story department store. An eighth-floor restaurant, with moderate to expensive prices, offers a lovely view of St. Patrick's Cathedral and the Rockefeller Center Promenade and ice rink. Restrooms are located on the sixth floor for men and the fourth floor for women.

Standing in front of Saks, looking across Fifth Avenue, you are facing one of the finest commercial complexes ever built: **Rockefeller Center.** Not just buildings, but a commercial neighborhood that quickly became an integral part of the city that showed the twentieth century how to deal with the gargantuan scale of skyscrapers while maintaining intimacy. The center integrated mammoth buildings in a web of streets, promenades, gardens, and plazas that fully recognized the modern while nodding to the traditional. Expertly planned to handle masses of people, it always respects the individual.

In the early nineteenth century, New York State gave to Columbia University, then located near City Hall, a swath of countryside from 48th to 51st streets and from Fifth Avenue almost to Sixth. By the time the university was ready to move here in the 1850s, however, the countryside was ripe for development by the rich. Columbia relocated to Madison Avenue and 49th Street and filled this property with fashionable town houses to let. By World War I, Fifth Avenue and Columbia's brownstones had gone commercial. During Prohibition the brownstones became Midtown's speakeasy belt.

In the late 1920s, Columbia was approached by the Metropolitan Opera Company, which sought to develop the vast property. The Opera Company envisioned a city-within-the-city with a new Metropolitan Opera House, then located at Broadway and 39th Street, as its centerpiece. Unable to finance such a huge project by itself, the opera turned to John D. Rockefeller, Jr., who lived on West 54th Street. John D. went for it, leasing Columbia's property and laying plans for the new Metropolitan Square complex in 1929. A few months later, the Stock Market crash forced the Opera out of the project and John D. was stuck with the leases. Undaunted, he decided to build his own version of the plan as only a fortune like Rockefeller's could in the worsening years of the Depression.

In 1985 Columbia University sold the land under the original 1930s complex to the Rockefeller Group, the family's investment company leasing the property. The 11.7 acres went for $400 million (that's about $34 million per acre), at the time a record for Manhattan real estate. More recently, stories have swirled that Japanese business interests—such as Sony and Matsushita—had bought control of Rockefeller Center. Actually, Japanese business interests have a stake in the holding company that owns the center, nothing more.

The best view of the Center is where you are standing, in front of Saks opposite the Center's **Promenade**—or, as it is officially known, the **Channel Gardens**, providing a sweeping vista of the entire complex and especially its centerpiece, the former RCA Building (renamed the **GE Building** in 1990), at 30 Rockefeller Plaza. The RCA Building (as it continues to be known), rising where the opera house would have been, is a masterful achievement combining enormity with sensitivity. When the seventy-story skyscraper opened, it was the largest private office building in the world and headquarters to NBC and its parent company, RCA. A third family corporation, RKO, was enthroned atop the **Radio City Music Hall**, a building that represented the super-flash technology of twentieth-century communications. Radio City, as the entire complex was called, gave the radio, movie, and record industries an appropriate symbol of their power and New York was given an appropriate symbol of its strength in those industries.

Radio City Music Hall opened in the midst of the Depression, brainchild of Samuel L. "Roxy" Rothafel, a New York entertainment mogul who had developed the Roxy movie palace at Times Square. The original Rockettes, the famous leggy dancers with the trademark sky-high kick step, were first known as "Roxyettes." Roxy liked things done in a splashy way, and his music hall showed it. The entrepreneur talked big, too. The stunning proscenium before the stage resembled a rising sun, said

Roxy, because it was conceived while he was on a trans-atlantic cruise while viewing a stunning sunrise. Architectural evidence indicates it was likely lifted from European theater designs popular at the time.

When Radio City Music Hall opened, it had a luxurious lobby and a stage that could open and close at the push of a button, including a giant spinning section in the middle operated by hydraulics. In fact, it had everything that a modern theater could, except patrons. Roxy's idea of entertainment—a lavish extravaganza—turned out to have too high an admission price for New Yorkers in the middle of the Depression. The theater closed on opening night and the music hall was deemed a failure. Soon afterward Roxy died, some say from heartbreak.

But what was considered Roxy's failure eventually reopened as a venue for live entertainment, with simple shows within the budget of average theatergoers. It became a smashing success. Renovated in 1979, the theater is now considered one of the city's premier entertainment halls.

The striking style of the stage and lobby of Radio City Music Hall is echoed throughout the original Rockefeller Center complex. The imagery of the RCA Building is a German Expressionist vision of the city, which served as the prime spirit behind New York's skyscraper style of the 1920s. The movement saw the skyscraper as a secular cathedral dominating the modern city in the same way great cathedrals towered over medieval towns.

When architect Raymond Hood was chosen to design Rockefeller Center, the New York skyscraper was reshaped. Hood and Associated Architects, who designed the Center, listened to the Modernist voices coming out of Europe. Le Corbusier, Mies van der Rohe, and Walter Gropius wanted to open up skyscraper cities to sunlight and spaciousness. Hood and his team joined these ideas with the 1920s Expressionism. The result is pure American.

Crossing Fifth Avenue to the Channel Gardens, we

arrive at the center's "grand promenade," designed in the European manner but built to an American scale. This promenade, threaded through skyscrapers, was planned as a pedestrian "street" lined with shops so that it would simultaneously serve the public and profit the developer. This "street" began with the Promenade in front of you, then continued through the sunken plaza to the statue of Prometheus and on to the subway station. The idea was that commuters could pour through the Center, against a backdrop as dignified and civilized as the grand boulevards of Europe. In a country that had largely worshiped rural virtues and small-town living, Rockefeller Center was an astonishing achievement.

This public promenade and plaza were mind-boggling to a capitalist country whose cities were intensely cultivated for private development. Unlike Europe, America had no aristocratic tradition of public urban spaces. Typical of an American city, there was not one public square between the Public Library at 42nd Street and Grand Army Plaza at 59th Street. If you wanted to sit down you had to go into a coffee shop and pay for the privilege.

Rockefeller changed all that by providing for public spaces on private property. He did it, he said, for profit. Amenities like these, and others he included in the Center, allowed him to charge premium rents in the depths of the Depression, thereby setting a precedent that coaxed other private developers to do the same. It was a uniquely American way for our cities to provide the kind of public plazas Europeans took for granted.

The sunken plaza itself has been made famous by its wintertime ice-skating rink. When finished in 1932 it was intended as the shop-lined grand entrance to the RCA Building's shopping mall and subway station, but the station didn't open until 1940 and the plaza remained lifeless. Finally, at Christmastime 1936, out of desperation, the plaza's sunken floor was used as an ice-skating rink and a New York legend was born. Ironically the success of the skating rink foiled one of the planners'

Christmas angels at Rockefeller Plaza

original aims. People were meant to move *through* the Center from Fifth to Sixth Avenue. Instead, having reached and encircled the skating rink, visitors are more likely to return to Fifth. What had been meant as a grand east-west axis became a truncated cul-de-sac.

Rockefeller Plaza soon became New York's "town square," surrounded by skyscrapers much like a medieval square was bordered by its cathedral. Rather than dark and brooding, however, our modern square is light filled, open, and airy because Hood "streamlined" the skyscrapers, making them slender "slabs" in the Le Corbusier manner instead of the mammoth blocks of the typical Deco silhouette. Had the Plaza been surrounded by the likes of the Chrysler Building, hubcaps and hood ornaments notwithstanding, this inviting town center would have been cast in permanent gloom. Rockefeller's planners also included an extra north-south street, so necessary in a city chronically short of north-south avenues. The new street, Rockefeller Plaza, opened up the mid-block sections of the complex to better access—and higher rents.

The north-south passage was originally to terminate at the Museum of Modern Art's new building on 53rd Street, visually integrating a palace of culture into this high-rise compound of commerce. Unfortunately, a private property owner refused to sell, and the Center's north-south axis was cut back to West 51st Street. Had the plan succeeded, Rockefeller's Center's vistas, combining the corporate and artistic worlds, would have been a stunning tour de force.

The "slab" design of the Center's skyscrapers opened up not only the plaza, but the cross streets as well, making them feel distinctly different from the rest of Midtown. Inside the slab, no office space was more than twenty-eight feet from a window so that all office workers had access to open windows and sunlight. Unlike the Europeans, who wanted buildings on stilts like the Seagram Building (1959) on Park Avenue, Hood placed his new office slabs on a traditional solid base—but one that rose three stories, not sixteen. This made the Center's streets feel traditional with solid street walls, plenty of shop fronts, and a low-rise human scale; Rock Center's streets seem comfortable and familiar, with the skyscrapers almost "disappearing" from view.

The entire Center was placed on a multilevel service base. You're standing on the top "deck." The European Modernists wanted the base to be a podium in the manner of Le Corbusier's "Ville Radieuse" sketches of 1925. Rising above the city's streets the deck would be free of cars, like Lincoln Center or the World Trade Center in the 1960s. But, those car-free plazas were devoid of people as well as cars and their blank retaining walls made them stand aloof from the city. Rockefeller Center's deck is at street level with its "podium" sunk below ground so the Center melds seamlessly with the city around it. Though New Yorkers are always passing through Rockefeller Center, they never know where the city "ends" and the Center "begins," making it the friendly gray giant of Midtown.

Running through this base at the same level as the skating rink is an extensive underground street system, lined with shops, linking the Center's buildings and the subway line. The underground concourse was extended in the 1970s to the west side of Sixth Avenue and, after a recent remodeling, is being extended to Seventh Avenue via the 1986 Equitable Center. The skyscrapers plug into a veritable mall of approximately two hundred shops and thirty-five restaurants all accessible to any Rockefeller Center employee or visitor. Below the underground streets, under the skating rink, is a truck unloading dock that banishes trucks and their cargoes from the surface. No double-parked trucks mean fewer traffic jams, less horn honking, and easier maneuvering for pedestrians, another reason why Rock Center's streets feel so different from the rest of the city. The city below was created to civilize the city above. The Modernists in Europe may have sketched it, but it was the Americans who made it actually work. When its moment in history had passed Rockefeller Center's special lessons were forgotten, but in the 1980s the Center's principles are once more being studied and copied. Manhattan's newest "city," Battery Park City near the World Trade Center, has been designed to carefully follow Rockefeller Center's civilized example. Above and below ground, Rockefeller Center is a pleasant exploration that can last hours.

Keeping pace with the tour, however, now walk north to 50th Street and Fifth Avenue to **St. Patrick's Cathedral.**

New York's first Catholic cathedral opened in 1815 at Mott and Prince streets in Little Italy. Its modest size reflected the status of Catholics in an overwhelmingly Protestant country. Massive waves of Irish Catholic immigration beginning in the 1830s changed that. By the 1850s half of New York City's population was foreign born, and half of those were Irish. The Irish were changing the city and in 1858 they began building a new cathedral.

When completed in 1877, St. Patrick's Cathedral immediately dominated this stretch of the avenue, creating an ironic situation. Here, above the chateaux of New York's rigidly Protestant society, soared a Catholic cathedral representing the power of a burgeoning immigrant population. The Cathedral's architecture has ironies as well. The neo-Gothic style became popular here in the 1840s in a nation of Yankee businessmen who tended toward a severe, deritualized congregationalism. In a country without its own Gothic age or the medieval outlook, nineteenth-century American neo-Gothic looks like a cutout from a doll's book. When used for smaller churches it could be charming, but inflated to the size of St. Patrick's, the eleventh-largest church in the world in 1870, the style's stiffness becomes more apparent. The granite exterior, whose hardness adds to that stiffness, was cleaned in 1979. There's a booklet about the church just inside the entrance.

Detail of door, St. Patrick's Cathedral

Walking east on 50th Street, on the south side of the cathedral, across the street—above and behind Saks—is the headquarters of **Swiss Bank Corporation**, designed by Lee Harris Pomeroy in 1990, which used air rights from the landmark-designated (likely to be preserved) Saks building. Set back from the avenue, its presence is discreet to pedestrians on Fifth, while its carefully articulated facade firmly anchors the vista from Rockefeller Center's Channel Gardens.

At Madison Avenue and 50th Street, we reach another amalgam of old and new, the **Villard Houses**, by McKim, Mead & White, at 451–57 Madison Avenue between 50th and 51st streets, topped by the Helmsley Palace Hotel. Although this may look like one giant palace, there were originally six different residences that made up the Villard Houses. If you look closely, you can notice the segmentation in the facade that demarcates each house. The residences were designed to look like a single, grand Italian Renaissance palazzo for Henry Villard, Bavarian-born owner of the New York *Evening Post* and founder of the Northern Pacific Railroad. Building an ensemble of middle-class row houses and disguising them to look like a single aristocratic palace was an old and showy architectural trick, dating from eighteenth-century English "terraces." But the ostentatious ploy backfired on Villard. Shortly after the houses' completion Villard went bankrupt, ruining his stockholders, who—thinking that the entire complex was his alone and built with their lost money—almost stormed his house to extract revenge. The houses, created by the first generation of professionally trained American architects, mark a milestone in American architectural history, launching the Beaux Arts era in New York.

Villard's own house was in the south wing of the U-shaped complex. Augustus Saint-Gaudens and John LaFarge, America's premier sculptor and painter, worked with architect Stanford White to create triumphant interiors.

In 1969 the owner of the property, the Catholic Church, looking to redevelop the site, began working with builder Harry Helmsley, who proposed demolishing the building for a new hotel. When preservationists threatened battle on the plan, a compromise emerged that preserved much of the Villard Houses. The Fahnstock house in the north wing was leased to the Municipal Art Society for the Urban Center, and the hotel was built behind the facade of the central three houses, with the courtyard retained as a grand entrance. Enter the hotel on 50th or 51st Street between Madison and Park avenues. The interiors are open to the public only for the stiff price of a stiff drink at the bar (which is a little stiff, too: a dress code is enforced) located in Villard's former dining room. The hotel's lobby (new, but designed to look antique) includes a mezzanine-level fireplace by Saint-Gaudens, rescued from Villard's town house. One thing you will notice at the Palace is that service has been refined to an art and you will be treated royally.

Leaving the lobby at 51st Street, return now toward Fifth Avenue to the **Olympic Tower**, 645 Fifth Avenue, designed by Skidmore, Owings & Merrill. Built in 1976, this was the swan song of the "glass box" in New York, and not a moment too soon. This bronze glass monolith looms over Fifth Avenue. The building actually has three parts: a two-story galleria at ground level; a seventeen-story office tower above with its entrance in the galleria; and a thirty-story coop apartment house. Enter the galleria at East 51st Street.

The galleria and the apartments were created as amenities because the tower is located in a special zoning district, approved in 1971, that encompasses this stretch of Fifth Avenue. By adding the apartments and galleria, the developer earned a zoning bonus which allowed him to build a bigger building—in this case an extra eight or nine lucrative floors. But things did not go as planned. The galleria stood empty for five years (after the developer balked at holding up his end of the zoning bargain) and the arcade was not completed until 1981, after the city threatened legal action.

Finally, the arcade opened and it appeared to be a success. An extension of the Rockefeller Center "idea" into the 1980s, the Olypmic galleria was a light-filled, tree-lined indoor street that the public could enjoy winter or summer. Public seating was available for "brown-bagging" a lunch or one could take advantage of the cafés and bars to meet a friend. However, by 1991 that had all changed again. Perhaps to discourage street people and the homeless from congregating here, most of the public seating had disappeared, except for the tables and chairs by the waterfall; the galleria became lackluster.

Exit now through the northern 52nd Street exit of Olympic Tower. Turning left, toward Fifth Avenue, we pass **Cartier** on the southeast corner of 52nd and Fifth, occupying two modest survivors of a row of millionaire's homes that once stretched along this block. The corner house was built for Morton F. Plant, a wealthy New Yorker. It and its neighbor were sold in 1917 to the French jewelry firm, Cartier, for their American base. In a story not unlike that of the purchase of Manhattan by the Dutch for beads and trinkets worth $24, legend has it that the price of the Cartier building was one pearl necklace—then worth $1 million. Ironically, soon after Cartier's barter, cultured pearls made their debut, drastically lowering the value of the necklace.

Retracing your steps, enter the HarperCollins Building at 52nd Street almost directly across from where you exited Olympic Tower. This covered pedestrian walkway is a convenient way to cross to 3 East 53rd Street, where you will encounter **Paley Park**, officially known as Samuel Paley Plaza.

The park is built on the site where the original Stork Club stood. Sherman Billingsly, owner—some would say "czar"—of the nightclub, ran the Stork Club like his own fiefdom during the 1950s, with a door policy that set a standard for exclusion unmatched until the appearance of the city's 1970s clubs, such as Studio 54. No amount of money or fame could pull back the velvet ropes of the Stork Club unless Billingsly said so. In a particularly infamous refusal, he denied Josephine Baker entrance.

The urban retreat that occupies the space today was a 1967 gift from the head of CBS, the late William Paley, and named for his father. Its inauguration was a breakthrough: for the first time since the opening of Rockefeller Center, New Yorkers were given a humanely-designed public space in Midtown to use and enjoy, and, again, it was provided by a private entrepreneur. Using a waterfall to mask the city's noises, trees to blot out the sky-scrapers, movable chairs to allow us to create our own conversation groups, and a small café for munching, Paley Park was instantly popular. After years of skyscrapers fronted by empty plazas—à la the 1959 Seagram Building at Park Avenue and 52nd Street—Paley Park proves that urban spaces *can* be lively and people-filled.

The civility of Paley Park induced the city in 1971 to revise its 1961 zoning code. The newer skyscrapers on our tour were all designed under this revised code and that's why most of them sit atop a galleria, parklet, or atrium. Paley Park, updating the best elements of Rockefeller Center, was the original model for this 1980s generation of skyscrapers.

Return now, via 53rd Street, to Fifth Avenue. At the northwest corner is **St. Thomas's Protestant Episcopal Church and Parish House**, 1 West 53rd Street, designed in 1914 by Cram, Goodhue & Ferguson. The original St. Thomas's opened at Broadway and Houston Street in 1826, but as its parishioners began moving uptown in the mid-1800s, the church building followed in 1870. That building burned down and was replaced with the present sanctuary in 1914. Architect Bertram Goodhue was a master at updating and personalizing ecclesiastical designs. Unencumbered by allegiance to nineteenth-century notions of Gothic design, Goodhue's relaxed proportions and brilliance at integrating decorative elements breathed life into his personalized Gothic style. He managed, on this cramped site, to create a powerfully accented corner with the upward sweep of the south tower showing skillful architectural play. Check for organ and choral recitals on Sundays and Wednesdays; the setting couldn't be finer.

Head west now on 53rd Street to the **Museum of Modern Art (MOMA)** at 11 West 53rd Street, designed over the years by a virtual colonnade of pillars in the temple of twentieth-century architecture: Edward Durell Stone and Philip L. Goodwin (1939), Philip

Johnson (1962), and Cesar Pelli with Gruen Associates (1979–84).

MOMA was founded in 1929 to innovate and set trends in design—not merely to "collect" as other museums did. It indeed set a trend when one of its first shows, the 1931 "International Style" exhibition, brought to the United States the radical architectural ideas of the young European Modernists. The show's curators, Henry-Russell Hitchcock and Philip Johnson, went on—the former through his writings and the latter through his buildings—to have an enormous influence on postwar American architecture. The show's title was soon applied to the Modern movement itself, and when the museum finally built its own home in 1939 the building was used as a sounding board for the new "International Style" by embracing the style itself, with geometric shapes and undecorated flat surfaces used to make it look something like a machine-made product with a no-nonsense functional design. The museum's 1939 facade was just the right scale. Modern buildings larger than the original MOMA can present an oversized geometry and undecorated severity that overwhelms. Set down in a row of 1880s brownstones, its brusque Modernism stood out boldly—like an Isadora Duncan among fussy Victorian matrons. But all that has changed. Since its opening, the museum has progressively consumed its neighbors with low-rise additions and, finally, its own high-rise tower.

The Museum Tower was conceived in 1979 to insure MOMA's financial stability in an age of shrinking subsidies and fewer patrons. MOMA sold its air rights to a private developer for $17 million so that a 53-story luxury condominium apartment house could be built over the new west wing. The condo owners' real estate taxes do not go to the city. Instead, they are paid, via a special New York State–approved fund, directly to the museum. The fund can be used by other museums for the same purpose. It was in the service of this "good" cause that MOMA bulldozed one of Midtown's low-rise side streets

Viewing a Picasso at the Museum of Modern Art

for this monolithic tower, in much the same way that Tower 49 obliterated the pre–World War II East 49th Street and the IBM/Trump/AT&T complex (which you'll see later) erased low-rise East 55th Street. Critics grumbled that the museum was acting like an ordinary developer out to maximize profit. The museum argued that if it didn't build the tower, what were the alternatives for such a lucrative guaranteed income?

The tower's glass mosaiclike decoration is composed of twelve subtly different colors that are used to visually separate the floors and to pick out the different types of apartments. Can you? The coloring job was Mr. Pelli's Postmodern bid to bring back decoration to skyscraper design fifty years after MOMA's famous show made such decoration absolutely taboo.

The museum's collection is world renowned, including such masterpieces as Dali's *Persistence of Memory*, Picasso's *Head of a Bull* (the one made of a bicycle seat and handlebars), and a design collection that includes the Movado watch, an Olivetti typewriter, and a Sikorsky helicopter. The new western wing doubled MOMA's exhibition space, allowing more than 80 percent of the museum's holdings to be displayed. The museum film series are excellent and its enlarged sculpture garden facing West 54th Street is one of New York's better retreats. Don't forget the gift shop; like many other museums today, MOMA is aggressively marketing its "wares."

Across the street and slightly to the west of MOMA, you come upon the **The American Craft Museum**, 40 West 53rd Street, which houses an intriguing collection of Americana and has a reputation for hosting compelling exhibits. Started in 1957, the museum serves as a repository for a collection of post–World War II American arts and crafts. Included in the huge permanent collection are ceramic, metal, glass, and fiber used in both applied and fine arts. Next door, at **31 West 52nd Street**, is the museum's humbled neighbor, the former E. F. Hutton Building. How the mighty do fall! E. F. Hutton, the venerable Wall Street brokerage house, planned this new headquarters at the height of the 1980s boom, only to be consumed in a corporate takeover and then dismembered in the 1990s bust. Architects Roche & Dinkeloo gave the lobby here (entered at the far southern end of the plaza that fronts the building's west side) a neo-Deco/Assyrian theatricality that plays off well against the austerity of the CBS Building next door to the west. The lobby becomes even more dramatic at dusk when the high ceiling lights come on. Though not popular with the design cognoscenti around town, this reminiscence of 1920s architecture-as-theater is certainly more enjoyable than MOMA's pompously sterile lobby-as-art. The tower itself, with its jagged edges and "splayed" mansard on top, adds a dash of personality to the skyline. And check out the plaza, a comfortable space to stroll or sit for a break. Note that the plaza and its neighbor, CBS's plaza, meet but don't talk—an opportunity to merge the two was lost when they were designed to exist at two different levels, joined only by a small stairway.

At the south end of the plaza, at 52nd Street, look eastward, toward Fifth Avenue, to the new **Museum of Radio and Television** (formerly the Museum of Broadcasting) at 25 West 52nd Street, designed by Philip Johnson in yet another homage to the great buildings of the past. The museum, devoted to our newest media, specializes in exhibits and screenings of vintage TV shows: Sid Caesar, *Leave It to Beaver*, and *M*A*S*H* are available for viewing in one of eighty carrels. Next to the museum is the famed **21 Club.** When the Stork Club was at its prime, the 21 Club was its main competition, but unlike its exclusionary competitor, the 21 Club let in anyone properly dressed and carrying sufficient funds. A similar policy holds today.

Now go to Sixth Avenue, officially Avenue of the Americas, walking one block west along 52nd Street. On the northeast corner of the avenue stands the **CBS Building** at 51 West 52nd Street. This building is very much a monument to the man who conceived it, CBS's late chairman, William S. Paley, the media pioneer whose egomania set the tone for how network television was run from its inception until the late twentieth century. Paley's patronage can be seen throughout the neighborhood. Besides opening Paley Park, he donated the land for both the old and new homes of the Museum of Broadcasting and was MOMA's chairman throughout its latest expansion. For this 1965 shrine to TV, Paley contracted one of America's great postwar architects, Eero Saarinen, to give CBS a corporate classic. Saarinen, practicing in the Modern era, tended to be an un-Modern architect, preferring the sculpted and solid to the glass boxes of the day. Here, in his only constructed skyscraper, he fused the old-fashioned need for solidity with the prevailing desire for functionalism by eliminating the steel cage of beams and supports, opting for a relatively new kind of skyscraper construction. Affectionately known as "Black Rock," the CBS Building is a giant tube of reinforced concrete piers elegantly clad in black granite. The rigid structural frame of the exterior piers, with an elevator core in the building's center, supports the entire building, so that what appears to be decorative vertical piers on the exterior are actually functional. Thus, CBS's office floors are open and column-free spaces. Unfortunately, the building does not seem to relate to street-level dynamics, with a sunken plaza that offers little for the pedestrian—a case of "plaza-itis": too much empty space, not much purpose.

At this point on Sixth Avenue, take a moment to look up and down this broad boulevard. Even for opponents of the International style, there is something stunning about this row of monumental buildings that stand along the avenue like so many oversized books on a broad urban shelf. Proceed north to 54th Street and turn right at the **Warwick Hotel.** This is the hotel The Beatles called home when they played New York in the mid-1960s. Thousands of teens would flock to the Warwick, hoping for glimpses of the Fab Four. Often, the groupies—mostly girls—would prowl nearby buildings looking for the secret passages that supposedly allowed the Liverpool boys to enter and exit unnoticed. The fact that the passages don't exist didn't discourage the hunt.

Walking east to 17 West 54th Street, you encounter the **Rockefeller Apartments.** The Rockefellers have been associated with this street and this neighborhood since 1885, when John D. Rockefeller, Sr., bought a freestanding brownstone mansion on the south side of the block. After being raised in that house, John D., Jr., built his own house next door and there brought up his five children, including Nelson (who became governor of New

York and U.S. vice president) and David (head of Chase Manhattan Bank). When John D., Sr., died in 1936, John D., Jr., who was then developing Rockefeller Center "in the neighborhood," gave his family's homes to the Museum of Modern Art as the site for its new museum.

Wallace K. Harrison, in charge of Rockefeller Center's plans after Raymond Hood's death and soon to marry into the Rockefeller family, designed this intimate apartment house in an early expression of the International Style, at the time a shocking departure from traditional practice. Its minimalist detailing, functional beige brick and glass bays, emphasis on light and air, and willingness to give up rentable interior space for an open courtyard, wider sidewalks, and street-side landscaping broke new ground in urban design. MOMA's opening three years later would make this part of the city a hotbed of Modernism.

Harrison went on to become the Rockefeller's "court architect," having an important role in the design of the United Nations Building (1950), Lincoln Center (1965), and the Albany Mall (1978)—all Rockefeller-inspired projects.

At **13–15 West 54th Street** are twin houses designed by the architect of the Plaza Hotel, Henry J. Hardenbergh, in 1895. Nelson Rockefeller, who grew up across the street, died in 1979 at his office at no. 15 while in the company of an assistant. Circumstances suggest "Rocky" enjoyed his life to the end.

Next on our walk is **U.S. Trust Headquarters** at 9–11 West 54th Street. This neo-Georgian double town house, built in 1896 by McKim, Mead & White, was built for James J. Goodwin, a partner of J. P. Morgan. The wider no. 11 was Goodwin's own house, while no. 9 was built for income—a posh example of the simple two-family house. His son, Philip Goodwin, was coarchitect of MOMA's 1939 building a block away.

Continuing east on 54th, you come to **5 and 7 West 54th Street**. The entire stretch of town houses on West

54th Street were built in 1900 on St. Luke's land and remain miraculously intact today. Their survival gives us only a hint of what this neighborhood was like when it was New York's residential Gold Coast at the turn of the twentieth century. These two houses were built for Philip Lehman, a banker whose empire would eventually become today's Shearson Lehman Brothers. His son, financier Robert Lehman, inherited the house and filled it with a remarkable collection of paintings that in 1976 became the Lehman Wing of the Metropolitan Museum of Art.

As you walk along this stretch, peek through the iron rail fence of MOMA and glimpse the sculpture garden. The changing exhibits here make good use of the light and air and provide a tranquil setting for the likes of Marc Chagall stabiles and Anthony Bladen sculptures. You may hear the strains of a cello or violin as you stroll: The garden sometimes serves as a concert setting.

You are now approaching the **University Club**, 1 West 54th Street, built in 1896–1899 by—yes—McKim, Mead & White. The club's home was created by the same brilliantly restrained hands that created the Villard Houses (1885), the Morgan Library (1906) on East 36th Street, and a dozen-odd other classical parfaits. When the University Club was built, private clubs, founded and patronized by the city's richest men, had grown to the size of hotels. Charles McKim used his knowledge of proportion, scale, and history learned at the École des Beaux-Arts to create the illusion of a "small" Italian palazzo that was really a skyscraper clubhouse. The club's interiors are among the most handsome in the city. Unfortunately, except for members and their guests, one can only see them from the sidewalk when the house lights go on at dusk.

As you reach Fifth Avenue, note the **Aeolian Building** on the northeast corner, at 691 Fifth Avenue. This twelve-story gem from the avenue's classic age of commercial architecture features a limestone facade, rounded corner, and delicate eighteenth-century detailing and cornice line that reinforce the avenue's feeling as a grand boulevard for commerce and retailing as compared to the stand-alone statements of Trump and Olympic towers. Across the street, one door east of the southeast corner, is the former Famolare Shoe Store at **4 East 54th Street**, another McKim, Mead & White masterpiece. Cross Fifth Avenue here and head east on 54th Street. At 3 East 54th, **Bice Ristorante**, which has been offering alfresco dining since 1926, offers a good place for people watching over an espresso or a Campari and soda.

As you reach Madison Avenue, you see the **Continental Illinois Center**, 520 Madison Avenue, on the southwest corner of Madison and 54th Street. Of the 1980s crop of Midtown skyscrapers, this may be the worst. It's big and clumsy with a sloped base breaking the street wall of Madison Avenue for no apparent purpose, and a red-and-black granite facade that is poorly detailed and cheap looking. There is one bit of relief, however. Puncturing the building's pomposity is Reidy's, a restaurant popular with the Midtown business crowd. Originally part of a five-story townhouse, the restaurant was cut down to two stories and integrated into the skyscraper's mezzanine level. Owned and operated by the Reidy family at this location since 1947, the restaurant, which includes a bar, features a friendly staff and serves moderately priced home-style food.

On the northeast corner, at **535 Madison Avenue**, is an Edward Larrabee Barnes building. Barnes, architect of the IBM Building up the avenue, created a small Postmodern skyscraper here with notches at both the top and the bottom. Its streamlined aluminum-clad tower feels light, but its solid base provides a strong street presence. On the east side of the building's 54th Street frontage is a slightly larger version of Paley Park, including a fifty-foot waterfall.

Go north now on Madison Avenue to 55th Street. On the northwest corner stands the triumphant **AT&T Building** (soon to be the Sony Building), perhaps the greatest achievement in Philip Johnson's career. One of the most outstanding features of this building is the public space at its base. When the weather's warm, it's hard to find a place to sit, perhaps the best possible compliment for a public space. Inside, the 1916 gold-leaf statue *Spirit of Communication* by Evelyn Longman was removed from AT&T's old downtown headquarters at 195 Broadway and made the lobby's centerpiece. The building's broken pediment top—resembling a Chippendale highboy—became an instant landmark on the city's skyline.

Turning left at Madison onto 55th Street, head toward Fifth Avenue to the **St. Regis–Sheraton**, 2 East 55th Street, at the southeast corner of Fifth. The St. Regis was one of the "Astor" hotels built by the old New York family near the turn of this century. Another "Astor" hotel, the Knickerbocker, at Broadway and 42nd Street, was popular with the theater crowd. The Knickerbocker, known as the "country club of 42nd," hosted such guests as Enrico Caruso and George M. Cohan, both of whom lived there. It had gold service setting for parties of sixty. Its grand bar, which fronted a 1908 mural by Maxfield Parrish, *Old King Cole*, served as the main watering hole for the city's turn of the century high society. After the Knickerbocker closed, the mural was moved into the St. Regis and for many years served as the backdrop for the hotel's handsome King Cole Restaurant.

When it opened, the St. Regis featured the latest in American gadgetry: air-conditioning and a centralized vacuum cleaner system with outlets in every room. The lobby floor was once threaded with elegant dining rooms but the cafés were replaced by shops (such as Bijan menswear store) when Fifth Avenue went commercial. After a recent renovation, the St. Regis now claims to be among the city's most expensive hotels, with rooms beginning at $350 per night. The enormous Maxfield Parrish painting can be seen in the newly created—although antique-looking—bar at the far eastern end of the lobby.

Walking to Fifth Avenue and turning right, you come

to 711 Fifth Avenue, **The Coca Cola Building,** formerly the headquarters of Columbia Pictures. This is another great building from the avenue's classical period. Like the Aeolian Building, its scale, detailing, and limestone facade preserve Fifth Avenue's "boulevard" elegance without sacrificing function or modern amenities.

Look now across Fifth Avenue to the southwest corner of Fifth and 55th to **The Peninsula Hotel,** originally the Gotham Hotel, at 2 West 55th Street. The Gotham was a Renaissance palazzo stretched to twenty-one stories, then embroidered with an un-Renaissance flamboyance. In 1981, the Gotham was bought by the Nova-Park group, a Swiss hotel chain that restored the exterior, gutted the interior to create a "grand hotel" in the Continental tradition, and then sold the hotel to its current owners. Renovations included two new stories added for a health club, skating rink, restaurant, and garden terrace—all open to the public.

As you look across to the west side of Fifth Avenue between 55th and 56th streets you see the **Fifth Avenue Presbyterian Church** at the northwest corner of 55th and Fifth, followed by a small series of exquisite storefronts. In the late 1980s a developer planned to demolish these two smaller buildings at **712 and 714 Fifth Avenue** to make way for another blockbuster skyscraper. Preservationists fumed that more of Fifth Avenue's prewar elegance would be lost. When it was discovered that the windows on the upper floors of the **Coty Building** (no. 714) were the work of French glass designer René Lalique, the buildings were immediately designated city landmarks over the objections of the owner, who was forced to incorporate the smaller buildings into the new development. The historic facades (for everything behind them was demolished) front a new version of the Henri Bendel specialty store that was formerly on West 57th Street. At the southwest corner of Fifth and 56th Street is Harry Winston, the jeweler who bedecked Madonna in $20-million worth of diamonds when she performed at the 1991 Oscars.

Fifth Avenue Presbyterian Church

At 56th Street, turn right and walk east. Here, on this block between Fifth and Madison, you will see what some call the Big Three, three buildings that occupy spaces where over two dozen once stood. The display of architectural virtuosity is dazzling, but what has resulted is a Midtown more overpowering, congested, and expensive than ever before. Retail space in the new **Trump Tower**, which is before you on the northeast corner of 56th and Fifth, is over three times the price of lofts on West 56th Street.

Like Olympic Tower, Trump Tower is a three-part skyscraper consisting of a twenty-story office building and a forty-story condominium apartment building over a dazzling six-level shopping center. The luxurious shops are wrapped around a skylighted atrium lined with exquisite (some would say gaudy) rose-colored Italian marble and polished brass and bronze tinted mirrors and dominated by a sixty-foot waterfall. The entire package, both tower and atrium, is wrapped in reflective glass and is stepped at the base.

There are two outdoor public gardens, a tiny one at the fourth level facing East 56th Street and a larger one at the top floor with tables for brown-bagging a lunch and a small café for drinks. The upper garden lays out a spectacular view of East 57th Street. All said and done, though, the bulk of this "public" atrium is an upscale shopping center. The look—too much marble and too much brass in too narrow a space—lends a display-case feeling to this monument to the ultraconsumerism of the late twentieth century. But the building has proven to be one of the most popular tourist stops on Fifth Avenue, with jaunty touches such as the high-hatted doormen adding a bit of humor to the corner.

As you proceed to 56th Street and Madison Avenue, you come upon the **IBM Building**, designed by Edward Larrabee Barnes, at the northwest corner. The IBM Building's granite-clad tower looms over a public space that contrasts starkly with the Trump Tower atrium. Nature, rather than retailing, is the centerpiece here. A bamboo-filled atrium, a small outlet for the New York Botanical Gardens, leads to the IBM Gallery for traveling art exhibitions. The twenty-foot-tall bamboo plants that remain green all year, the rotating planters whose floral displays change seasonally, the movable chairs for tailoring individual arrangements (echoes still of Paley Park), and the glass greenhouse enclosure make this a part of the Midtown scene while at the same time removed from it. Although everyone is welcome to the bamboo garden and IBM Gallery, don't expect kind treatment if you attempt to go upstairs uninvited. IBM takes its security very seriously and is rigorous on who may use the elevators. You can be sure that the security technology on display in the lobby (visible from the bamboo garden) is some of the tightest in the city.

On the southwest corner, across 56th Street, you can again see the AT&T Building. Now that you've seen Trump Tower and the IBM Building, it becomes evident how the AT&T building was stylistically the most controversial of the Big Three because of its conscious throwback to the neoclassical skyscrapers of the prewar years.

Before heading north on Madison Avenue, spend a moment at the low, powerful fountain on the northwest corner of Madison and 56th at the base of the IBM Building. It is one of the most dramatic uses of a small space you will see along this walk. You might also want to try your hand at deciphering the marks on the edge of the fountain. Hint: the lines are coded references to surrounding street numbers.

Next, walk north along Madison to the southwest corner of 57th Street. Look up and witness the stunning architectural trick of the IBM Building, an entire skyscraper floating above your head!

On the northeast corner is the 1929 **Fuller Building**, 41 East 57th Street. This is the "new" home of the construction company whose former headquarters was the landmark Flatiron Building at Fifth Avenue and 23rd Street, seen in tile in this building's lobby floor. An excellent example of the Art Deco era, in its base are huge art gallery windows dictated by 57th Street's role as an art gallery "boulevard." The sculptures by Elie Nadelman over the two-story-high entrance are of two construction workers against a New York skyline—as built by Fuller, of course.

You are now on New York's vibrant 57th Street. After the Civil War this was the finest address in the city, home to the Vanderbilts, Whitneys, and Roosevelts. But the wealth and political power of its residents could not prevent the inevitable: the invasion of commerce following World War I.

The art galleries and smart shops of the street have a long tradition, including Carnegie Hall (1896), Aeolian Hall (1911), and the Art Students League (1891). By the 1920s, 57th Street was one of the centers of New York's cultural life. In the 1930s, 57th Street at Fifth became the retail hub for the city's most posh "specialty" department stores when Bergdorf Goodman (1930), Tiffany's (1940), and, later, Henri Bendel's (1955) opened their doors. Despite the intrusion of skyscrapers and the changes of commerce, the specialty stores here at 57th have held their own. This is still one of the world's most prestigious addresses for retailing.

Walk west on 57th Street—past boutiques for Burberry's, Hermès, and Chanel—to Fifth Avenue, and you will see a parade of the world's most beautifully dressed women and elegantly attired men strolling along the street. In a 1986 real estate survey it was estimated that 36 million people a year pass through this intersection. It's a corner to be savored.

On the southeast corner stands the streamlined Art Deco granite box that houses one of the city's oldest retail establishments. **Tiffany's** was founded in 1837 on Broadway opposite City Hall when that was New York's retail hub. Since then, the firm has moved north five times,

Street of fashion dreams: the Chanel window

reflecting the historical movement of the city's retail core up Manhattan Island.

At one Tiffany's location, Charles Tiffany, the firm's founder, had a local ship's carpenter carve a statue of Atlas out of wood, which was then hoisted above the store's entrance. Ever since, when Tiffany's has moved, Atlas has gone with it. Today, in a bronze coat, he looks out over Fifth and 57th and people assume he's made of solid bronze—after all, this *is* Tiffany's. The windows of Tiffany's let us get as close as we may ever come to the exquisite jewels that have rightfully earned the store its incredible reputation. The displays show off precious stones in charming miniature dioramas. Don't let the name Tiffany's scare you off from making a shopping foray. There are still some bargains to be found here, particularly on the third floor, where place settings and craftware are sold. Check the "bargain" table of odds and ends at the far corner. A Limoges espresso cup and saucer, for example, can be yours for less than $20. Also, expect to be waited on in the grand tradition: sales clerks who ask you to be seated when you make your purchase and who never touch money (special runners do that) and, of course, complimentary gift wrap in the famous Tiffany's blue boxes.

Across the avenue, on the southwest corner, is **The Crown Building**, 730 Fifth Avenue. The first skyscraper on this stretch of Fifth Avenue and the first to be completed after New York's landmark 1916 zoning code requiring setbacks for massive buildings so as to preserve street-level light, this clunky building with a boxy silhouette was not well received by the critics. Today, however, with its facade cleaned in 1982 and its spandrels freshly gold leafed with 23-karat gold and its top sensationally illuminated by lighting genius Douglas Leigh, it is a handsome facet of the skyline.

Across 57th on the northwest corner with Fifth Avenue is **Bergdorf Goodman**, 2 West 57th Street. Here once stood one of New York's most grand mansions, the home of Cornelius Vanderbilt II, a grandson of the "Commodore." Constructed in stages, the final cost for the 130-room mansion was $5 million at completion in 1893—and, in 1893 dollars, that's a lot. Built to last forever, it was demolished within thirty-two years for the building Bergdorf's now occupies.

Farther west on the north side of the street, at 9 West 57th, is the **Solow Building**, built in 1974 by Skidmore, Owings & Merrill. A heavy-handed addition to 57th Street, this fifty-story skyscraper's sloped facade appears like a science fiction monster gobbling up the street. Its travertine marble plaza and sidewalk had to be chemically roughened when it was discovered that the marble surface turned into a giant banana peel in wet weather, sending pedestrians flying. Many, though, find the building fascinating. The only thing that seems to have universal appeal here is the building's "address," a giant red 9 by Ivan Chermayeff set into the sidewalk.

Return now to Fifth Avenue, turning left and walking one block north to a two-block plaza, one of the city's most splendid public spaces, Grand Army Plaza, which reaches north to Central Park.

When Central Park was built, Americans readily understood the idea of an urban park: a slice of the American countryside set in the center of town. When Frederick Law Olmsted and Calvert Vaux created Central Park in the late 1850s, the idea caught on immediately and soon urban parks were being built across the nation. But if we understood the American idea of the park, we never understood the European idea of the public square. Creating a true public plaza—an outdoor room for the free use of the public—went against the American instinct for private enterprise. Grand Army Plaza is one of Manhattan's few places that create a plaza in the European sense.

The northern half of the plaza, which seems to merge with Central Park, is focused around Saint-Gaudens's 1903 statue of William Tecumseh Sherman, the Union general who led the murderous March to the Sea from Atlanta. The statue was regilded in 1990 and the resulting brightness of the gold leaf caused quite a stir. Researchers swore the statue originally looked as bright and that the mellower gold color of recent memory was the result of years of grime and exposure. But the surrounding corporations and landlords—who helped pay for the restoration—winced at what they perceived as the nouveau riche vulgarity of the offending color. One can't predict the outcome of this imbroglio, but certainly the generation that created this statue was not shy about parading its wealth.

The southern half of the plaza is centered on the Pulitzer Memorial Fountain topped by Karl Bitter's statue of

Abundance. Both halves of the plaza were never knit into a single unit like, for example, the place de la Concorde in Paris. The buildings around the plaza only accidentally give it the form and unity it has, including the fairly foreign presence of the General Motors Building, built in 1968. This black-and-white-striped, fifty-story building, by Edward Durell Stone, replaced the Savoy Plaza Hotel and was not particularly liked when built. It has acquired few fans in the intervening years. The owners fulfilled the zoning requirements of the day by including a plaza in exchange for a bigger building. But who needs a plaza on Grand Army Plaza? The plaza's visual tightness was punctured and this sunken plaza has never worked. The GM Building lobby, however, is a great place to look at top-of-the-line vehicles from the nation's largest automaker—without the pressure of a salesperson.

Another nice part of the GM Building that does work is home of **F. A. O. Schwarz**, "the palace" of the toy world. F. A. O. Schwarz, like Tiffany's, has moved several times since it was founded in 1862, opening this new headquarters as recently as 1986. This was the setting for the famous toyland scene in Tom Hanks's movie *Big*.

We now move to the culmination of our tour, the **Plaza Hotel**. The Plaza, grande dame of Grand Army Plaza's west side, replaced an earlier low-rise hotel built here in 1890. In a city whose grid plan arranges buildings like merchandise on a shelf, the Plaza was a rarity: a building that could be savored as a whole. Architect Henry Hardenbergh, who had designed the Dakota Apartments on Central Park West twenty years before, rose to the occasion and created a true landmark. Its granite base, brick and terra-cotta facade, and green tiled roof are expertly pulled together in this stunning Americanization of a French Renaissance chateau. The two-story dining room, the Oak Room, is the only original interior to remain intact. The bar, with its Everett Shinn murals, took its present shape in the 1940s. The original basement grill is now a movie theater, and the Palm Court lost its Tiffany glass ceiling in the 1940s when the hotel was part of the Hilton chain. In the much-ballyhooed divorce settlement of Donald and Ivana Trump, the former Mrs. Trump kept her job as manager of the hotel, a position that has allowed her to surprise critics with her ability to keep the hotel running smoothly. Step inside the lobby around the corner at Central Park South. Note the painting of Eloise, the little six-year-old who served as the main character of a children's book series created by Kay Thompson. Thompson immortalized Eloise as the scamp who charmed the Plaza's guests and staff with her impish ways. The painting is an indication of the affection the hotel holds for its fictional resident brat.

It's time to end our walk. The grassy expanses of Central Park offer a beautiful respite from the pavement, stone, and glass that dominate this part of New York. Even a brief visit will make the city seem so very far away, but for those who haven't quite had their fill of this consummately New York experience, check your watch. If it's ten, two, or four, there's nothing like high tea at the Plaza.

Barry Lewis is an architectural historian specializing in nineteenth- and twentieth-century architecture for the New York School of Interior Design. He also teaches the "City Transformed," covering New York's architecture and urban planning, for the 92nd Street Y. He is a contributing writer to the 1991 *Berlitz Guide to New York*, the Municipal Art Society's *Juror's Guide to Lower Manhattan*, and to the Society's newsletter, *The Livable City*. A native of Manhattan, he has conducted walking tours for the 92nd Street Y for fifteen years.

Walk · 5

MMMMMMMMMMMMMMMMMMMMMMM

Millionaire's Mile

MANHATTAN'S MONEYED
UPPER EAST SIDE

JOYCE MENDELSOHN

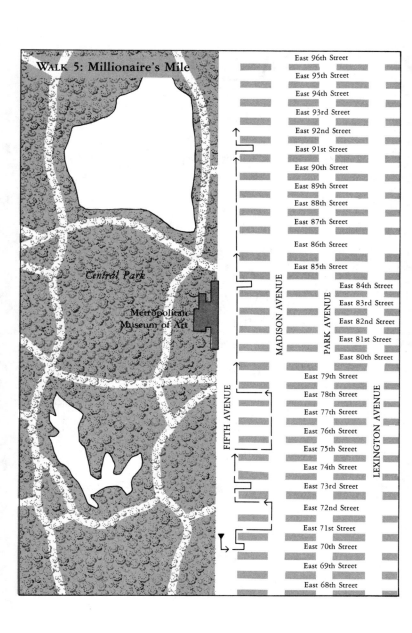

WALK 5: Millionaire's Mile

Central Park

Metropolitan
Museum of Art

FIFTH AVENUE

MADISON AVENUE

PARK AVENUE

LEXINGTON AVENUE

East 96th Street
East 95th Street
East 94th Street
East 93rd Street
East 92nd Street
East 91st Street
East 90th Street
East 89th Street
East 88th Street
East 87th Street
East 86th Street
East 85th Street
East 84th Street
East 83rd Street
East 82nd Street
East 81st Street
East 80th Street
East 79th Street
East 78th Street
East 77th Street
East 76th Street
East 75th Street
East 74th Street
East 73rd Street
East 72nd Street
East 71st Street
East 70th Street
East 69th Street
East 68th Street

Starting Point: Fifth Avenue and East 70th Street
Walk Length: 2½ hours
Subway Stop: 68th Street (6 train); walk two blocks north and three blocks west

An aura of privilege envelops Manhattan's Upper East Side, a wealthy enclave of elegant mansions and town houses, luxury apartments and preeminent cultural institutions. It is the city's—perhaps the nation's—most prestigious address. A genteel commerce of choice restaurants, hotels, art galleries, and fashion boutiques fits sedately into this quiet neighborhood. This is a walk through history, architecture, culture, and lots and lots of money.

The tour guides you up a moneyed stretch of Fifth Avenue, with occasional explorations onto side streets and along upscale Madison Avenue. This walk will also bring you back in time to the late nineteenth century when the first mansions rose here and New York's elite began living on the grand scale for which the area is still known—an area that was a rural slum little more than one hundred years ago.

It's hard to believe that in the 1850s this part of New York was a wasteland inhabited by thousands of impoverished squatters living in makeshift shanties. At the time, the city's richest families lived only as far north as Madison Square Park at 26th Street. Rapidly expanding commercialization of Manhattan and the press of new immigrants, however, pushed the well-heeled north.

The clearing of land for Central Park began in 1857, but the Civil War and the Financial Panic of 1873 impeded the area's development. Despite these setbacks, though, the Upper East Side was slowly becoming the city's Gold Coast.

Brownstone row houses for the middle class were built in the area beginning in the mid-1860s, with transportation to lower Manhattan provided by horsecar. The opening of the Third Avenue elevated railroad line in 1878 and the Second Avenue El two years later led to a building boom. By the 1880s palatial mansions began to appear on Upper Fifth Avenue facing the newly completed Central Park, extending the line of wealth from the Astor homes on 34th Street past the Vanderbilt mansions in the East 50s, transforming the Upper East Side into the gilded realm of New York society.

The New York Central Railroad, which since the 1830s had sent locomotives chugging up Fourth Avenue (later renamed Park Avenue), electrified and went completely underground in 1907, paving the way for the construction of homes and offices with elite Park Avenue addresses.

A large number of these opulent residences designed by outstanding architects were demolished for the construction of luxury apartment houses, but many survive as private schools, businesses, cultural institutions, consulates, and diplomatic missions. The Upper East Side continues to be the neighborhood of choice for New York's wealthiest, but today their sumptuous lifestyle is discreetly hidden behind the understated facades of apartment houses, their privacy protected by zealous doormen.

* * *

To begin your tour, stand next to the gray stone wall that bounds the eastern edge of New York's famous Central Park, a half block north of East 70th Street, on the west side of Fifth Avenue in front of the **Richard Morris Hunt Memorial**, commemorating one of America's most influential architects. Hunt's better-known buildings include the base of the Statue of Liberty, the Fifth Avenue facade of the Metropolitan Museum of Art, New York's first apartment house—which stood at 142 East 18th Street from 1869 to 1957—and numerous mansions.

Hunt (1827–1895) was the first American architect to be trained at the École des Beaux-Arts in Paris, which instilled in him a design sensibility based on Renaissance forms. For the World's Columbian Exposition of 1893, held in Chicago, Hunt—together with Charles Follen McKim, Daniel Burnham, Stanford White, and other influential architects—created what was dubbed the "White City," a dazzling metropolis of exhibition halls designed in the classical manner, decisively turning American architecture toward visions of European splendor.

To honor Hunt, a founder of the Municipal Art Society and the American Institute of Architects, colleagues erected the memorial in 1898. Daniel Chester French sculpted the two female figures as well as the bronze bust of Hunt at the center of the classical alcove. The bust gazes across Fifth Avenue at the ghost of what was considered one of Hunt's outstanding buildings, the Lenox Library, destroyed in 1912.

The library, opened to the public in 1877, was commissioned by bibliophile James Lenox. When his father, Robert Lenox, a prosperous merchant, died in 1840 he left to his son the thirty-acre family farm that stretched from 68th to 74th streets between Fifth and Fourth (later named Park) avenues. James Lenox, more interested in books than real estate, collected rare volumes and manuscripts that included Shakespeare, Milton, early printed Americana, and over 4,000 Bibles, the most outstanding of which was the first Gutenberg Bible in the United States. In 1895, fifteen years after Lenox's death, the li-

The Richard Morris Hunt Memorial

brary merged with the collections of the Tilden Trust and the Astor Library to form the New York Public Library, which stands on Fifth Avenue between 40th and 42nd streets.

Across the avenue from the memorial and a few steps back will bring you to East 70th Street. At 1 East 70th, on the site of the Lenox Library, stands the **Frick Collection**, formerly the Henry Clay Frick residence, completed in 1914 from plans by Thomas Hastings.

Frick, who amassed a fortune from iron, steel, and processed coal and who ran the Carnegie Steel Company, is notorious in the history of the American labor movement because of the cruelty of his actions in the Homestead Strike of 1892. In that bitter labor dispute with coal miners in Pennsylvania, Frick hired three hundred armed Pinkerton guards to quietly row up the Monongahela River to a Carnegie company town, where striking workers and their families had refused to move. Hoping to instill fear in anyone who dared defy the wishes of his powerful corporation, Frick instructed the guards to do whatever it took to remove the strikers.

What resulted was a massacre. The guards killed twelve workers and wounded twenty-five, outraging the nation.

Reacting to the tragedy, Alexander "Sasha" Berkman, the twenty-one-year-old lover of anarchist Emma Goldman, decided to assassinate Frick—the symbol of capitalist oppression—but needed money to carry out his plans. Berkman had the $15 it would take to buy a train ticket from New York to Pittsburgh, but needed an additional $20 to buy a suit—so that he could inconspicuously get close to Frick—and a gun.

Goldman supported her lover's plans, but the $4 a week she made as a seamstress was insufficient to cover the costs of the operation. Having recently read Dostoyevsky's *Crime and Punishment*, Goldman decided to raise the money—like Dostoyevsky's character Sonya—by prostituting herself, but the nervousness of the twenty-three-year-old anarchist doomed her efforts. A kindly old man, however, feeling sorry for Goldman, gave her $10, a sizable sum in the 1890s.

Finally, Berkman had the money he needed for his plan. Wearing his new suit, carrying a gun and a knife dipped in poison (as a backup) and with an explosive capsule wedged between his teeth, Berkman talked his way into Frick's private office. He fired several shots into Frick and then stabbed him, but Frick somehow survived. When the capsule failed to detonate, Berkman was immediately captured, tried, convicted, and sentenced to a long prison term.

Frick recovered and retired to New York, where he concentrated on buying immortality by collecting splendid art from the fourteenth through the nineteenth centuries, acquired for him by Joseph Duveen, an Anglo-Jewish art dealer. Duveen bought works by Rembrandt, Vermeer, Velázquez, Titian, and other great masters to hang in Frick's mansion, but the magnate would live in his palace for only a few years before his death in 1919.

The Frick Collection, one of the nation's great private art collections, is open to the public Tuesday through Saturday from 10:00 A.M. to 6:00 P.M. and Sunday from 1:00 P.M. to 6:00 P.M. Admission is $3 for adults and $1.50 for students and senior citizens.

Leaving the Frick Collection, return to Fifth Avenue and walk north to 71st Street, turn right, and proceed to 10 East 71st. Here you will find the **Frick Art Reference Library**, designed by John Russell Pope in 1935.

The library was founded by Helen C. Frick in honor of her father, Henry, in 1920. Originally, the library was housed in the former bowling alley in the Frick mansion's basement. The library contains over 235,000 books and materials dealing with European and American art from the fourth through the twentieth centuries. It is open to members and others with photo identification from 10:00 A.M. to 4:00 P.M., Monday through Friday, and Saturday from 10:00 A.M. to noon.

Across the street, at **9 East 71st**, is a town house designed in 1930 by Horace Trumbauer for Herbert Straus, son of Ida and Isador Straus, who drowned together in the sinking of the *Titanic* in 1912. In 1888 the Straus family acquired a half interest in R. H. Macy and Co. and became sole owners ten years later. Their holdings also included the Abraham & Straus Department stores, now known simply as A&S. (Both stores are located in Herald Square at Broadway and 34th Street.) Herbert Straus died in 1933 without ever having lived in the home he had commissioned.

It appears that a lingering merchandising karma still hovers over the mansion. In 1990 Leslie Wexner, the "Bachelor Billionaire" founder and chief executive of The Limited apparel chain—which includes Henri Bendel, Lane Bryant, and Lerners—purchased the home. The retailer reportedly paid $13 million for the building and is investing $8 million in renovations, including advanced communications and security equipment.

Across the street at **no. 18** is a home that was built in 1911 from plans by architect John Duncan. In 1987 television star Bill Cosby purchased the home for $6.2 million. His $1.2 million rehab includes a four-story rear addition housing a solarium and garden, a top-floor entertainment center, and six bedroom suites.

Continuing to the northeast corner of 71st Street and Madison Avenue, you come upon **St. James Episcopal Church**, founded in 1810 as a rural summer church for New York's oldest and wealthiest families. Members included the Schermerhorns, Astors, and Rhinelanders.

Jacob Schermerhorn came to New Amsterdam in 1636 and worked as a peddler, selling guns to Native Americans in upstate New York. Generations later, his descendants had become wealthy shipowners and merchants who became richer when Peter Schermerhorn filled in the "water lots" adjoining his landholdings at the South Street Seaport and created a sizable new chunk of Manhattan real estate.

In 1853, Caroline Schermerhorn married William Backhouse Astor, Jr., and, disregarding her own descent from a peddler, established herself as the arbiter of who was who in society. Because the ballroom in the Astor mansion could hold only four hundred people, Mrs. Astor's party invitation list became *the* Four Hundred—an American equivalent to royalty.

The Rhinelanders were French Huguenots who came to America in 1686 and established the Old Sugar House in Lower Manhattan, an important building because it supplied the sugar for the making of rum, an essential item in hard-drinking early New York. During the Revolutionary War, the British used it as a jail to house patriot prisoners.

St. James Episcopal was originally designed in a High Victorian Gothic style, but in the 1920s the present neo-Gothic facade was added. In the 1950s, the metal steeple replaced a crumbling stone tower. The interior contains stunning Tiffany windows, a magnificent (although not by Tiffany) rose window, an English hammerbeam ceiling, and a Spanish gilt and polychromed reredos.

Walking up Madison Avenue to 72nd Street, you arrive at one of the avenue's major intersections. Madison Avenue was not included in the original New York City Commissioner's Plan of 1811—which laid out Manhattan's street grid from Houston Street to 155th Street—but was added in 1836. As the Upper East Side developed, Fifth Avenue's wealth spilled over to Madison, with a series of town houses built along the avenue and large mansions sited at important street intersections, such as 72nd Street.

The Charles Tiffany house, designed by Stanford White, stood on the northwest corner of Madison and 72nd Street until 1936, when it was demolished to make way for the understated apartment house that stands there today.

On the diagonally opposite corner of the intersection, at **867 Madison Avenue**, fortunately, an early mansion remains. Completed in 1898, the house was designed by Francis H. Kimball and George Thompson for someone who would never live there, society matron Gertrude Rhinelander Waldo. Several of her family members, however, did live in the home, including Police Commissioner Rhinelander Waldo, made famous by James Cagney in the film *Ragtime*, based on the novel by E. L. Doctorow.

The mansion reflects the architecture of sixteenth-century chateaux of the Loire Valley in France. The style was introduced to New York City by Richard Morris Hunt, who broke with the brownstone tradition in 1879 when he designed a chateau worth $3 million (in 1870s dollars!), on the site of what is now a skyscraper, for William Kissam Vanderbilt at 660 Fifth Avenue. The François I style appealed to New York's millionaires and numerous chateaux were built on the Upper East Side in what has often been called the "Fifth Avenue Style."

The Rhinelander Waldo mansion is a five-story, symmetrical building, richly carved and ornamented, crowned with a steep mansard roof pierced by chimneys and wall dormers. This was a home meant to dominate this important corner, and it does.

In 1986 the building was sensitively renovated at a cost of over $14 million after it was leased to **Polo/Ralph Lauren**. Lauren, born Ralph Lifshitz in 1940 in the Bronx, created his fortune by marketing casual but elegant clothing reflecting the tastes of the British aristocracy. In 1989 an Irish investment group bought the mansion for $43 million from a development firm that had purchased it five years earlier for $6.4 million.

Turning left on 72nd Street toward Fifth Avenue, you pass two elegant French Beaux Arts mansions on the north side of the street at **nos. 7 and 9**. The École des Beaux-Arts, founded by Napoleon I as a national school of art and design, stressed the unity of painting, sculpture, and architecture. Beaux Arts buildings have a lush quality and sculptural elements are integral to their design. The buildings are monumental and formal, and emphasize

Detail of the Rhinelander Mansion

clarity and logic in their interior layouts. Grand Central Terminal, the New York Public Library, and the Customs House in Lower Manhattan are first-rate examples.

The mansions at nos. 7 and 9, built a few years apart by different architects, make a striking pair. At no. 9 is the **Henry T. Sloane residence**, built in 1894–96 by John Carrère (1858–1911) and Thomas Hastings (1860–1929), architects of the New York Public Library and graduates of the École des Beaux-Arts. Sloane, a member of the retailing family of W. and J. Sloane, was a patron of the Metropolitan Opera House who donated maroon carpeting and gold seating to its first building at 39th Street and Broadway.

Number 9 was later occupied by James Stillman, banker and art collector, whose Paris home was converted to a hospital during World War I. At the same time, Stillman loaned this building to the French Mission to the United States.

Next door at no. 7 stands the mansion of oil and steel magnate Oliver Gould Jennings, built in 1898 from plans by Ernest Flagg (1857–1947) and Walter Chambers.

These two mansions possess a true Gallic flavor, French designs by French trained architects for Francophiles. In an appropriate link to the past, the houses are currently occupied by the **Lycée Français**, a private school offering instruction in French to the children of elite New York families.

Continue along 72nd Street to Fifth Avenue, turn right, walk past three twentieth-century apartment houses to 73rd Street, and turn right again. At **11–15 East 73rd Street** is the **Joseph Pulitzer residence**, completed in 1903 from plans by Stanford White for the Hungarianborn publisher of the *St. Louis Post-Dispatch*, which became the basis for what is today a media empire of television, radio, and newspapers.

Pulitzer (1847–1911) entered the fray of East Coast journalism in 1883 when he bought the New York *World* from Jay Gould. The *World* and William Randolph Hearst's *Journal* were pitted in frenzied competition, outdoing each other in "yellow" journalism—a seamy journalistic tradition of sex and sensationalism. The style Pulitzer helped create is largely eschewed by the prestigious Pulitzer Prizes, named for the publisher and awarded annually since 1917 for excellence in literature, journalism, and history.

The Pulitzer house is based on two specific Venetian palazzi. The palazzo style, historically linked to the great banking families of Italy, was especially appealing to New York's millionaires. Because Pulitzer was almost totally blind when his house was planned, Stanford White, rather than rely on fine drawings, used heavy plaster models of the house that Pulitzer evaluated by feel.

Pulitzer was a somewhat quirky individual. Not only was he nearly blind, he was phobic about sounds. He spent a great deal of time on his yacht, which had one squeaky door posted with a sign that said, "Not to be opened while Mr. Pulitzer is asleep." In his home, Pulitzer had the master bedroom, measuring thirty-two by thirty-six feet with a sixteen-foot ceiling, completely sound-proofed to block all outside noise. To test the room, Pulitzer's secretaries went into the room, closed the door, and jumped and screamed—but those outside could hear nothing. Unfortunately, a water-pump heating system installed in the basement sent heartbeat throbs through the double walls and Pulitzer judged the house "a wretched failure." In the 1930s the mansion was converted to apartments, and Pulitzer's bedroom is now some lucky New Yorker's extremely quiet living room.

Returning back to Fifth Avenue and heading north, you come upon 1 East 75th Street, the 1909 **Edward S. Harkness house.** This elegant five-story mansion of fine Tennessee marble is surrounded by a splendid decorative iron fence. It is believed that the fence was a gift by the emperor of Japan in gratitude for the supply of fuel given to the Japanese Navy by Standard Oil, for which Harkness was an executive, during the Russo-Japanese War.

Harkness, the son of one of John D. Rockefeller's six original partners in Standard Oil, was an alumnus of Yale and a generous patron of both Harvard and Yale, employing his mansion's architect, J. G. Rogers, to design ten of the residential colleges at Yale. Harkness's wife, Mary Stillman Harkness, collected art and rare manuscripts, leaving her collections to museums, universities, and the New York Public Library.

The Commonwealth Fund, a philanthropic organization established by the Harkness family and dedicated to a broad range of social issues, has occupied the house since the early 1950s.

On the south side of East 75th Street at **no. 4** is a neo–French Renaissance mansion built in 1895–96, a house once owned by Thomas J. Watson, Jr., founder of IBM.

In 1965 the residence was converted to the Harkness House for Ballet Arts, founded by Rebekah West Harkness (1916–1982). Rebekah married William Hale Harkness, a grandson of the Standard Oil partner, in 1947. When William died in 1954 he left his grieving widow with $75 million, which Rebekah used to promote herself as a patron of dance.

A reveler in exhibitionism and excess, Rebekah Harkness studied music and dance and was a frequent performer—on and off the stage. She founded the Harkness Ballet Company and converted an old movie house on the Upper West Side to the short-lived Harkness Theater. The company traveled extensively and was booed in some of the finest theaters of Europe.

Later Harkness funded the Jerome Robbins Ballet, as well as the Pearl Primus and José Greco companies, and supplied money for several seasons of free summer dance programs in Central Park. In 1961 she became the generous sponsor of the Joffrey Ballet, underwriting tours and showering the dancers with extravagances. A few years into her sponsorship, though, Harkness—stung by Robert Joffrey's refusal to allow her artistic control—suddenly and capriciously withdrew her support, stunning the dance community and leaving the company in chaos.

The mansion at no. 4 was renovated by Harkness to provide studios, dressing rooms, and a small theater on the second floor, reached by a marble staircase and an open-cage elevator surrounded by a shaft painted with allegorical figures. In the lobby, open to the public as an art gallery, was a glass case containing an eighteen-inch goblet called *The Chalice of Life*, designed by Salvador Dali and purchased by Harkness for $250,000.

The chalice, decorated with diamond-, emerald-, and ruby-winged butterflies, sat on a rotating pedestal. After Harkness's life of drugs, alcohol, and failed artistry ended in 1982, a daughter schlepped her cremated remains in a Gristedes shopping bag to the mansion, where a portion of the ashes was placed in the chalice so that Rebekah West Harkness could pirouette into eternity.

The building, purchased in 1987 by Jaqui Safra of the

Safra National Bank, will soon be converted back to residential use. No one seems to know exactly what became of the chalice or its contents.

Now proceed east on 75th Street to Madison Avenue. On the southeast corner is the **Whitney Museum of American Art**, a concrete fortress faced with dark gray granite, designed by Bauhaus architect Marcel Breuer and constructed in 1963–66 to house an extensive twentieth-century art collection established by Gertrude Vanderbilt Whitney (1875–1942).

Gertrude was a great-granddaughter of Cornelius Vanderbilt, a Staten Island farmer who ran ferries to Manhattan in the early 1800s. The business later expanded to long-distance steamships (earning Cornelius the sobriquet "Commodore") and, still later, to a vast network of railroads. Gertrude, the daughter of Cornelius Vanderbilt II, grew up in a one-hundred-room mansion on the site of what is now Bergdorf Goodman at Fifth Avenue and 57th Street. Her marriage to Harry Whitney took place at The Breakers, the Vanderbilts' seventy-room Newport "cottage."

Whitney, mother of four children and the aunt of "Little Gloria" Vanderbilt, was a figurative sculptor who maintained a studio on MacDougal Alley in Greenwich Village. Two of her sculptures are permanent features of the city landscape: the Washington Heights–Inwood War Memorial—a heroic grouping of World War I soldiers—and a statue of Peter Stuyvesant, New York City's last Dutch governor, in Stuyvesant Square Park on Second Avenue and 16th Street.

Whitney, foremost a patron of American art, bought and exhibited painters such as John Sloan, Edward Hopper, and Stuart Davis early in their careers. By the 1930s her private collection contained over six hundred twentieth-century paintings. The Whitney Museum's open, airy interiors exhibit such artists as Maurice Prendergast, Jasper Johns, Willem de Kooning, Alexander Calder, Mark di Suvero, David Smith, and Louise Nevelson.

As with most of the city's museums, the Whitney suffers from a severe shortage of space. To alleviate the crunch, the Whitney has established several satellite minimuseums in office buildings around New York and one in Fairfield, Connecticut, raising questions about excessive corporate influence.

Currently, the museum plans to demolish the row of 1870s neo-Grecian brownstones next door on Madison Avenue to build an expansion designed by Postmodernist Michael Graves. Controversy has met all of Graves's proposals. Many people reason that since Breuer's design created a bully on the block, no new building, whether one designed to preserve the integrity of the original or to sit comfortably next to it, would be a welcome addition to the avenue.

The museum is open from 11 A.M. to 6 P.M. on Wednesdays, Fridays, Saturdays, and Sundays; 1 P.M. to 8 P.M. on Thursdays; and closed Mondays and Tuesdays. Admission is $5 for adults, $3 for senior citizens, and free to everyone after 6:00 P.M. on Tuesdays. Children under twelve with adults and all students with valid identification are admitted free at all times.

Walking north along Madison Avenue, across from shops for Givenchy and Delorenzo, you come next to the **Carlyle Hotel**, between 76th and 77th streets. Built in 1929 for Moses Ginsberg, an enterprising Brooklyn real estate developer who lost the hotel to bank foreclosure two years after its opening, the hotel's name was suggested by Ginsberg's daughter, who had read author Thomas Carlyle in college.

A transient and permanent residential hotel, the Carlyle's first occupant was composer Richard Rodgers. The hotel has always catered to heads of state, celebrities, and the very wealthy, who expect and receive exceptional service, security, and privacy. Presidents Truman, Kennedy, and Johnson favored the Carlyle during their New York visits. Rumors have held for years that Kennedy and several film stars used a secret labyrinth and secret exits from the hotel to avoid the Carlyle's public entrance. Ever loyal to its clientele, the hotel denies it all.

The Carlyle has hosted such guests as Imelda Marcos,

whose huge bills were always settled in cash, ex–King Peter II of Yugoslavia, who couldn't meet his bills, and Elizabeth Taylor, who overwatered an orchid in her room, ruining a $14,000 carpet for which she graciously paid.

The hotel lobby is tiny to encourage privacy and prices are high to discourage all but the very well-to-do. The Art Deco building is crowned with a conical tower brushed with 23-karat gold leaf and illuminated, making a distinctive mark on the nighttime sky.

To get a taste of the Carlyle, stop in at the bar with its charming murals by Ludwig Bemelmans or treat yourself to an evening with cabaret legend Bobby Short, a fixture at the Cafe Carlyle since the late 1960s.

Next, walk north on Madison to 78th Street. Here, on the northwest and southwest corners of the intersection, we have two McKim, Mead & White mansions, both reflecting the classical tradition, but expressed in very different styles.

McKim, Mead & White was one of America's most influential architectural firms, founded in 1879 by three very different personalities. Charles Follen McKim (1847–1909), methodical and scholarly and trained at the École des Beaux-Arts, designed in the grand manner. Stanford White (1853–1906), exuberant and vibrant, produced elegant buildings with exquisite detailing. William Rutherford Mead (1846–1928), possessing a command of architectural planning and a cool business judgment, anchored the firm. For almost thirty years the partners worked in harmony, producing close to eight hundred designs, many inspired by Italian Renaissance buildings. Some of their more outstanding work in New York includes the University and Metropolitan clubs, the Washington Arch, the Villard Houses, the Low Memorial Library, and the now-demolished Pennsylvania Station.

Although the firm continued into the 1930s, the partnership was shattered in 1906 by the murder of White by Harry K. Thaw, the deranged husband of former showgirl Evelyn Nesbit. At age sixteen Evelyn had been seduced by White in his erotic hideaway near Madison Square and their liaisons continued prior to her marriage to Thaw. The murder took place during a performance of an Eddie Foy musical on the roof garden of one of White's own creations, the 1890 Madison Square Garden at 26th Street and Madison Avenue. While White sat at his table, watching the musical, Thaw approached, drew a pistol, and killed the architect in front of a stunned audience. The orchestra, in the middle of a rendition of "I Could Love a Million Girls" and ever mindful that the show must go on, played through the murder, never missing a beat.

Stanford White designed the 1898 palazzo-style mansion that stands on the northwest corner of 78th Street for railroad executive Stuyvesant Fish and his wife Mamie.

The outstanding feature of the interior of the mansion at **25 East 78th Street** is the large second-floor ballroom where Mamie Stuyvesant Fish lavishly entertained New York society. Mamie broke the tradition of stiff high-society parties with a wacky sense of fun. She was the first to invite offbeat entertainment to formal dinners, bringing circus acts and their animals to her mansion to charm her guests. On one occasion she sent invitations to her elite friends for a formal dinner—served on a three-hundred-piece gold Tiffany service—for Prince del Drago. After the guests arrived, Mamie presented the prince, who turned out to be an elegantly dressed monkey.

Across the street is another Stanford White mansion, the 1902 neo-Georgian **Philip Rollins house** at 28 East 78th Street.

Next door are three slim row houses at **26, 24, and 22 East 78th Street** built by speculator Silas M. Styles in 1871. After their completion, the houses stood alone on the block for ten years because of the financial impact of the Panic of 1873.

Speculators typically purchased several 25-by-100-

Detail of mansion at 25 East 78th Street

foot lots on which they squeezed narrow row houses. Here, two 25-foot lots are really squeezed, holding three houses. Originally these housefronts were faced with thin layers of brownstone covering a core of common brick. In the last half of the nineteenth century, a brownstone row house was the favored dwelling of the respectable New Yorker. So pervasive and monotonous was the style that author Edith Wharton once characterized the city as "this little low-studded rectangular New York cursed with its universal chocolate-coloured coating of the most hideous stone ever quarried."

Today, only the house at no. 22 retains its brownstone facade and stoop. After Richard Morris Hunt and colleagues unveiled their vision of the dazzling White City, brownstones were suddenly "out" and the wealthy rushed to give their homes a new classical look. Number 26 was painted white and its stoop removed, while no. 24 underwent a radical facelift with a classically detailed limestone facade added on top of the old front, extending the building forward.

Continuing along East 78th Street to Fifth Avenue, you come to the **James B. Duke residence** at 1 East 78th. Duke was born in 1865 near Durham, North Carolina, on a modest farm decimated by the Civil War, save for a small patch of leafy tobacco. His family cultivated the patch and began manufacturing cigarettes on newly invented rolling machines. By the age of twenty-nine, Duke was sent to New York to set up a branch factory.

Eventually, Duke consolidated several large tobacco companies into the American Tobacco Company. In 1911, in a charge led by Teddy Roosevelt, the "tobacco trust" was broken into four separate companies; but by this time Duke was secure in his wealth. In 1924 he made tiny Trinity College in Durham an offer it couldn't refuse, donating $40 million in exchange for renaming the school Duke University.

Duke lived in the mansion with his wife and their only child, Doris, and a staff of fourteen servants. Doris was twelve when her father died in 1925, leaving the girl a fortune of over $100 million. In 1958 she gave the mansion to New York University. After the donation, architect Robert Venturi—in one of his earliest commissions—helped in the building's renovation. Some of Doris Duke's other favorite philanthropies include the Newport, Rhode Island, Restoration Foundation, the Duke Gardens of Somerville, New Jersey, and her 1988 posting of $5 million bail for her friend Imelda Marcos.

The residence was designed by the office of Horace Trumbauer (1868–1938) and completed in 1912. Trumbauer's firm produced some of the nation's most spectacular mansions for America's wealthiest families. For over three decades, the chief designer in Trumbauer's office was a black architect, Julian Francis Abele (1881–1950), the first African American to graduate from the École des Beaux-Arts. As an undergraduate at the University of Pennsylvania, his classmates awarded him their highest honor by electing him president of the Architectural Society in his senior year.

After graduation, Abele met Trumbauer, who, impressed by Abele's extraordinary talent, encouraged him to enter the École des Beaux-Arts and financed his four years in Paris. Abele returned to Philadelphia with a

French wife and joined Trumbauer's firm in 1906, becoming chief designer in 1909.

Abele worked on all the firm's major commissions, including the Duke mansion, the Free Library of Philadelphia, the Philadelphia Museum of Art, and the Widener Memorial Library at Harvard. Duke commissioned Trumbauer's firm to plan the new Duke University, with Abele designing the school's splendid neo-Gothic chapel. Abele did not, however, supervise the chapel's construction on the southern campus, leaving that to a white architect. After Trumbauer died in 1938, Abele became a partner in the firm until his death in 1950.

Around the corner at **972 Fifth Avenue**, between 78th and 79th streets, is a 1906 residence designed from plans by McKim, Mead & White for Payne Whitney, son of William Collins Whitney and Flora Payne. William, a prominent Democratic politician and a businessman involved in oil, tobacco, and street railways, was secretary of the navy under President Grover Cleveland.

Flora was the sister of another Standard Oil partner, Oliver Hazard Payne. When "Colonel" Payne died a bachelor in 1917, he left the bulk of his fortune to one nephew, Payne Whitney. Payne was a favorite of his uncle because he had opposed his father's remarriage after the Colonel's sister, Payne's mother, died. His brother, Harry Whitney, supported his father's remarriage, and so was slighted by the bachelor uncle. No worry for Harry, though, since he ended up marrying art patron and sculptor Gertrude Vanderbilt.

Payne married Helen Hay, daughter of John Hay, Lincoln's private secretary and secretary of state for Presidents McKinley and Theodore Roosevelt. Two Whitney children grew up here: John Hay "Jock" Whitney, the sportsman, publisher, movie producer (*Gone With the Wind*), diplomat (U.S. ambassador to Britain), and philanthropist who died in 1982, and Joan Whitney Payson, late owner of the Mets and an art collector who bought Van Gogh's *Irises* in 1947 for $84,000. (The painting sold for $53.9 million in 1987.)

Adjoining the Payne Whitney mansion is the **Henry Cook house** at 973 Fifth Avenue. Stanford White designed both mansions to appear as one continuous facade.

Walking up Fifth Avenue to the north side of East 79th Street and facing south, you get a full view of the exuberant French chateau style of the **Fletcher-Sinclair residence** at 2 East 79th Street, designed by Charles Pierrepont H. Gilbert (1860–1952) and originally owned by Isaac D. Fletcher, a businessman and art collector. The second occupant, Harry F. Sinclair, was a pharmacist-turned-oil-tycoon who gained notoriety in the Teapot Dome scandals of the 1920s.

The picturesque mansion was purchased in 1930 by Augustus van Horn Stuyvesant, a recluse who lived here with his sister, Ann Stuyvesant, until her death in 1938. Augustus then lived alone, rarely going out of doors, until his death twelve years later. The siblings were the last direct descendants of Peter Stuyvesant and when they were interred with the governor in the family vault at St. Marks-in-the-Bowery Church in the East Village, the vault was sealed forever.

C. P. H. Gilbert also designed a home for five-and-dime retailer Frank Woolworth that stood on the northeast corner of East 80th Street and Fifth Avenue until the mid-1920s, and three adjoining houses for the Woolworth daughters that still stand at **2, 4, and 6 East 80th Street**. The last stop on this tour, the Jewish Museum at 92nd Street and Fifth Avenue, was also designed by Gilbert, a prolific but relatively unknown architectural star.

Behind you at **985 Fifth** is a 1968 apartment house designed by Paul Resnick and Harry F. Green on the site of what was once the Brokaw mansion. Completed in 1888 from plans by Rose & Stone for businessman Isaac Brokaw, the mansion—solid and severe—was surrounded with three other homes commissioned for his children.

In the mid-1960s, preservationists, concerned about the possible demolition of the mansions, mounted a campaign to save them. But in February 1965, in a move that outraged New Yorkers, three of the four Brokaw mansions were quickly demolished in a surprise weekend attack that left very little to save. The protests that followed, coupled with the loss in 1963 of the Pennsylvania Station, led to the establishment of the New York City Landmarks Preservation Commission, signed into law by Mayor Robert F. Wagner in 1965. The impact of the commission can be seen on this tour, which encompasses three Historic Districts running from 59th to 96th streets, with extensions being considered as far north as 99th.

Perhaps now is a good time to cross Fifth to the park side of the avenue. As you've strolled along Fifth Avenue, you've walked beside what many consider to be the greatest treasure of New York City, **Central Park**. Designed by Frederick Law Olmsted and Calvert Vaux and completed in 1873, this vast and beautiful public space extends from 59th to 110th Streets, bounded by Fifth Avenue and Central Park West (Eighth Avenue).

It is important to emphasize what the park is *not*. It is not a piece of Manhattan preserved with a wall around it. Nor was it intended as a front yard for the mansions of Fifth Avenue. The park was envisioned by its planners as a place where people from all walks of life could leave the city behind and enter into a world of nature.

New York in the 1840s was experiencing rapid growth of industry and a mass influx of new immigrants jammed into squalid housing, workers who drudged long hours to eke out a living. A group of idealistic New Yorkers—including newspaper editors Horace Greeley and William Cullen Bryant—proposed a large public park, providing a healthy alternative to slum living, that would serve as common ground for the enjoyment of all segments of society. Bryant, a Transcendentalist, also favored the plan on spiritual grounds, believing that God could be found in nature.

The proposal drew support from politicians who could provide patronage jobs to unskilled immigrants and from property owners and developers who envisioned rising real estate values on the park's periphery. In the mid-1850s, the state legislature approved and financed the proposed park and workers began clearing the site of over 5,000 squatters living in wretched, unhealthy conditions in the quarries and swamps. A competition for the park's design drew thirty-three entries, with Olmsted and Vaux's "Greensward" plan declared the winner in 1858.

Olmsted (1822–1903), who became the nation's foremost environmental planner, and English architect Calvert Vaux (1824–1895) created ponds, lakes, and a palette of landscapes linked by winding paths and iron bridges, from the wild forest of the Ramble to the open Sheep Meadow, where sheep grazed in a bucolic setting.

In an original engineering stroke, Olmsted and Vaux designed four east-west sunken transverse roads, creating the first traffic underpasses in America. They created separate bridal, carriage, and pedestrian paths to segregate traffic. The park, at 843 acres, is larger than Monaco.

Fourteen million people visit Central Park annually. A pastoral refuge from the city and yet an integral part of it, the park provides minivacations for bird watching, fall foliage touring, bicycling, picnicking, horseback riding, jogging, skating, walking, and just plain relaxing. Cultural activities include the New York Shakespeare Festival's free Shakespeare productions and rock, ethnic, and classical music concerts in the summer.

The park is best enjoyed during the day and in the company of others. Visitors have been cautioned since the 1870s to avoid the park at night. The exception is the free evening event (well-lighted and policed) when often hundreds of thousands of people enjoy music and drama in incomparable surroundings.

Walking now to the southeast corner of Fifth Avenue and 81st Street, you will be in front of the **Stanhope Hotel**, constructed in 1925–26 from plans by Rosario Candela. The 274-room hotel went through an extensive renovation in the 1980s. The Stanhope holds the first New York City sidewalk café license and is a popular, if pricey, spot for refreshments and people watching.

On the north side of 81st Street stands **998 Fifth Avenue**, an apartment house designed by William Kendall in the office of McKim, Mead & White, built in 1912 after the death of the two major partners and commissioned by developer James T. Lee, maternal grandfather of Jacqueline Bouvier Kennedy Onassis.

This was the first apartment house built on Fifth Avenue above 59th Street and the first to lure the very wealthy from their mansions into apartments. At a time when New York millionaires occupied their very own châteaux or palazzi, it took the marketing genius of real estate agent Douglas Elliman to offer discounted rentals of $15,000 per year (a saving of $10,000) to open the doors of apartment-house living to the upper class.

The building, designed in the Italian Renaissance palazzo style, has a prominent midsection and an elaborate cornice. Here, the Italian palazzo has been adapted as a multidwelling by stretching the midsection, a device that would later become quite popular in apartment house design. The original apartments were extraordinary, some duplexes, but typically one apartment per floor, organized around a central court. One floor plan shows a seven-bedroom apartment with an enormous reception room, salon, living room, and dining room. To hold a corps of servants, the plan shows nine maids' rooms that were anything but enormous.

Once the very wealthy discovered they could continue their lavish lifestyles in sumptuous apartments at lower cost and with less maintenance, they left their mansions and moved to elegant addresses such as no. 998. By the 1930s most affluent Upper East Side families lived in apartments. Number 998 was converted to coops in the 1950s and the apartments subdivided.

Continue north to **1001 Fifth Avenue**, a 1979 apartment house built for real estate developer Peter Kalikow, publisher of the *New York Post*. Although Philip Birnbaum designed the building, Philip Johnson designed the Fifth Avenue facade. The apartment house replaced three town houses that stood between 998 Fifth Avenue and the Benjamin N. Duke residence on the southeast corner of Fifth and 82nd Street, across the street from the Metropolitan Museum of Art.

While the apartment house was in the planning stages, the Landmarks Preservation Commission was considering, but had not yet designated, the Metropolitan Museum Historic District. Preservationists, fearing a banal building on this important site, brought legal action to save the last remaining town house. Responding to public pressure, Kalikow commissioned Johnson to design a facade that would relate to the neighboring buildings and enhance the prestigious location.

For the apartment building at no. 1001, Johnson chose to use a limestone facade with a strongly rusticated base and horizontal moldings, all of which relate to the design elements in the adjacent McKim, Mead & White apartment house to the south. Just to the north of Johnson's building at **no. 1009** is the five-story, mansard-roofed **Benjamin Duke house**. In a gesture to its French-inspired neighbor, Johnson topped 1001 Fifth Avenue with a mansard of its own, but only a false front, looking like a billboard but lacking a coherent message. Viewed from Fifth Avenue, no. 1009—completed in 1901—is a small, five-story limestone house with graceful bay windows and a cheerful red-tile mansard topped with copper cresting. Walk around the corner to 82nd Street, however, and you will see that the house is actually a large Beaux Arts mansion decorated with limestone carvings and surrounded by a moat.

The house was first occupied by Benjamin Duke, brother and business associate of tobacco tycoon James Duke, whom we met earlier on East 78th Street. Benjamin's son, Angier Buchanan Duke, married Cordelia Biddle and the couple became parents of Angier Biddle Duke, who became a diplomat and philanthropist. Benjamin's daughter, Mary, married A. J. Drexel Biddle. Their daughter, Mary Duke Biddle Semans, and her husband, Dr. James Semans, own the mansion, which was converted to apartments in the 1960s, and maintain a pied-à-terre in the former family residence.

Across the street stands one of the world's greatest art institutions, the **Metropolitan Museum of Art**, a magnificent collection spanning over 5,000 years of art ranging from ancient Egyptian, Greek, and Roman to the twentieth century. The museum was founded in 1869 by the art committee of the Union League Club—an organization that included William Cullen Bryant and Central Park Commission President Andrew Haswell Green, who urged the museum to locate in the park.

The first building was a small Victorian Gothic structure designed by Calvert Vaux and Jacob Wrey Mould with the entrance facing Central Park. A few years earlier, Vaux and Mould had collaborated on the first building of the American Museum of Natural History, constructed on the west side of Central Park on what had been Manhattan Square. Both original buildings still stand. To find the original Vaux and Mould building when you visit the Met, walk west through the museum to the Robert Lehman Collection, enter the glass diamond that juts into the park, and turn around. You will see the red brick wall with pointed arches of alternating black and white bands from the 1880 building. As is evident from the massiveness of the museum, there have been many additions, including one in 1902 that turned the museum's back on Central Park with a monumental, triple-arch Beaux Arts facade on Fifth Avenue, designed by Richard Morris Hunt.

The Metropolitan Museum of Art not only holds great art, it is one of the city's most popular places and visitors should allow ample time for a return visit. For some visual perspective, the roof sculpture garden offers a stunning view of the city. In good weather, massive crowds sit on the broad steps to watch the parade of New Yorkers and tourists go by.

The Metropolitan Museum of Art

The museum's cafeteria offers fare from a cup of coffee to a hot dinner. The museum, open from 9:30 A.M. to 5:15 P.M. Sunday and Tuesday through Thursday and 9:30 A.M. to 8:45 P.M. Friday and Saturday (closed Mondays), has a suggested entrance fee of $6 for adults and $3 for students and seniors and is free to children under twelve. The prices are only suggestions, however, and if you want to go to the cafeteria it is common to pay a minimum amount, say $1, to enter the museum.

Restrooms, hard to find elsewhere on this tour (and in most neighborhoods in the city), are available in the museum and can be used without paying any entrance fee. Enter on the ground floor at Fifth Avenue and 81st Street, go as far left as you can past the coat check, and you will find large, clean bathrooms.

Leaving the museum, cross Fifth Avenue and proceed to **3 East 84th Street**, a 1928 Art Deco apartment house by John Mead Howells (1868–1959) and Raymond Hood (1881–1934) for Joseph Medill Patterson, founder of the *Daily News*. Patterson began the *Illustrated Daily News* in 1919, copublishing it with Colonel Robert R. McCormick of the *Chicago Tribune*. By 1924, with a feisty combination of sex, sensationalism, and extensive use of photography, the *News* became the largest circulation paper in America.

When the *Tribune* held a competition for the design of its new Chicago headquarters in 1922, architects from around the world entered. Of the 281 drawings that reached the finals, Howells and Hood won first place with a neo-Gothic tower topped with a crown. This architecturally retrogressive tower, rejecting the pioneering skyscrapers of Louis Sullivan (1856–1924) and the Chicago School, was erected in 1925.

Second place in the competition went to Finnish architect Eliel Saarinen, who expressed the modern European aesthetic by turning his back on Classicism and submitting a design calling for a sleek tower with ornamental setbacks. The tower was never built, but the plan exerted a profound influence on future skyscraper design.

After Hood and Howells built their Tribune Tower, they did a complete turnaround and embraced the modern aesthetic. Their 1930 Daily News Building, also commissioned by Joseph M. Patterson, alternates tan brick verticals with darker recessed windows and spandrels to achieve a soaring volume on East 42nd Street.

This gem of an apartment house at no. 3, only nine stories tall but with a strong vertical emphasis, claims an important place in architectural history. Devoid of classical references, the asymmetrical limestone facade is enlivened by geometric motifs recalling Mayan designs. The recessed metal spandrels, later used as a critical feature of the Empire State Building, appear for the first time in this building.

Returning now to Fifth Avenue, walk to **1040 Fifth Avenue**, a seventeen-story luxury apartment house designed by Sicilian-born Rosario Candela (1893–1953), architect of the Stanhope Hotel. Candela set the standard for the way the very wealthy lived in apartment houses, with subdued exteriors housing grand interiors of generous dimensions. Currently, Jacqueline Onassis occupies a five-bedroom, sixteen-room apartment on an upper floor facing the park.

Walking north on Fifth Avenue to the southeast corner at 86th Street you come to the 1914 **William Starr Miller residence** at 1048 Fifth Avenue, designed by the firm of Carrère and Hastings. Miller's wealth came from railroads and banking, with his 1935 obituary in *The New York Times* describing him as a "retired capitalist." Richmond H. Shreve, a young architect at Carrère and Hastings, was active in this building's construction and design. Shreve, William Lamb, and Arthur Loomis Harmon formed their own firm in 1920 and became famous as architects of the Empire State Building, the city's venerated icon that you can see by looking south down Fifth Avenue to 34th Street. This striking limestone and red-brick mansion, designed in the Louis XIII style, reflects a period between Francois I chateau style and the French neoclassic styles of the Louis XV and XVI eras.

In 1944 the mansion was purchased by Grace Wilson Vanderbilt, widow of Cornelius Vanderbilt III, brother of Gertrude Vanderbilt Whitney. After Grace's death in 1953, the YIVO Institute for Jewish Research acquired the building.

From 1925 until the Nazi invasion of Poland in 1939, YIVO accumulated a vast collection of materials dealing with Jewish life in Eastern Europe, assembled in New York after heroic Jews had them smuggled out of the Vilna archives after the city's occupation by Nazis. In 1989 an estimated half of YIVO's original materials, long thought to have been destroyed in the war, were discovered in Lithuanian archives. YIVO, the world's leading organization for the perpetuation of Yiddish culture, offers frequent exhibitions and lectures open to the public.

As you continue up Fifth Avenue you will see, almost regardless of the weather or time of day, joggers who enter the park at various locations on the avenue. Often decked out in expensive designer togs, but sometimes wearing common sweats, the joggers provide an interesting contrast to the staid, conservative look of most of the neighborhood's residents. Many runners do their laps on the 6.2-mile path around the Central Park Reservoir, an integral part of New York's clean and plentiful water supply. A view of the reservoir is considered to be an enhancement to an Upper East Side address.

At Fifth Avenue and 88th Street stands Frank Lloyd Wright's (1869–1959) only significant building in New York City, the **Solomon R. Guggenheim Museum**, completed in 1959. It was established by one of seven sons of Swiss-born Meyer Guggenheim, whose shrewd purchase of Colorado mining property in the 1880s and even shrewder expansion into smelting and processing became the foundation of a family fortune. With the active management of strategically-placed sons, the Guggenheim fortune grew into a worldwide industrial empire.

The middle son, Solomon (1869–1949), collected avant-garde twentieth-century paintings in the 1920s, showing them at his apartment in the Plaza Hotel and later at a rented gallery space. He commissioned Wright in 1943 to design a permanent home for the collection. Although Guggenheim lived to approve the design and Wright saw the museum almost to completion, neither patron nor architect lived to see the museum open.

Wisconsin-born Wright's only formal training was in civil engineering at the University of Wisconsin, after which he worked in the architectural offices of Adler and Sullivan. In 1893, the same year as the pivotal Chicago Exposition, Wright completed his first significant design on his own, the Winslow residence in River Forest, Illinois, a structure that hinted at his nascent "Prairie" style. Although the Chicago Exposition introduced the classical White City based on Roman models, Wright took a new approach, creating an indigenous American architecture based on natural materials and horizontal forms.

Wright broke through the rectilinear street wall on Fifth Avenue with the Guggenheim's compelling circular form. Viewed from the outside, it appears as a giant sculptural form facing Central Park, but the essence of the museum is the flowing interior space contained in the concrete shell. The continuous, cantilevered spiral ramp gently moves visitors through the museum and expresses the sculptural quality of poured concrete. On a subliminal level, its construction relates to Central Park, articulating Wright's philosophy of organic architecture based on forms found in nature. The cantilever recalls the natural principle of tree branches, and the spiral ramp plays on the interior of a chambered nautilus. A visit to the museum provides an opportunity to view art *and* to experience an exhilarating architectural masterpiece. It is open from 10 A.M. to 8 P.M. every day except Thursday.

The museum's permanent holdings have grown substantially from Guggenheim's original collection of nonobjective paintings to over 5,000 paintings and sculptures. Many of the works have never been displayed due to lack of space. A controversial ten-story annex designed by

Gwathmey Siegel & Associates, begun in 1990, will provide a much-needed expansion, although many feel it detracts from the original building.

Around the corner at 3 and 5 East 89th Street—and at 1083 Fifth Avenue—is the **National Academy of Design**, founded in 1825 by Samuel Finley Breese Morse, inventor of the telegraph and Morse Code and a prominent nineteenth-century painter. The academy is the oldest art school in New York and has occupied this location since 1940. The Fifth Avenue building was altered to its present French neoclassical facade in 1915 by Ogden Codman, Jr. In 1897 Codman and budding author Edith Wharton wrote *The Decoration of Houses*, a book that shunned traditional Victorian interiors in favor of designs embracing light and harmony.

Number 1083 was occupied by the stepson of railroad magnate Collis P. Huntington, Archer Milton Huntington, and his sculptor wife, Anna Vaughn Hyatt Huntington. Collis adopted Archer after marrying his mother, Arabella Yarrington, two weeks after the death of Collis's first wife. When Collis died, he left Arabella a fortune of $150 million, making her the richest woman in America. Uninterested in smaller matters, Arabella once left ten strands of pearls—worth $3 million dollars—on the desk of the art dealer Joseph Duveen. Duveen helped Arabella acquire such masterpieces as Gainsborough's *Blue Boy* and Rembrandt's *Aristotle Contemplating the Bust of Homer*. After Collis's death, Arabella married his nephew, becoming Arabella Yarrington Huntington Huntington.

Next on your walk up Fifth Avenue you pass the **Church of the Heavenly Rest** on the southeast corner of 90th Street, completed in 1929 from plans by Hardie Philip of Mayers, Murray & Philip. Curiously, this modern Gothic church is similar to the Guggenheim Museum both in structure and materials. The limestone-faced ex-

Detail of the Church of the Heavenly Rest

terior gives no hint, but the church is designed on the same cantilever principle as the museum and, like the museum, is built of reinforced concrete. The striking figures of Moses and St. John the Baptist flanking the entrance are the work of Lee Lawrie, sculptor of *Atlas*, which stands in Rockefeller Center across from St. Patrick's Cathedral. Malvina Hoffman carved the graceful female figure inside on the pulpit, "Vision." Serving an affluent Episcopalian congregation, the church operates an extensive community outreach program for the less fortunate.

Walking around the corner to **2 East 91st Street**, you arrive at the Andrew Carnegie mansion, home of the **Cooper-Hewitt Museum**.

Carnegie (1835–1919), born in Dunfermline, Scotland, came to Pennsylvania with his impoverished family at the age of thirteen and began working in an Allegheny County cotton mill. The industrious Carnegie became a telegraph operator, a secretary, and, later, superintendent for the Pennsylvania Railroad, where he began investing in stock. By the age of thirty he owned a construction company that replaced wooden railroad bridges with ones of iron. Realizing the limitations of iron, he turned to steel, recently made practical and cheap by Henry Bessemer's process in England. As America entered the age of great steel bridges, skyscrapers, railroads, and machinery, Carnegie became one of the wealthiest men on earth. By 1899 his steel company's output topped Great Britain's. In 1901 he sold his empire to J. P. Morgan and retired on $44,000 a day.

Carnegie regarded himself merely as a trustee of money and felt it his duty to give away large portions for good causes. He enunciated this philosophy in an article called "The Gospel of Wealth" in which he declared it was the noble obligation of the rich to give away their fortunes in their lifetime, a philosophy that conveniently did not extend to decent wages for steelworkers. By the time of his death, 90 percent of his wealth had been donated to causes such as the Peace Palace at the Hague,

Carnegie Tech (now Carnegie-Mellon University) in Pittsburgh, and colleges and libraries across America. He is particularly remembered for the great concert hall that bears his name on West 57th Street.

When Carnegie purchased land for his mansion at 2 East 91st Street in 1898, the area was semirural and completely unfashionable, inhabited by squatters and dotted with such well-meaning institutions as the New-York Magdalen Asylum (for "fallen women") and the New York Christian Home for Intemperate Men. Carnegie had to settle this far north because he wanted land for a spacious garden in the rear of his mansion. Soon, other wealthy families followed to "Carnegie Hill."

Carnegie directed the architects Babb, Cook and Willard to build "the most modest, plainest and most roomy house in New York." He got a sixty-four-room, neo-Georgian country house with a large garden surrounded by a handsome iron fence. Entering under a Tiffany copper and glass canopy, visitors are treated to hand-carved Scottish oak paneling, wood ceilings with gilded leather, and stained glass windows creating a warm, handcrafted atmosphere with a disregard for classical formalism that surely would have distressed Edith Wharton.

This "old-fashioned" house was built in 1901 with the most advanced technology of the day, including a structural steel frame, temperature and humidity control, a form of air-conditioning, and a water-purifying system.

Carnegie, who promised his mother that he would never marry during her lifetime, finally tied the knot in his fifties. After his death in 1919, his widow lived in the house until her death in 1946. The building opened in 1977 as the **Cooper-Hewitt Museum**, the Smithsonian Institution's National Museum of Design.

The museum was founded by Sarah, Amy, and Eleanor Hewitt, granddaughters of Peter Cooper and daughters of Sarah Amelia Cooper Hewitt and Abram S. Hewitt, an associate of Cooper in iron manufacturing. Hewitt was a prominent Democratic politician who defeated both

Teddy Roosevelt and Henry George to become mayor of
New York from 1887 to 1888.

The Hewitt sisters traveled Europe extensively, buying
decorative arts such as textiles, glass, wallpaper, and silver-
ware. In the 1960s their 300,000 objects spanning a period
of 3,000 years were transferred from their grandfather's
tuition-free school, Cooper Union, to the Smithsonian and—
in 1977—installed in the Carnegie mansion. Visitors not
only see an outstanding design collection, but can enjoy the
ambience of an authentic baronial mansion.

The museum is open from 10:00 A.M. to 9:00 P.M. on
Tuesdays, 10:00 A.M. to 5:00 P.M. Wednesday through
Saturday, and noon to 5:00 P.M. on Sundays (closed Mondays). Admission is $3 for adults, $1.50 for students and
senior citizens, and free to children under twelve. The
museum is free to everyone after 5 P.M. on Tuesdays.

On the northeast corner of 91st Street and Fifth Avenue stands the **Otto Kahn mansion** at 1 East 91st,
completed in 1918 from plans by J. A. Stenhouse and
C. P. H. Gilbert, now occupied by the Convent of the
Sacred Heart, a private girls' school. Kahn (1867–1934),
financier and patron of the arts, was born to a wealthy
German Jewish merchant family and showed an early
interest in music, art, and literature. By age twenty-one
he was working for the Deutsche Bank in London where
he transformed himself into an Anglophile complete with
British citizenship, clipped British accent, and a love for
fine English tailoring.

After six years in London, he moved to New York
and married Adelaide Wolff, daughter of Abraham Wolff,
partner in Kuhn, Loeb & Co. Kahn soon firmly established himself in the international banking firm and
worked closely with railroad genius Edward Harriman. In
twenty years they had built the world's largest railroad
fortune.

Becoming the major stockholder and later chairman
of the board of the Metropolitan Opera, Kahn steered the
Met from a socially pretentious exclusiveness to a new

life as a major cultural institution, bringing Toscanini, Gatti-Casazza, and Caruso to New York. He financially backed Diaghilev, Stanislavsky, Eva LeGallienne, and the Provincetown Playhouse and became known as a leading supporter of the arts.

Kahn lived on a grand scale in a 126-room French chateau in Cold Spring Harbor, Long Island, and here on 91st Street in this magnificent Italian palace. Designed in the High Renaissance style, it is based on the fifteenth-century palazzo in Rome that today houses the Chancellery of the Holy See.

The neighboring mansions at 7 and 9 East 91st Street, on property once owned by Carnegie, were built for the daughters of Emily Vanderbilt Sloane, granddaughter of William H. Vanderbilt, and William Douglas Sloane of the W. & J. Sloane furniture stores.

Number 7, the **Burden house**, was completed in 1905 from plans by Warren & Wetmore, architects of Grand Central Terminal, for Florence Adele Sloane and her husband James Burden. The Burden wealth derived from an iron company in Troy, New York, that manufactured horseshoes for the Union Army and railroad spikes. Their extravagant wedding cost $1 million in 1895.

Next door, at no. 9, is the **John Henry Hammond house**, designed by Carrère and Hastings. The house was built for Emily Vanderbilt Sloane and her husband, lawyer and banker John Henry Hammond. Their son, John Hammond (1911–1987), legendary talent scout and record producer, exerted a major influence on the direction of American popular music during a fifty-year career. Young Hammond first developed a taste for music in the servants' hall and during his frequent forays uptown, sneaking out of the mansion to hop a trolley to Harlem where he explored the neighborhood's street music.

Dropping out of Yale, he continued to frequent Harlem and its jazz clubs and traveled to southern roadhouses, discovering and recording artists such as Billie

Holiday and Count Basie. It was Hammond who convinced Benny Goodman (who later married Hammond's sister) to form his own band, the first racially integrated big band. Always an advocate of racial equality, in 1939 Hammond produced the "Spiritual to Swing" concert at Carnegie Hall, bringing blues and gospel to the American concert stage for the first time. As an executive at Columbia Records his genius for discovering and nurturing new talent led to his recording Bob Dylan and Bruce Springsteen. Hammond's son, John, continues his father's music legacy today as a blues singer.

The mansions at nos. 7 and 9 permitted the two Vanderbilt-Sloane sisters and their families to live in an opulent setting, their homes connected by a garden. Look for the aedicule, a miniature temple, designed with Ionic columns framing handsome French windows at no. 9.

In 1975 the Soviet Union converted the Hammond mansion into a consulate, turned the garden into a parking lot, installed a clutter of security devices on the mansion, and surrounded it with a high fence. Five years later, in retaliation for the invasion of Afghanistan, they were asked to go home. The building remains vacant.

Return now to Fifth Avenue and cross to the Central Park side of the block, halfway between 91st and 92nd streets. Looking east you can see a tall Palladian window, centered near the top of the 1926 apartment house at **1107 Fifth Avenue**, which replaced a town house owned by Marjorie Merriweather Post and her husband at the time, E. F. Hutton. In return for permitting their home to be demolished to build the apartment house, an apartment on three levels overlooking the park was constructed for the Huttons.

The Post family wealth was based on breakfast cereal. In the late nineteenth century Marjorie's father, Charles W. Post, who had been a patient in the private Kellogg's sanitorium—the birthplace of cornflakes—went a step further and created a cereal-based coffee substitute called Postum, advertised for its curative powers. Grape Nuts, Post Toasties, and a merger with the General Foods Company followed.

Marjorie married four times. One husband, Joseph Davies, served as ambassador to the Soviet Union. Her 118-room Mediterranean-style home, Mar-a-Lago, in Palm Beach, Florida, was purchased by Donald Trump in the mid-1980s.

The now-subdivided Hutton apartment was a fifty-four-room affair, opulent as any mansion, and included a private elevator. Rented for $75,000 per year, it had amenities such as a wine room, a room for the silver, a flower room, and a special closet for Marjorie's gowns. A small army of servants, consigned to live in tiny cubicles, kept the household running.

At **1109 Fifth Avenue**, on the corner of 92nd Street, you come to the **Warburg mansion**, completed in 1908. This French chateau was home to Frieda Schiff Warburg and Felix Warburg and their five children until the death of Felix in 1937. Frieda was the only daughter of Jacob Schiff and Therese Loeb, daughter of Fanny Kuhn Loeb and Solomon Loeb, a founder of Kuhn, Loeb & Company. Married to Therese in 1875, Schiff became a full partner and within ten years was in complete control of his father-in-law's banking house.

Schiff was an unbending, stern, pious man, but a generous philanthropist, giving away vast amounts of his fortune—often anonymously—largely to Jewish causes. A domineering father and husband, he closely controlled every aspect of the lives of his children, Mortimer and Frieda. When young Felix Warburg fell in love with the beautiful Frieda, Schiff rigidly directed the courtship. Despite Schiff's reservations about the handsome, witty Warburg, the marriage took place soon afterward.

Warburg had admired the Fletcher-Sinclair chateau on Fifth Avenue and 79th Street and commissioned its architect, C. P. H. Gilbert, to build this family residence in the same style. The mansion reflects the Warburgs' family-centered life and their love of music and art. A gallery for displaying etchings was located on the ground floor. The second floor held a music room complete with pipe organ. The third floor was private family space. On the fourth floor, the children's bedrooms featured an electric railroad that snaked in and out of their rooms. Guests stayed on the fifth floor, which also had a squash court. The servants shared small quarters on the top floor.

In 1944 Frieda Warburg donated the mansion to the Jewish Theological Seminary of America to house the **Jewish Museum**, currently undergoing a $24.4-million renovation and expansion. Established in 1904, the museum holds more than 14,000 artifacts and works of art spanning 4,000 years of Jewish history, including archaeological treasures, ceremonial objects, paintings, and drawings. It is the largest museum of its kind in America and one of the largest in the world.

We are now at the end of our tour. If the walk has made you hungry, stop off at **Sarabeth's Kitchen**, 1295 Madison Avenue between 92nd and 93rd streets, a casual restaurant serving an American menu at reasonable prices. The fact is, while a million dollars may be a prerequisite to live in this neighborhood, visitors require substantially less.

Joyce Mendelsohn, a teacher in the New York City Public Schools for twenty-five years, educates teachers on the history of the city for the New York Teacher Centers Consortium. She also teaches two courses—"Ethnic New York" and "Literary New York"—at the New School for Social Research. She has studied nineteenth-century art and architecture with the Victorian Society in London. A contributor to the Encyclopedia of New York City, a project of the New-York Historical Society, she has conducted tours for ten years.

Walk · 6

▯▮▯▮▯▮▯▮▯▮▯▮▯▮▯▮▯▮▯▮▯▮▯▮▯▮▯▮▯

Brooklyn Heights

THE SOUL OF NINETEENTH-CENTURY AMERICA

JAMES S. KAPLAN, ESQ.

View of the Brooklyn Bridge at Old Fulton Street

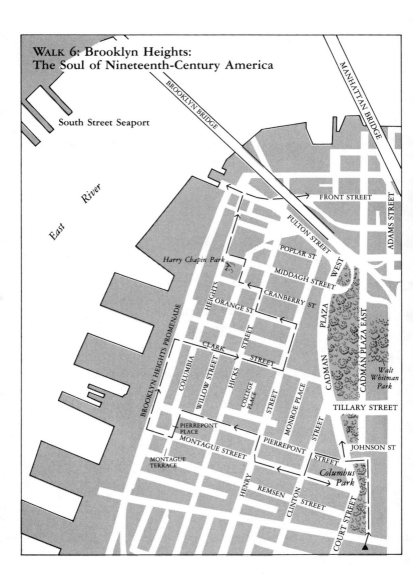

WALK 6: Brooklyn Heights: The Soul of Nineteenth-Century America

MANHATTAN BRIDGE

BROOKLYN BRIDGE

South Street Seaport

East River

Harry Chapin Park

ADAMS STREET

FRONT STREET

FULTON STREET

POPLAR ST

MIDDAGH STREET

CRANBERRY ST

ORANGE ST

CLARK STREET

STREET

HEIGHTS

BROOKLYN HEIGHTS PROMENADE

COLUMBIA

WILLOW STREET

HICKS STREET

COLLEGE PLACE

MONROE PLACE

PIERREPONT PLACE

MONTAGUE STREET

MONTAGUE TERRACE

PIERREPONT STREET

STREET

HENRY

REMSEN STREET

CLINTON STREET

COURT STREET

WEST

PLAZA

CADMAN

CADMAN PLAZA EAST

Walt Whiman Park

TILLARY STREET

JOHNSON ST

Columbus Park

Starting Point: Brooklyn Borough Hall, Cadman Plaza
Walk Length: About 3 hours
Subway Stop: (2, 3, 4, or 5 train) Borough Hall; exit at Borough Hall

Brooklyn Heights, a residential and commercial neighborhood of diverse brownstones, Gothic churches, a beautiful promenade, and architecturally eclectic government and private buildings, has a unique character that is simultaneously urban and suburban. While many residents proudly consider the area separate and distinct from both the rest of Brooklyn and the rest of New York City, the "Heights" is actually intimately linked historically and architecturally with both.

To understand Brooklyn Heights, one must understand its origins as New York's archetypal suburb. Prior to the Greater Consolidation of 1898, Brooklyn was a separate city from New York (which then consisted only of Manhattan). As a result of New York's tremendous economic boom during that era, Manhattan was destined to be the city's urban industrial center. The original developers of Brooklyn Heights, by contrast, sought to create a more tranquil setting across the East River, in which the upper middle class—Protestant Yankee businessmen and professionals—could be assured that their families could safely grow and prosper. In the Heights, they would be close to churches and far from the foreign and worldly influences encountered at places of business in Lower Manhattan. As a result, residential property in the Heights would have an elite cachet that would cause it to sell at premium prices.

Prior to 1810, Brooklyn Heights had a population of less than 5,000 and was a small farming community like thousands of others on the Eastern seaboard. It was part of the village of Brooklyn (originally named *Breuckelen* by the Dutch)—one of the six original Dutch villages founded by the Dutch West India Company prior to the seizure of New York by the English in 1664. (The others were Flatbush, Flatlands, Bushwick, Gravesend, and New Utrecht). The area had changed little in the 150 years since its founding.

In the first two decades of the nineteenth century, however, there were two seminal technical and political developments that caused a cataclysmic change in the physical and demographic character of Brooklyn Heights, as well as the rest of the city of New York.

First, Robert Fulton, with the financial and political backing of Robert Livingston, a Brooklyn Heights land-owner, successfully developed the steamboat, and in 1814 the Fulton Ferry Company inaugurated steam ferry service from the old Brooklyn ferry slip (today called Fulton Landing) to South Street in Manhattan.

Second, and even more important, in 1825 the state of New York, under the leadership of Governor DeWitt Clinton, successfully opened the Erie Canal, which linked the port of New York with the Great Lakes, thereby insuring that New York would be the nation's preeminent commercial center. As a result, the population of the borough of Brooklyn grew from 8,300 in 1810 to 279,000 in 1860, and land value in Brooklyn Heights skyrocketed.

The families that owned tracts of land in Brooklyn

Heights, such as the Livingstons, the Remsens, the Jorale-
mons, the Hickses, and the Pierreponts (all have streets
named for them today), soon found that their land was
much more valuable if used for *residential housing* rather
than for farming. Thus, in a process that would be repeated
in the twentieth century, as farm land in Long Island,
Westchester, and ultimately even Dutchess County would
give way to suburban communities such as Manhasset,
Larchmont, and Scarsdale, these nineteenth-century Protestant Yankee farmers soon found themselves in the much
more lucrative business of real estate development. In fact,
almost half of the buildings standing today in Brooklyn
Heights, including most of the brownstones, were originally
built between 1820 and 1860 as part of this initial wave of
residential development.

Ultimately, the Heights would become nationally recognized as the intellectual, religious, and political center
of upper-middle-class Protestant thought. It is thus no
accident that the two leading religious and literary figures
of that epoch—Henry Ward Beecher and Walt Whitman—lived and worked in the Heights for most of their
active careers.

One of the reasons the Heights is so interesting is
that while twentieth-century urban development is clearly
evident in parts of the area, it has not completely obliterated the nineteenth-century development. It is this con-
fluence of the urban and the suburban, this tension
between the aspirations of the nineteenth century and the
modern demands of the twentieth century, that gives
Brooklyn Heights its unique character, and makes a walk
through it so rewarding.

Our tour begins in front of **Brooklyn Borough Hall** at
the south end of **Cadman Plaza**, a narrow park created
by an urban renewal project of the 1950s. (If you have
exited the subway at Joralemon Street, walk to the other
side of Borough Hall.)

The cupola-topped Brooklyn Borough Hall is one of Brooklyn's finest public monuments. Completed in 1849, about forty years after Manhattan's City Hall, its opening coincided with the emergence of Brooklyn as a world-class city, as opposed to a small farming village. Like Manhattan's City Hall, Brooklyn's Borough Hall (its city hall until 1898) is built in the Greek Revival style, and is in many ways even more austere and imposing than its Georgian/Greek Revival cousin across the East River.

When the construction of Brooklyn's Borough Hall began in 1836, the economic impact of the opening of the Erie Canal was beginning to be felt in full force. Optimism about the future swept through New York's commercial community. Furthermore, since the Erie Canal—a government project—had created this prosperity, belief in the democratic system of government became very strong, particularly among Brooklyn's rising upper middle class. At a time when most of the world was under the rule of aristocracies and kings, the residents of Brooklyn had a very strong belief that, internationally, democracies were the wave of the future, and this was reflected in their public architecture. Buildings like Borough Hall looked very consciously to the democratic Greek city-states as models. The citizens of Brooklyn saw themselves as the spiritual descendants of the citizens of Athens, and their erstwhile farming village was now seeking to project itself on a grand, classical scale.

When it was finished, Brooklyn civic leaders could not but view Borough Hall with extreme pride and as a physical example of the triumph of democratic government. The architect of the building, Gamaliel King, was listed in the Brooklyn city directory as a grocer until 1830. Thereafter, he was listed as a carpenter. Brooklynites believed that in nineteenth-century democratic America any man of ability could aspire to and achieve great artistic and scientific distinction without noble

Brooklyn Borough Hall

birth or specialized academic training or degrees from elite universities.

Borough Hall has been renovated several times, most recently in the late 1980s under the direction of the architectural firm of Conklin and Rossant. The 1980s renovation was one of the most expensive in New York City history and was subject to long delays and cost overruns. Nevertheless, its completion was an occasion for considerable civic celebration. At its public opening, Jacqueline Kennedy Onassis personally presented the Municipal Art Society's award for urban improvement to New York City Department of General Services Commissioner Hadley Gold, whose agency had been responsible for the renovations.

Now walk north up Cadman Plaza (named after Rev. Parkes Cadman, America's first radio preacher), toward the Brooklyn Bridge in the distance. Directly in front of Borough Hall, in a small semicircular plaza, on your left is the black rectangular marble **monument to John Cashmore**, borough president of Brooklyn during the 1950s Downtown urban renewal that created the park.

There are widely differing views as to the success of this project. To understand it, we must understand the position of downtown Brooklyn at the time it was built. The Greater Consolidation of 1898, narrowly approved by Brooklyn voters despite vigorous opposition from factions arguing that Brooklyn should remain independent, did not achieve the goal of making Downtown Brooklyn New York's second main business district (after Lower Manhattan), even though this had been cited as a major reason why Brooklyn voters should support the consolidation. Midtown Manhattan, with its proximity to Grand Central Terminal, soon eclipsed Downtown Brooklyn as the business location of choice, and by 1950 the neighborhood, like downtown areas in many smaller cities, was in serious decline, with older buildings along Fulton Street up to Borough Hall in serious disrepair and unsightly elevated tracks keeping sunlight from the streets.

Cashmore and his associates in Borough Hall undoubtedly sought to create a new Brooklyn Civic Center that would return Downtown Brooklyn to the classical grandeur that existed when Borough Hall was newly constructed. If you look straight ahead at the open park, with the orderly row of state and federal court houses on your right, to the distinctive U.S. Post Office Building—looking like a medieval castle in the distance—and to the outlines of the spires of the Brooklyn Bridge still farther beyond, you can see that, to some extent, the 1950s urban renewal achieved this objective. The dark and decaying downtown was replaced with this clean park. The park is at times widely used, with a TKTS booth selling discount tickets to Broadway shows and a greenmarket at which fresh produce is sold on weekends.

However, the development is not without its critics. The most frequently voiced complaint is that the plaza stands as a largely self-contained unit with no relationship to the surrounding areas and no anticipation of future commercial development. Cadman Plaza Park in fact cuts a swath that separates Brooklyn Heights from the rest of downtown Brooklyn to the east, leading some critics in the 1960s and 1970s to compare the park to the Demilitarized Zone in Vietnam. It physically separated wealthy Brooklyn Heights from the poor of central Brooklyn, thereby reinforcing the cultural and economic segregation of Brooklyn society.

Now walk past the Cashmore monument to a sculpture **memorial to Robert Francis Kennedy**, who was assassinated in 1968 just after winning the California Democratic Presidential primary. This is one of the few public monuments in New York City to Robert Kennedy, who at the time of his death was a senator from New York.

It is appropriate that this monument should be in Downtown Brooklyn. In 1964, one year after the assassination of his brother John, Bobby Kennedy needed a place from which to advance his career toward the pres-

Robert F. Kennedy Memorial in Cadman Plaza

idency. Although the Kennedy family had always been politically associated with Massachusetts, and Robert Kennedy
at the time was living in Virginia, he took the somewhat
unusual step of announcing (with the encouragement of
several local Democratic leaders) that he would challenge
New York's incumbent Republican Senator Kenneth Keat-
ing. The Republicans immediately charged that he was a
carpetbagger, and facetiously offered him a road map to find
out where places like Brooklyn were located. However,
Kennedy quickly proved the adage that anyone who has
lived in New York for more than two weeks can claim to
be a New Yorker. He defeated the Republican incumbent
by more than a million votes.

As you walk farther you come to a sign that marks a monument to another adopted son of Brooklyn, **Christopher Columbus**. Although Columbus never set foot in North America, he is more revered in New York City than in many Latin American countries. The sign indicates that this stretch of the plaza is Columbus Park and the 1867 statue of Columbus by Emma Stephens (which until 1971 stood in Central Park) is clear evidence that Brooklyn, with its large Italian population, considers Columbus one of its heroes, notwithstanding any revisionist views to the contrary.

Now walk up to the **statue of Henry Ward Beecher**, just in front of the Post Office building. This statue by John Quincy Adams Ward, who also did the statue of George Washington over Federal Hall on Wall Street, was made from the death mask of Beecher and is considered, not surprisingly, his best likeness.

To nineteenth-century residents of Brooklyn, there was no one who was more important in the United States than Beecher. As pastor of Brooklyn Heights's Plymouth Church for more than forty years, Beecher was a leading religious advocate in the movement to abolish slavery and a key supporter of Abraham Lincoln before his election to the presidency and during the Civil War. The son of a Congregationalist minister, Beecher's ministry was the essential component to the growth of the newly founded Plymouth Church, which is located nearby and which you will see later on your walk.

Facing the statue, on Beecher's left, is a statue of the slave girl Pinky, who was auctioned off by Beecher in 1854 from his pulpit, to dramatize the plight of slaves and to buy the girl's freedom. Symbolizing Beecher's love for children are two other youngsters portrayed on his left. Although Beecher's sister, Harriet Beecher Stowe, author of *Uncle Tom's Cabin*, is better known today, Brooklynites of the 1800s considered the preacher a much more significant figure.

Behind the statue of Beecher is the Brooklyn central

office of the **U.S. Post Office**, which you saw earlier from Borough Hall. Designed by Miffin Bell in 1885 in the Romanesque Revival style, the work was later assumed by William A. Freret, supervising architect for the Treasury Department, and the building was completed in 1891.

Some Heights residents consider the fortresslike structure to be one of the most unusual and distinctive public buildings in the city. The Romanesque style of the post office is certainly interesting when contrasted with the Greek Revival style of Borough Hall behind you. When it was built, the United States had become much more certain of itself. No longer were the citizens of Brooklyn content to view themselves as austere members of a Greek city-state. The federal government, which commissioned the building, projects itself on a grand, Roman scale, and the architecture of this post office reflects it.

To the north of the post office, and attached to it, is a 1931 extension built by James Wetmore during the Depression. Wetmore was a partner in the firm of Warren & Wetmore, which was involved in the building of Grand Central Terminal. Here, the attempt is to harmonize the 1930s addition with the earlier style of its 1890s neighbor. You will have to judge for yourself the success of this effort at harmonization.

Turn left now and walk out of Cadman Plaza to **Pierrepont Street**, named after Hezekiah Pierpont, the patriarch of the Pierrepont family (the spelling was changed by Hezekiah's son), whose descendants became leading citizens of Brooklyn Heights throughout the nineteenth century. Pierpont originally had a gin distillery here in the Heights, but, like many of his neighbors, he became more and more interested in real estate development. He foresaw the potential for the Heights as an upper class bedroom community for the emerging commercial centers of South Street and Wall Street in Manhattan, and was one of the creators of the Heights as a suburban

An unusual branch of the U.S. Post Office

residential community. As early as 1820, Pierpont advertised his newly erected houses as suitable for a man of business seeking a quiet residential area "only seven minutes by ferry" from his office in lower Manhattan.

The Pierreponts, like their neighbors the Livingstons (Livingston Street is one block to the south of Borough Hall), were enthusiastic backers of Robert Fulton's desire to run ferry service from what today is Fulton Street in Manhattan to Fulton Street in Brooklyn. Henry E. Pierrepont, a descendant of Hezekiah, was associated with the operation of the Brooklyn ferries for almost fifty years, during which time they were critical to the neighborhood's success. It is a testament to the Pierreponts' foresight that even today apartments in Brooklyn Heights rent or sell at much higher rates than other residential property in Brooklyn.

You're now standing on the corner of Cadman Plaza West and Pierrepont Street. Walk to the right to the redbrick skyscraper, **One Pierrepont Plaza**. This 600,000-square-foot office building was one of the greatest economic development triumphs of Mayor Ed Koch's administration. The building was erected in 1986 by the developer Forest City with a heavy investment of New York City capital budget funds, and was successfully able to lure the "back office" operations of Morgan Stanley and Goldman Sachs as tenants. The success of the project laid the groundwork for other downtown Brooklyn projects such as MetroTech, which is undoubtedly Brooklyn's most ambitious urban development to date.

Although MetroTech is to some extent cut off from the Heights by Cadman Plaza, if you look carefully past the Beecher monument and behind the massive New York State Supreme Court building, you will see the outlines of several towers of this 4,700,000-square-foot commercial and academic project, which is expected to create 14,500 new jobs in Downtown Brooklyn. In contrast to the design of Cadman Plaza's 1950s urban renewal that separated the Heights from the rest of Brooklyn, truncating Brooklyn's downtown, the design of MetroTech consciously seeks to integrate the

Cadman Plaza, looking toward Borough Hall

poorer residents of central Brooklyn with the more affluent commercial and academic institutions of modern
Brooklyn's dynamic and emerging downtown.

Take a walk into the ornate lobby of One Pierrepont
Plaza, which can be viewed either as an exquisite example of Postmodernism or as a copy of a tacky powder
room. A plaque on the wall states that the building marks
the beginning of Downtown Brooklyn's role (again) as
the city's third business district. A century after this hope
was first advanced, it remains to be fully realized; but,
after all, neither Rome nor Brooklyn were built in a day.

Leaving the lobby, proceed right up Pierrepont Street to
Clinton Street, named after DeWitt Clinton, a Manhattan

politician who served at various times as mayor of New York City, governor of New York State, and numerous lesser offices. He was the original secretary of the Tammany Society (the forerunner of the nineteenth-century political organization that controlled the city's politics, and—ironically—later became his bitter political enemy) and is sometimes alleged to be the founder of Tammany's system of political patronage. However, Clinton was no ordinary hack politician. He was a visionary who, after having been rebuffed by the federal government, stubbornly fought to convince New Yorkers that the state of New York, on its own, could construct the 362-mile Erie Canal linking Lake Erie at Buffalo with the Hudson River at Albany.

The success of this "upstate" project, begun after Clinton's election as governor in 1816 and completed nine years later in 1825 (two years behind schedule), marked a political, social, economic, and psychological turning point in the history of Brooklyn Heights and New York City. It created for the first time a national market for produce from the Midwest using New York Harbor as its eastern terminus, and caused New York City and Brooklyn to expand exponentially in the early nineteenth century, far outstripping all other ports on the Eastern seaboard. At the tumultuous celebration of its opening, it was declared that not since the Egyptian pharaohs had irrigated the Upper Nile Valley three thousand years earlier had such an important public water works project been undertaken at any time, anywhere in the world.

At the southeast corner of Clinton and Pierrepont streets, look at the white Italian palatial bank. This building, with its unusual black lamps and detailed interior and a sign that says **Manufacturers Hanover Trust** (soon to be merged into Chemical Bank), was built by the architectural firm of York & Sawyer.

The building effectively demonstrates the success of the Italian palatial style for use in bank buildings and is the precursor of the larger and better-known Federal Reserve Bank on Maiden Lane in Lower Manhattan, built

Detail of Brooklyn Historical Society building

by the same architects ten years later. Look at the top of the building and read the names of the old Brooklyn farming towns—Flatbush, Flatlands, New Utrecht, Bushwick, New Lots, etc.

Across the street is George B. Post's **Brooklyn Historical Society** building on the southwest corner. For many years, the society that occupies this building was known as the Long Island Historical Society. After a somewhat bitter debate, it was recently renamed the Brooklyn Historical Society as if to emphasize that, fundamentally, modern Brooklyn Heights looks west to Manhattan, rather than east to Long Island. Post's neo-Romanesque style contrasts sharply with the York & Sawyer design of the bank building nearby and aggressively informs Brooklynites that this is a building of importance.

The museum contains an exhibit area with fascinating displays on Brooklyn history, including Coney Island, the Brooklyn Navy Yard, and the Brooklyn Dodgers. The inscription on the outside of the building says *Historia Testes Temporium*—"History is the witness to our time."

On the northwest corner of Pierrepont and Clinton is the former Crescent Club, today **St. Ann's School**. On the northeast corner is the backside of Pierrepont Plaza. From 1962 to 1986, this site was a parking lot and an eyesore for Brooklyn Heights, a monument to the folly of tearing down the past before being ready to proceed into the future.

Prior to 1962 it was the site of the graceful Anglo-Italian Brooklyn Savings Bank Building by the architect Frank Freeman, one of Brooklyn's greatest nineteenth-century architects. Its 1962 owners tore it down to make way for a more "commercially viable" building, which they were subsequently unable to construct.

After Pierrepont Plaza was finally erected, some members of the New York City Law Department's Economic Development Division, who had worked on the lease of the property to the developer, argued that the building's lobby should contain a retrospective on the work of Frank Freeman, who also designed many other architecturally distinctive buildings in the Heights. The developer, Forest City, which has received millions of dollars in city subsidies, recently funded a photography exhibit of old Brooklyn buildings, held in the Pierrepont Plaza lobby, and has indicated that a Frank Freeman retrospective may, at last, be forthcoming.

From this corner, turn left onto Clinton Street and come to the **Church of St. Ann and the Holy Trinity** on the northwest corner of Clinton and Montague streets. The church was begun in 1843 and completed in 1847 by the architect Minard Lefever. If St. Ann's is open, step inside and look at the fine William Bolton stained glass windows.

As a young man in his twenties, Bolton created these windows at a factory in Pelham, New York. They are among the first stained glass windows made in the United States, and are considered some of the best. After creating the windows (according to the late Reverend Howard Mellish, longtime pastor of the church), Bolton gave up the practice of window making and went to England. There he married, had a family, and never mentioned his life in America again. Seventy years later, his daughter, an old woman in failing health, found references to his earlier career as a stained glass window maker in America and made a pilgrimage to New York to find his work before her death. Supposedly, the discovery that her father had made the windows so moved her that it helped restore her health.

For some years there was a dispute over the direction of the congregation, as the church pastor ran into conflict with the more conservative members and the building closed in 1957. The church fell into disrepair and there was fear that the windows might be lost forever. The building reopened in 1969, and in the 1970s and 1980s an extensive effort was made to raise funds for the restoration of the windows to their original condition, an ongoing task.

One of the leading figures in the founding of St. Ann's and raising the capital to build it was Edgar Bartow, son-in-law of Hezekiah Pierpont. Its location and financial backing made St. Ann's *the* establishment church of the Heights. By design, Protestant churches are found on almost every block in this area. Hezekiah Pierpont and other developers not only were religious, they also understood that surrounding property values would rise with a church nearby. They also helped stress the image of Brooklyn as a refuge from the worldly influences of Manhattan with its immigrant hordes, street gangs, crime, noise, poverty, and Catholics—exactly the sort of thing that the upper middle class, nineteenth-century Protestant New Yorker wished to avoid. (If you have time when the tour is over, return to Montague and Hicks and walk two blocks south on Hicks, past Remsen Street, to Grace Court and Grace Court Alley to experience true suburban tranquility in the shadow of **Grace Church** of Brooklyn.)

As you look east, the block on the northern side of

Montague Street between Clinton and Court streets presents an interesting mélange of different architectural styles. The aggressive lack of contextual relationship between the buildings is so striking as to make the street incongruously interesting.

First, there is York & Sawyer's bank building at 177 Montague Street, which you saw from Pierrepont Street. Next door is Mowbray & Uffinger's **Citibank building** at no. 181. This is in the Greek Revival style but is a bit more gaudy than Brooklyn Borough Hall. Nevertheless, its looks very much become its function as a bank. The ornate frieze at the top would be quite attractive standing alone, and even in this eclectic selection holds its own.

Next door, at no. 185, is the 1929 Corbin, Harrison & McMurray **Municipal Credit Union**. This building is a precursor to these architects' work as part of the team on Rockefeller Center, the famous Midtown Manhattan landmark, just as York & Sawyer's building at no. 177 is the precursor to their work on the landmark Federal Reserve Bank on Maiden Lane in Lower Manhattan.

Next is the nine-story former **Real Estate Exchange** at nos. 189–191. Originally built in a Renaissance style, you would hardly recognize it today beneath its new modern glass skin. Hidden beneath this awkward exterior is the work of Frank Freeman. The ultimate indignity to the original design is the installation of the boxy, fake colonial doorway of the present ground floor occupant, the European American Bank.

At no. 195 is the building that, since 1962, has been the headquarters of **Brooklyn Union Gas Company**. It is in the Modern or International style of glass and steel facades. This style, pioneered by Lever House and the Seagrams Building on Park Avenue in Manhattan, has been copied throughout the city with less than complete success.

Turn around and walk west up Montague Street, past St. Ann's. You are now entering a district that is Brooklyn's rival to Manhattan's Columbus Avenue. The clatter of shoppers and visitors on this block of boutiques and restaurants between Clinton and Hicks streets makes this one of the trendiest and friendliest areas of Brooklyn Heights. The notoriously high rents on Montague Street have been cited as a cause of significant turnover in the restaurants and shops here.

The block—often in flux—contains, in addition to fast-food and ice cream franchises, a number of individually distinctive restaurants such as, on the north side, the **Grand Canyon**, an excellent and relatively inexpensive burger joint with Western-style decor featuring Texas longhorns over the bar. More expensive is **Armando's**, a higher-priced classical Italian restaurant. On the south side of the block is **Leaf and Bean**, a tea and coffee emporium that also sells an enormous array of ceramics and housewares and has a busy small restaurant in the back. Farther east, toward Clinton Street, is a brownstone with a Japanese restaurant, **Nanatori**, upstairs, and downstairs a Chinese restaurant, **Lichee Nut**, which claims to have "the best food of the East in Brooklyn Heights." Also not to be missed is **Happy Days**, a recently renovated 24-hour, seven-days-a-week 1950s juke-box diner that is in the basement of the brownstone at 148 Montague Street. This is Brooklyn Heights's answer to Ellen's Stardust Diner in Manhattan, and is especially known for its chicken pot pie. If you want to get a bite to eat, or use a bathroom, this is one of the best opportunities to do so throughout the walk. On the next block are the **Montague Street Saloon**, a local bar with saloon decor, and **Slades**, a yuppie restaurant and singles bar with an outdoor café.

Montague Street has been one of the main arteries of Brooklyn Heights since the mid-nineteenth century. Prior to the building of the Promenade, which you'll soon see, it sloped down to the East River past a small bridge called the Penny Bridge (so named because it cost a penny to cross) to the Montague Street terminal of the Wall Street ferry. Montague Street is intimately linked with the name of Brooklyn's world famous baseball team—the Dodgers. In the late nineteenth century, electric trolley cars would take residents down the Heights to the ferry terminal. Since residents of Brooklyn became used to dodging the trolleys, Brooklyn's major-league ball team became known as the Brooklyn "Dodgers." By the mid-twentieth century the Dodgers were considered the soul of Brooklyn and as much a part of the borough as the Brooklyn Bridge itself. Who can forget Gil Hodges, Pee Wee Reese, pitcher Sandy Koufax, or the Dodgers defeat of the hated Yankees in the 1955 "subway" World Series? In 1958, when Dodgers owner Walter O'Malley—who had sought a bigger and more modern stadium than Ebbets Field—was not satisfied with the response of Brooklyn's political leaders, he moved the team to Los Angeles. Brooklyn has yet to recover fully from the departure of the famous baseball team that took the name given to it by the borough it left behind. Ebbets Field, site of the stadium where the Dodgers played, is now a city housing project.

Continue walking west toward the East River on Montague and turn right on **Henry Street**, named for Thomas W. Henry, a Brooklyn physician of the early nineteenth century. Proceed north to the southwest corner of Henry and Pierrepont streets to one of Frank Freeman's greatest residential buildings—the **Herman Behr House**.

Designed in 1890, this building is one of the best examples in New York of the Romanesque Revival style as applied to a residential structure. Popularized by the Boston architect Henry Hobson Richardson, the Romanesque style reflects the prosperity of 1890s America. The style is exuberant while classical, befitting the *nouveau riche* merchant for whom it was designed. The house was later enlarged with a six-story addition to become the Hotel Palm, and later a house of ill-repute. It was subsequently acquired by the Catholic Church, and then sold for conversion to its present use—cooperative apartments—in 1976. The opulence of this Romanesque Revival style is a marked contrast with the extreme austerity of other homes, such as 80 Pierrepont Street, between Henry and Clinton streets.

On the block of Pierrepont Street between Henry and Hicks there is a range of architectural styles, including Greek Revival, Romanesque, and Federal. You will also notice, on the north side of the street, some twentieth-century apartment buildings. At one time, it was feared that all of Brooklyn Heights would become high-rise apartments. With the increasing urbanization of twentieth-century Brooklyn, a high-rise apartment building would afford a residential landlord a greater return than a group of brownstones.

Because Brooklyn had largely missed out on the economic booms that transformed Manhattan in the 1920s and 1950s, there was much more to lose in Brooklyn Heights than in other areas of the city. Furthermore, in the 1940s and 1950s, Brooklyn Heights had also suffered, like other inner-city neighborhoods, from long-time residents fleeing to newer, more spacious suburbs farther from the central urban core. This was a particularly ironic trend for the Heights, since it had been built as a suburban haven from the city in the first place. Many of the fine row houses became single room occupancy (SRO) rooming houses and preservationists feared that either through deterioration or redevelopment the nineteenth-century brownstones would be destroyed and the community would lose its link to a past that had sustained it for more than a hundred years.

Then a Brooklynite came to the rescue. A young lawyer named Otis Pratt Pearsall, who was living in a basement apartment on Willow Street, began a movement to retain the historic character of Brooklyn Heights. With the backing of the Brooklyn Heights Association, Clay Lancaster, a former teacher in the Department of Fine Arts at Columbia University, was retained to survey the Heights and publish a guide book of the historic homes.

This effort culminated in the publication of Lancaster's *Old Brooklyn Heights: New York's First Suburb* in 1961, a book influential in the naming of Brooklyn Heights as New York City's first historic district and the passage of the city's landmark preservation laws. Saving Brooklyn Heights from the wrecker's ball proved the viability of landmark preservation as a political and intellectual movement, not only for New York City but for other cities of the nation as well.

Walk now to the intersection of Pierrepont Street and Pierrepont Place to the **Pierrepont playground**, just before you reach the promenade. (You will be walking west on Pierrepont Street, past Hicks Street toward the East River.) This small, state-of-the-art playground, with separate areas for toddlers and older children, is a widely-used amenity in an area that lacks a major park (other than Cadman Plaza). The playground is built on the site of what was once 1 Pierrepont Place, the mansion of Henry E. Pierrepont, Hezekiah Pierpont's descendant. Author of a privately published history of the Fulton Ferry Company, Henry Pierrepont argued that the ferries were as important and charitable an institution to Brooklyn as its hospital. The house was demolished (unfortunately, before the landmarks preservation law) in 1946.

Next door to the playground, you arrive at **2 and 3 Pierrepont Place**—two residences that *did* survive. These buildings are the true "kings" of Brooklyn Heights brownstone architecture. Number 3 was occupied originally by the tea merchant Abiel Abbott Low. A. A. Low and Company was a significant importer and exporter on Manhattan's South Street and a key participant in nineteenth-century New York's booming trade with China. His son Seth Low was the mayor of Brooklyn in the 1880s, and in 1901 was elected mayor of all of New York City. After he was defeated in 1903, he served as president of Columbia University. Seth Low's career as a good government leader was unquestioned, but good government isn't always good enough for New Yorkers.

Pierrepont Street

Seth lost his bid to be reelected mayor after his first term because of his aristocratic bearing and tendencies, which left him out of touch with the average New Yorker, who seemed much more comfortable with the backslapping—if corrupt—style of the slate of candidates backed by Tammany Hall, the regular Democratic Party. Number 3 was built for Alexander M. White, a fur merchant whose son, Alfred Treadway White, was a businessman and philantrophist also active in Brooklyn's civic activities.

Around the corner, walking south and to the right after no. 2, you will see a tablet that marks the lane where stood the **Four Chimneys**, the house where George Washington lived during the Battle of Long Island.

What the plaque doesn't fully explain is that during the American Revolution, Brooklyn was the site of what was probably the most disastrous battle for the Continental Army in the entire war. George Washington, after the Battle of Bunker Hill, decided that he would mass his troops in Brooklyn to face the British Army, which was set to arrive in New York Harbor. But Washington wasn't ready for the onslaught of 30,000 British soldiers under the command of brothers Richard and William Howe. Unfortunately for the Americans, the Howes' chief aide, General Henry Clinton, knew Brooklyn much better than the officers in George Washington's Continental Army— most of whom were from New England or Virginia! Clinton, son of the British governor of Long Island, had grown up in Brooklyn.

In one of the greatest blunders in American military history, a small road near Flatbush was left undefended by the American commanders. The bulk of Clinton's army passed through the road, encircled the continental forces, and almost captured the entire American army before it could retreat to fortifications in Brooklyn Heights. It was 1776, and the war was almost over before it began.

Washington was lucky. A fog covered the East River

and a significant number of American troops were able to escape to Manhattan, where they were again badly defeated by the British and again fled, this time to New Jersey, and later to Valley Forge. The army of 30,000 British troops represented over five times Brooklyn's entire population in 1776.

You are now about to enter the **Brooklyn Heights Promenade**. Behind you is Montague Street. Walk past the flagpole at the entrance to the Promenade to the railing. If you like, sit on one of the benches nearby, and you will see why it is said that the view of New York Harbor from the Brooklyn Heights Promenade is one of the most breathtaking views that New York has to offer. Here the resident and visitor alike have the sense that they have found a unique vantage point from which to view one of the world's greatest cities. Straight ahead is the tip of the island of Manhattan, featuring the South Ferry terminals. The smaller, white ferries carry Coast Guard personnel to **Governors Island**, the island in the foreground to the left. The larger ferries, usually orange, are run by the city's Department of Transportation and carry commuters from lower Manhattan to **Staten Island**, the large land mass somewhat to the left in back of Governors Island. The Staten Island Ferry has carried commuters from Staten Island, New York's smallest borough, to Manhattan since the days of Cornelius Vanderbilt, the famous railroad and shipping magnate who began his career as a penniless Staten Island ferryman and was the richest man in America when he died in 1877. In the distance at the extreme left you can catch a glimpse of the **Verrazano Narrows Bridge**, which connects Brooklyn and Staten Island. Looking straight ahead, again slightly to the left, you see an island with a massive red building on it. This is **Ellis Island**, the recently renovated national monument through which millions of immigrants passed in the heyday of American immigration. Slightly to the left is the unmistakable green lady in the harbor, the **Statue of Liberty**, renovated in 1986. Designed and promoted by Auguste Bartholdi, a French sculptor who believed large monumental sculptures could be a vehicle to promote Republican government in France, the Statue of Liberty has become the ultimate symbol of America and its people.

The Promenade in many ways creates the defining vision of Brooklyn Heights and its place in the city. As you will see, it is widely used by people from all walks of life. To have created a public amenity of this quality has to be considered one of the greatest achievements of the urban planning of Robert Moses, New York's great master builder.

Moses ran public work projects in New York from the 1920s to the 1960s with a power that has yet to be matched. His early success in the 1920s came when, as a protégé of Democratic Governor Al Smith, he built Jones Beach and the Long Island parkways that made the beaches accessible to city residents. As a result, he obtained considerable sway over public works in the city. Moses firmly believed that in the twentieth century New York's future lay with automobiles. In order to efficiently move cars from one place to another in the New York metropolitan area, he devised an extensive network of superhighways.

An early base of his power after Governor Smith left the political scene was the Triboro Bridge and Tunnel Authority, which built the Triboro Bridge and had the authority to control the tolls collected. Moses used these funds to push a series of highway projects. As a result, almost all of the island of Manhattan, as well as this part of Brooklyn where you are now standing, is ringed by highways.

Walk north on the promenade for several blocks toward the Brooklyn Bridge. As you've no doubt noticed, this is one of the most stunning vistas of the skyscrapers of Manhattan. Besides Lower Manhattan, the Promenade offers an extraordinary view of the **Brooklyn Bridge**, set against a backdrop of the **World Trade Center**, the

Empire State Building, the **Citicorp Center**, and the other glass and stone monuments of Manhattan. The red pier complex you see directly across the river to the south of the bridge is one of New York's most successful economic development projects of the 1980s: **Pier 17** of the **South Street Seaport**. As you get closer to the bridge, look to the right and notice the ornate ironwork on the back of nos. 2 and 3 Pierrepont Place visible through their backyards.

The Brooklyn Bridge, the first suspension bridge built in New York City, is not only an icon of Brooklyn and beloved by its residents, but is also a structure with a history to match its architectural beauty. After the opening of the Erie Canal, Manhattan and Brooklyn became one of the world's major commercial centers because of their broad waterfronts where goods could land by ship and barge. But after the nation became laced with railroads following the Civil War, the water that divided Brooklyn from the rest of the United States became a liability, because goods had to be loaded off and on barges to connect to New Jersey and beyond.

Concern grew that Brooklyn would die economically. The local Brooklyn business community began toying with the idea of building a bridge to connect Brooklyn with Manhattan. The only problem was that never in history had a bridge been built over a body of water as wide and as deep as the East River.

John Augustus Roebling, a wire maker from Trenton, New Jersey, believed that the suspension principle could be used to construct a bridge connecting Manhattan and Brooklyn. His concept was met with considerable skepticism since other suspension bridges that had been built in Europe had collapsed as soon as any significant weight had been put upon them. But, through dogged persistence, Roebling convinced the New York and Brooklyn city councils that he could do it. Work began in 1869.

Shortly thereafter, Roebling's foot was crushed by a moving construction crane in a freak accident as he stood watching the bridge construction from a distant pier. Several days later he died, apparently from a tetanus infection. Work was continued by Roebling's son, Colonel Washington Augustus Roebling. But Washington Roebling soon had maladies of his own.

One of the problems in the bridge's construction was the need to dig down into the East River to lay the caissons—the foundations for the twin supports from which the roadway is suspended. The one on the Manhattan side required work more than one hundred feet beneath the river surface. Workers were lowered in great dumbbells filled with heavily pressurized air that rested on the river bottom. Some men soon began suffering severe physical impairment, developing what was then called caisson disease, in which nitrogen bubbles stop the supply of oxygen to the bloodstream because of rapid decompression, now known as "the bends." Because of his fervor to participate in all aspects of the work, the younger Roebling insisted on going down on almost every shift with the construction workers to oversee the progress. Soon he was crippled by the disease, and confined to a bed in his home in nearby Columbia Heights. His wife Emily had to take over the day-to-day management of the bridge's construction, transmitting Roebling's instructions from his bedside to his men.

As the work continued, there were scandals about payoffs and shoddy construction. Although Roebling was never personally implicated in the scandals, Brooklyn's mayor, Seth Low, insisted that Roebling resign, citing health considerations. Roebling refused, and saw the bridge through its completion in 1883. He later partially recovered and returned to Trenton, New Jersey, where he died forty-three years later in 1926 at the age of eighty-seven.

When it opened, there was fear that when a large number of people walked across it, the mighty bridge would collapse. More than a century later it is still stand-

View from the Brooklyn Heights Promenade

ing, and has surely attained a mythic status to residents of Brooklyn who revere it as not just a bridge but also as an important public monument. In 1983, there was a huge fireworks celebration to commemorate the hundredth anniversary of its opening.

As you approach the end of the Promenade walking north, take one last look at the beauty before you. In addition to the skyscrapers already mentioned, you can see the Gothic spire of the **Woolworth Building**, one of the architect Cass Gilbert's finest works, and New York City's **Municipal Building**, designed by the architects McKim, Mead & White and one of the city's finest classical Beaux Art structures. At the top is the statue of "Civic Fame" by Adolph Weinman, surrounded by the five cupolas representing the five boroughs of New York consolidated into Greater New York City. You should also look at the brownstones of **Columbia Heights** behind you. A river view has always commanded the highest price of buildings in the Heights. Among the longtime residents of these houses is the writer and onetime may-oral candidate Norman Mailer.

You should now be at the northern end of the Prom-enade, near the unmarked entrance to **Clark Street**, which leads back toward the Heights residential section. Turn right. You are now going back into the oldest section of Brooklyn Heights, home of two of the leading intellectuals of nineteenth-century America—Henry Ward Beecher and Walt Whitman.

Clark Street takes us uphill and east from the Prom-enade. Stopping at the corner of **Willow Street**, you can look right (south) and see a beautiful collection of brown-stone styles, including a wooden Dutch house and sev-eral Federal-style homes. On the left is the **Towers Hotel** designed by Starret & Van Vleek, which was opened in 1928 as one of Brooklyn's last luxury hotels.

Continue along Clark Street, heading east up a gentle slope, to **Hicks Street**. Take a short right on Hicks head-ing south and look at the row of brownstones on the east side of the street at mid-block. The plaque at **no. 131** describes the residence as one of the few remaining ex-amples of the Gothic Revival design so popular a century ago. Note the tudor arch doorway and elaborate cornices. This home was built for Henry C. Bowen, the merchant who founded the pivotal institution Plymouth Church and the abolitionist newspaper *The Independent*, edited by Henry Ward Beecher. Bowen was a Congregationalist of firm beliefs and backed his sympathies with money.

Backtrack to the corner of Clark and Hicks and, turn-ing right onto Clark, walk past the **Hotel St. George**. Hicks Street is named after the Hicks family, who owned a farm in the north Heights. Reportedly, the use of the word *hick* to describe a farmer comes from early nineteenth-century New York when produce from the Hicks farm would be transported to Manhattan and the more sophisticated urban Manhattanites would say "here come the Hicks." The name stuck. In any event, the Hotel St. George, at one time, was the premier hotel of Brooklyn. Built in 1885 by William Turnbridge, a retired sea captain, it grew piecemeal and by 1929 was the largest hotel in New York City. This is where the Brooklyn Dodgers and the Brooklyn Democratic machine held their annual dinners and where every young Brooklyn girl hoped to have her storybook wedding.

After World War II the hotel lost some of its luster and became more and more seedy until in the 1960s it had devolved into a "welfare hotel"—a warehouse for the city's poor. As part of a city economic development project, it was sold in the 1970s to be converted into condominiums, a project that is obviously still in progress.

Coming now to Henry Street, you see the residential towers of Cadman Plaza, which were built as part of the same 1950s urban renewal plan that created the park where we began our tour. These buildings are in the Le Corbusier modern style, but with a much more gentle touch than the New York State Supreme Court Building that borders Cadman Plaza park on the other side.

As you turn left on Henry Street you will come upon a number of streets with the names of fruits and trees. Supposedly, Mabel Middagh Hicks, who had married into the Hicks family, hated the practice of naming streets after wealthy landowners. She insisted, instead, that these streets have names such as Orange, Pineapple, Cranberry, Poplar, and Willow. Those streets, extant today, serve as monuments to Mabel Middagh Hicks's influence. Ironically, nearby Middagh and Hicks streets attest to the fact that she was able to preserve a little notoriety for herself.

When you come to Orange Street, take a left. Halfway down the block, on the north side of the street, is a centerpiece of American history, the enormous redbrick **Plymouth Church**. Designed by architect J. C. Wells, the building's relative simplicity is reminiscent of a New England meeting house. Much more significant than its architecture, though, are the events that occurred inside.

This was home of the pulpit of Henry Ward Beecher, whose statue stands in the courtyard next to the church.

In the 1840s, when Beecher came to the church, New York was undergoing a tremendous commercial boom. Poor farmers who had come to till the land had made a fortune from real estate and had prospered beyond their wildest dreams. The heart of that wealth revolved around the city's position as a major center of trade.

Unfortunately, one of the most important sources of trade was moving the cotton picked by the slaves of the American South, with New York serving as the intermediary between the cotton fields of America and the cotton mills in England. For New York Congregationalists, democratic to the core and believers that all humans were equal before God, the economic link created a terrible moral dilemma.

If, during the week, people made money from commerce based on a system of slavery, how could they then honestly attend church and swear to Christian ideals on Sunday—a debate not dissimilar to recent discussions in theological circles concerning South Africa or nuclear arms.

One can imagine the stir that arose in Brooklyn when this young inspirational preacher from Indiana (though originally from an old Connecticut family of Congregationalist preachers), Henry Ward Beecher, arrived at the pulpit of Plymouth Church in 1848. In his very first sermon, he announced to the citizens of Brooklyn that they could no longer justify this contradiction of intimate links to the slave economy while claiming strong moral beliefs. He stated that it was the duty of all Christians to oppose slavery as a moral evil, regardless of their economic interests.

That was not an easy message to deliver to the families of suburban merchants here in Brooklyn Heights. Other churches in the area had avoided this indelicate issue for fear of alienating their wealthy members, but Beecher began to attract a following. Before long, Plymouth Church had 3,000 active members and became a national center of the antislavery movement.

As a leading opponent of slavery, Beecher became increasingly well known throughout the country. He actively opposed the Compromise of 1850, by which President Millard Fillmore sought to avoid war by having one slave state admitted to the union for each free state admitted and enacting the Fugitive Slave Law, which required the return of runaway slaves captured in the North. Plymouth Church—as well as many others in Brooklyn Heights—militantly opposed the Fugitive Slave Law and became an important stop on the Underground Railroad that helped fleeing blacks escape to Canada.

When a relatively unknown antislavery politician from Illinois came to speak in New York on January 30, 1860, he was expected to speak at Plymouth Church. Beecher and the organizers of his speech, however, decided that the day's inclement weather would discourage Manhattanites from traveling on the ferries to get to the church, so Abraham Lincoln delivered his pivotal "Cooper Union Address" near Astor Place in Manhattan instead.

After the Civil War began, Beecher went on a speaking tour of England and was credited with turning English public opinion in favor of the North. At the end of the war, Abraham Lincoln personally insisted that Beecher give the invocation at the raising of the Union Flag at Fort Sumter. After the Civil War, the preacher was at the apex of his influence—something akin to Billy Graham, Norman Vincent Peale, Jimmy Swaggart, and Jim and Tammy Bakker combined.

Then, in 1871, Victoria Woodhull, writing in *Woodhull and Claflin's Weekly*, an avant-garde journal promoting free love and women's rights, broke the bombshell sex scandal of the century. "The immense physical potency of Henry Ward Beecher is one of the greatest and noble endowments of this great and representative man," she wrote. "His only crime is not to openly admit his having frequently indulged in the practice of free love." The good citizens of Brooklyn Heights, thoroughly steeped in Victorian morality, were stunned.

Beecher was accused of having an affair with Elizabeth Tilton, a parishioner married to Theodore Tilton, an editor of the church newspaper. Theodore Tilton sued Beecher in State Supreme Court for alienation of affection of his wife. Even though a hung jury allowed Beecher to escape liability, his reputation never fully recovered, although he remained prominent in public affairs until the 1880s.

Now walk west along Orange Street again to Hicks Street. Take a right on Hicks and walk to **Cranberry Street**, site of several residences of the neighborhood's other great nineteenth-century personality, Walt Whitman.

Whitman came to Brooklyn Heights from Huntington, Long Island, at the age of fourteen and essentially never returned to his family's homestead. He held many different jobs, including printer's devil, general contractor speculating in Heights real estate, and local politician. His first public mention came at the age of eighteen when he addressed a Tammany Hall rally in support of Martin Van Buren's candidacy for president in 1840. He later became editor of the *Brooklyn Eagle*, Brooklyn's Democratic party newspaper, until he was fired for reportedly throwing the publisher down the stairs after he refused to support the Free-Soil (i.e., antislavery) ticket headed by Martin Van Buren in 1848.

Whitman is believed to have set the type for his *Leaves of Grass* at a house near the southwest corner of Hicks and Cranberry streets. In the 1850s and 60s there was considerable debate as to who was going to be the great American poet. In the 1870s a review appeared in a London literary magazine, arguing that Walt Whitman was the leading American writer of the day. It was universally attacked by most of the literati of the time, but after the dust had settled, Whitman's position was enhanced tremendously. The anonymous review was written by Whitman himself.

Whitman's intense patriotism, his belief in the future of the country and his understanding of the poten-

tial of democratic government in a multiethnic society—
all of which permeates his writing—has today earned him
a place as a literary spokesman, not only for nineteenth-
century Brooklyn, but all of America.

Before his problems with the publisher of the *Brooklyn Eagle*, Whitman served as editor-in-chief of the
paper. His position required that he write most of the
articles. In this capacity, he chronicled life in Brooklyn,
which was then a rapidly developing suburban community. His writing is notable for its keen observations
of lifestyle nuances still prevalent today in our suburban
communities. On August 19, 1846, he wrote enviously
about a return from a trip to see the new homes on
streets around Myrtle Avenue (a rapidly developing
community farther down from the Heights in Central
Brooklyn, which is today the site of MetroTech and the
neighborhoods beyond):

> "What an agreeable picture of domestic life is it to
> see a pretty wife upon the piazza anxiously peering
> at intervals down the avenue in expectancy of the
> evening return of her husband while children ac-
> companied by the spaniel are bamboling out in
> front, ready to run in haste in the near approach of
> their father. While as you pass, your eye uncon-
> sciously peers in at the basement window and takes
> rapid inventory of deeply arranged furniture and a
> well spread board rejoicing in all the glories of
> pure white china and spotless table linen. These
> are the incidents which make life rationally agree-
> able and leaves me interested in abundance on our
> return."

Whitman, who was homosexual, never fully participated
in this picture of domestic tranquility, but he understood
and shared its pleasure. As a Brooklyn journalist (and
sometime real estate developer and investor), he actively
promoted the benefits of that newly emerging suburban

community to the delight of his subscribers and adver-
tisers.

Whitman did more than just write about Brooklyn. He
was such an ardent antislavery man that he went to Washington to help treat the wounded during Civil War battles
because, at the age of forty-three, he had been deemed too
old to fight; and in 1862 he made the two-day journey from
Washington to Brooklyn just so he could be sure to vote
for the Union ticket in local elections.

Continue on Cranberry Street toward the Promenade
two blocks in the distance, and you will pass some of
the oldest buildings in the Heights. Note the Queen
Anne–style windows on the house on the northeast corner of Cranberry and Willow streets. Now, turn right on
Willow and walk to **24 Middagh Street**, which some
refer to as the "Queen of Brooklyn Heights." This house,
sometimes called the **Eugene E. Boisselet House**, after
the 1824 owner, is one of the few surviving homes built
in the Dutch Federal style, and is said to be the oldest
house in the neighborhood. The two bottom stories plus
an attic are characteristic of the Federal style, but the Ionian
doorway columns and other touches give the home a jewel-
like quality.

Walk west down Middagh Street, where you are in the
part of the Heights that is oldest because it is closest to the
water. As Middagh meets Columbia Heights, head north—
that is, turn right. Walk down Columbia Heights past Vine
Street, Doughty Street, and the large Watchtower Building
on your right. Columbia Heights will become Everit Street
for one block, as you move downhill toward the Brooklyn
Bridge. You are now in the **Fulton Ferry District**.

Robert Livingston, a significant Brooklyn Heights
landowner in the early 1800s, realized that the ferries in
use at the turn of the century were too unreliable to assure commercial success for Brooklyn Heights. While
serving as ambassador to France, however, he met a

The Promenade at dusk

thirty-nine-year-old American entrepreneur, artist, and engineer in Paris who had been working on a steam ferry— Robert Fulton. Livingston had previously obtained exclusive rights to run a steam ferry in New York if he could build one capable of running from New York to Albany at a speed of four miles per hour. Having been previously unable to achieve this goal, Livingston insisted that he and Fulton go into partnership. Fulton, eager to return to America because he felt his genius had not been recognized in his almost twenty years in Europe, accepted Livingston's offer.

Fulton arrived in New York in 1806 and immediately began spending Livingston's money to build a steamboat that would meet the specifications to obtain Livingston's franchise. In 1807 the steam ferry *Clermont* successfully made the trip from New York City to Albany at a speed of four miles per hour, thereby establishing the world's first commercially successful steam-powered ferry. Worldwide, steam rapidly replaced sail as the primary method of waterborne locomotion, so that within sixty years Fulton's invention had made obsolete the method of ship propulsion used for the previous 2,000 years.

In 1814, after establishing ferry services from New York to Albany and Manhattan to Weehawken (New Jersey), Fulton and Livingston began regular commercial service on the run from what is today Fulton Street, Manhattan, to Fulton Street, Brooklyn. Fulton and Livingston envisioned a nationwide system of ferries, but it never came to pass.

In addition to running the ferry operations, Fulton was active in numerous civic activities. An ardent believer in American democracy, he developed the first steam-powered warship as part of his efforts as a leader in the defense of New York Harbor in the War of 1812, and sought unsuccessfully to convince the navy to build a submarine. He was also, with DeWitt Clinton, a vigorous proponent of the construction of the Erie Canal. In 1815, at the age of forty-nine, he contracted a fatal case of pneumonia after a trip to Weehawken from Manhattan with his lawyer, Thomas Addison Emmet. The ice on that freezing winter day made the river partially impassable, and the corpulent Emmet fell into the water, followed by Fulton, who was trying to pull Emmet out. Fulton's funeral was one of the largest in New York's history, with people from all walks of life in attendance. In a eulogy, DeWitt Clinton proclaimed, "like the self burning tree of Gambia, he was destroyed by the fire of his own genius and the ceaseless activity of a vigorous mind." Henry Pierrepont, onetime manager of the Brooklyn ferries whose house you saw earlier on Pierrepont Street, insisted that a statue of Fulton be erected over the main Brooklyn ferry terminal at Fulton Street. Sadly, the statue has not survived, but Fulton's influence lives on and you shall see it in this final part of the tour.

Continue, with the Brooklyn Bridge ahead and turn right up Old Fulton Street. Walk until you reach the Anglo-Italianate building on the left, at **1 Front Street**. Number 1, originally erected for the Long Island Safe Deposit Company, features a highly decorated facade, supposedly modeled after a Venetian Renaissance palace. The bank, closed in 1891, has since been home to a series of restaurants.

From the front of the old bank, look back across the street to the **Eagle Warehouse and Storage Company** building. As the plaque on the side of the building attests, this was the site of Walt Whitman's *Brooklyn Eagle*. The building was converted about ten years ago to a condominium residence. Also from here, you have another view of the **Watchtower Buildings**, owned by the Jehovah's Witnesses, an institution whose world headquarters is in the Heights and which has long been active in religion *and* Heights real estate. The Jehovah's Witnesses have from time to time run into conflict with the preservation community because of their desire to tear down brownstones for high-rise developments.

Double back down Old Fulton Street toward the East

River and the actual Fulton Ferry district. Walk past the red-wood former firehouse that once housed the Fulton Ferry Museum to the water's edge.

Pause at the ferry slip that separates the **River Cafe** on the right from **Barge Music** on the left. We have now come to the last stop of our tour. The Brooklyn Bridge is overhead on the right, dwarfing all that's beneath it. At one time this was one of Brooklyn's most vital commercial districts. From this site sailed the original Fulton Ferry, which became the incunabulum of modern commuter mass transit. Starting with the steamboat *Nassau* in 1814, there were five major ferry lines running from the Brooklyn Heights waterfront to Manhattan by the mid-nineteenth century. By the 1870s, 600,000 people crossed by ferry from Brooklyn to Manhattan every day. Throughout most of the nineteenth century the ferry slip and its revenues legally belonged to New York City because New York (i.e., Manhattan) claimed all rights to the Brooklyn waterfront to the high-water line of the East River. Notwithstanding periodic attempts by certain Brooklyn leaders to convince them otherwise, the New York courts have ruled that the ancient Dorgan charter of 1686 granted Manhattan the right to control all access to the East River. It was the bridge overhead that presaged the twentieth-century demise of the ferry landing. Ferry ridership declined from the time the bridge opened in 1883, and in 1924 the ferry ceased running altogether.

The area was virtually abandoned by the mid-1950s. Then came signs of revival. The River Cafe opened in the 1970s along with Olga Bloom's Barge Music, beginning the renaissance of this long-forgotten area. The River Cafe is one of the most romantic spots in the city and is the precursor of such other waterfront restaurants as Manhattan's Water Club. It has an unparalleled view of Manhattan and a proximity to the East River and the Brooklyn Bridge that makes it an ideal place for dinner on a special occasion with a friend or lover. Unfortunately, it is not cheap. Olga Bloom's Barge Music is known for quality classical recitals at popular prices.

The renovation of the Fulton Ferry district to its former glory still has some distance to go. Some of the recent improvement can be traced to Peter Stanford, one of the original founders of the South Street Seaport museum, who sought to prevent the destruction of the old maritime buildings of the South Street area in Manhattan and to create a living museum of old renovated buildings. However, such buildings couldn't generate sufficient rental or tax revenue and control of the South Street Seaport Museum passed to more commercial interests. Stanford established the National Maritime Historical Society and Ferry Museum in the old firehouse next to which we are now standing. Reportedly, he wanted to make the Fulton Ferry district into what he had hoped South Street Seaport was to have been prior to its overcommercialization. However, after Stanford began his Brooklyn work, the borough president and others began to urge more development. In the late 1980s there was even a brief attempt to revive ferry service to the South Street Seaport. This development, however, with the downturn of the 1990s, has yet to come and the city's Department of Ports and Terminals (recently reorganized into the Department of Business Services) has again put out a request for proposals for the building's renovation.

Look at the skyscrapers of lower Manhattan ahead. One cannot fail to be amazed at the architectural beauty as well as the sheer density of the twentieth-century city's central core and marvel at how far the city has come since its founding in 1624.

As we end our tour, it is appropriate that our last' image should be of the majestic Brooklyn Bridge framing the Manhattan skyline. Although Manhattan is and remains the center of New York's urban core, the importance of the Heights and its people as the soul of nineteenth-century New York and America cannot be overestimated.

James S. Kaplan, a lawyer, is a longtime student of New York's economic and political history. He serves as consulting special tax counsel to the New York City law department and special counsel to the Manhattan law firm of Siller, Wilk & Mencher. A Manhattan native, he has led tours for the 92nd Street Y, the Municipal Art Society, the Fraunces Tavern Museum, Friends of the Parks, and other groups. He is also a member of the board of directors of the Bowling Green Association and has written articles on New York's history for various publications, including New York *Newsday* and *Talking Turkey*.

Restaurants

The New York restaurant scene changes as fast as stars twinkle in the sky. The restaurants listed here have earned their reputations over the years, but are only a starting point for the New York culinary wonderland. Look at menus as you walk by restaurants, read the papers, and talk to New Yorkers for suggestions for other eateries. We recommend you call ahead to confirm hours, credit card/ traveler's check acceptance, reservations, dress regulations, and special parking arrangements before making a special trip to any restaurant.

Lower Manhattan

Windows on the World, One World Trade Center, 107th floor, tel. 938-1111. Spectacular views of Manhattan, Brooklyn, the Bronx, Staten Island, Queens, and New Jersey, plus an unusual choice of restaurants:
- The Hors d'Oeuverie
- The Cellar in the Sky

- The Restaurant
- City Lights Bar
- Statue of Liberty Lounge

Dancing nightly in City Lights Bar and Statue of Liberty Lounge. Jacket and tie required in certain facilities. Moderately expensive to expensive.

Minetta Tavern, 113 MacDougal Street, tel. 475-3850. A delightful restaurant in the style of "Old New York," with wonderful murals depicting Greenwich Village as it was in the 1930s. Northern Italian specialties. Moderate.

Fraunces Tavern, Broad and Pearl streets, tel. 269-0144. New York's oldest tavern, established in 1762 as the Queen's Head Tavern. It has played a prominent role in the history of the United States. George Washington was a good friend of Samuel Fraunces and a regular diner. Washington bid farewell to his officers here on December 4, 1783. American cuisine. Moderate.

Delmonico's, 56 Beaver Street, tel. 422-4747. One of the Wall Street area's oldest, established in 1838. Continental cuisine. Moderately expensive.

Harry's, One Hanover Square (tel. 425-3412) and 233 Broadway (Woolworth Building, tel. 513-0455). Keep your ears open for the latest financial and business gossip at these popular hangouts for Wall Streeters. American. Moderately expensive.

Little Italy and Greenwich Village

Grotta Azzurra (Blue Grotto), 387 Broome Street, tel. 925-8775. In the heart of Little Italy, one of New York's finest Italian restaurants. Moderate.

Grand Ticino, 228 Thompson Street, tel. 777-5922. A setting for the movie *Moonstruck*. Northern Italian menu. Moderate.

Ye Waverly Inn, 16 Bank Street, tel. 929-4377. A colonial American restaurant with a turn-of-the-century look, including two fireplaces and candlelight; in summer, there is an outdoor garden. Moderate.

White Horse Tavern, 567 Hudson Street, tel. 243-9260. Greenwich Village hangout of writers and artists. Moderate.

Lower East Side

Second Avenue Deli, Second Avenue and Tenth Street, tel. 677-0606. Typical kosher deli. Specialties are chicken in the pot and cholent, in addition to corned beef and pastrami. Ask for a tasting of the cholent. Moderate.

Ratner's Dairy Restaurant, 138 Delancey Street, tel. 677-5588. Open in 1918, kosher, dairy only (no meat products). Specialties are blintzes, pirogi, and gefilte fish. Moderate.

Gramercy Park

Pete's Tavern, Irving Place and 18th Street, tel. 473-7676. Old Gramercy Park landmark, made famous by O. Henry who sat there, writing. Sidewalk café, when weather permits. Moderate.

Midtown–East Side

Four Seasons, 99 East 52nd Street, tel 754-9494. Pool Room and Grill Room. Legendary power lunch and dinner restaurant, renowned as much for its patrons as its food. The restaurant, designed by architect Philip Johnson, changes decor with each season. American contemporary. Jacket required. Expensive.

Lutèce, 249 East 50th Street, tel. 752-2225. Often ranked as the country's top restaurant. Famous for its haute French cuisine and enclosed back garden. Jacket required. Expensive.

Waldorf-Astoria, 301 Park Avenue, tel. 355-3000. The famed hotel offers a choice of dining locations:

- Peacock Alley—A continental café, ritzy and colorful, with Cole Porter's grand piano. Jacket required. Expensive.
- Oscar's—Dining and snacks. Moderate.
- Waldorf Cocktail Terrace—Tea and cocktails, entertainment nightly.
- Bull & Bear—American cuisine. Jacket required.
- Sir Harry's Bar—Cocktails.

Oyster Bar and Restaurant, in Grand Central Terminal, tel. 490-6650. Oysters from all over the world are featured on the menu. A New York landmark since 1913. Moderate.

Serendipity 3, 225 East 60th Street, tel. 838-3531. Frozen hot chocolate and fabulous ice cream concoctions bring out the kid in anyone. Hot dogs and other food. Funky boutique in front. Moderate.

Upper East Side

Stanhope Dining Room, 995 Fifth Avenue, tel. 288-5800. Directly across from Central Park and the Metropolitan Museum of Art. Continental cuisine. Features Baccarat crystal chandelier. Jacket required. Also in the hotel: Le Salon, serving traditional English afternoon tea daily; and Girards, for cocktails and light fare. Expensive.

The Sign of the Dove, 1110 Third Avenue, tel. 861-8080. Romantic ambience abounding in flowers. American/French cuisine. Expensive.

Midtown–West Side

Rainbow Room, atop 30 Rockefeller Plaza, tel. 632-5100. One of New York's most famous. Art Deco furnishings that are very elegant, located on the sixty-fifth floor with breathtaking views. Continental cuisine. Jacket required. Dancing begins at 7:30 P.M. Expensive.

The Rainbow Promenade, atop 30 Rockefeller Plaza, tel.

632-5100. Jacket required. Cocktails and light snacks with panoramic views. Expensive.

Russian Tea Room, 150 West 57th Street, tel. 265-0947. Celebrity spotting is serious sport at this "in" place "slightly to the left of Carnegie Hall." Russian specialties featured. Jacket required at dinner. Expensive.

21 Club, 21 West 52nd Street, tel. 582-7200. Originally a speakeasy, this clublike restaurant has a loyal following. Frequented by many celebrities. Cozy atmosphere, imaginative American cuisine. Jacket required. Expensive.

Gallagher's Steak House, 228 West 52nd Street, tel. 245-5336. Originated the "New York Cut" steak. Tradition has it that charcoal broiling started here. Moderate.

Top of the Sixes, 666 Fifth Avenue, tel. 757-6662. Superb view of Manhattan skyline thirty-nine floors up. American/Continental cuisine. Moderate.

Carnegie Delicatessen, 854 Seventh Avenue, tel. 757-2245. An old-fashioned New York deli. A real treat for corned beef, pastrami, and blintzes. Moderate.

Hard Rock Cafe, 221 West 57th Street, tel. 489-6565. The greatest of pop culture ambience with burgers and fries for the rock-and-roll crowd. Adjoining souvenir shop. Moderate.

Upper West Side

Tavern on the Green, Central Park at 67th Street, tel. 873-3200. Located inside Central Park, several romantic dining rooms including the Crystal Room's beautiful setting. American cuisine. Moderately expensive.

Café des Artistes, 1 West 67th Street, tel. 877-3500. Beautiful room with famous murals make this lovely restaurant a legend. Jackets required after 5 P.M. Moderately expensive.

Sylvia's, 328 Malcolm X Boulevard at 127th Street, tel. 996-0660. The best soul food in Harlem. Moderate.

"Floating" Restaurants

World Yacht Dining Cruises, Pier 62 at West 23rd and the Hudson River, tel. 929-7090. New York's harbor-cruising restaurants offering an exciting view of the skyline. Lunch and dinner cruises. Music and dancing, parking on pier. Expensive.

Brooklyn

The River Cafe, One Water Street, under the Brooklyn Bridge, tel. (718) 522-5200. Fabulous views of the East River and the lights of Wall Street from the Brooklyn waterfront. American cuisine. Jacket required. Expensive.

Peter Luger, 178 Broadway, tel. (718) 387-7400. Legendary steakhouse since 1887. Expensive.

Gage and Tollner, 372 Fulton Street, tel. (718) 875-5181. In same location since 1879, where Diamond Jim Brady and Lillian Russell came by carriage. Famous for seafood and Charleston She-Crab Soup. Moderate.

Junior's, 386 Flatbush Avenue, tel. (718) 852-5257. Noted for prizewinning cheesecake. Moderate.

Hotels

New York has nearly 80,000 hotel rooms available in all price ranges, from dormitory-style accommodations to fabulously luxurious penthouses. The selection below is a sampling of the range available to visitors. All the hotels listed are in Manhattan.

Algonquin, 59 West 44th Street, tel. 840-6800. Charming Midtown hotel recently renovated, long associated with its neighbor *The New Yorker* and the Roundtable eating and drinking circle. Moderate.

American Youth Hostel, 891 Amsterdam Avenue, tel. 932-2300. New York branch of the International Youth Hostel network, located on the Upper West Side. Dormitory-style accommodations. Inexpensive.

Beverly, 125 East 50th Street, tel. 753-2700. Midtown suite accommodations with kitchenettes. Good for families or long-term stay. Moderate.

Carlyle, 35 East 76th Street, tel. 744-1600. Elegant hotel convenient to uptown museums. Bobby Short plays the piano and sings downstairs. Expensive.

Chelsea Inn, 46 West 17th Street, tel. 645-8989. Townhouse hotel with rooms and suites in the Chelsea neighborhood between Greenwich Village and Midtown. Moderate.

Drake Swissotel, 440 Park Avenue, tel. 421-0900. Large deluxe hotel convenient to Park Avenue offices and Fifth Avenue shopping. Expensive.

Embassy Suites, 1568 Broadway, tel. 719-1600. This all-suite hotel is located in the heart of the Theater District. Moderately expensive.

Empire, 44 West 63rd Street, tel. 265-7400. Located right across the street from Lincoln Center and convenient to Midtown. Moderate.

Grand Hyatt New York, Park Avenue at 42nd Street, tel. 883-1234. Enormous luxury midtown hotel adjacent to Grand Central Station. Moderately expensive.

Helmsley Palace, 445 Madison Avenue, tel. 888-7000. Luxury Midtown hotel across from St. Patrick's Cathedral, incorporating into the modern hotel the historic Villard Houses. Expensive.

Holiday Inn Crowne Plaza, 1605 Broadway, tel. 977-4000. Theater district hotel and one of few deluxe ones with swimming pool. Expensive.

Howard Johnson, 851 Eighth Avenue, tel. 581-4100. New York branch of this chain, located on edge of Theater District. Moderate.

Malibu Studios Hotel, 2688 Broadway, tel. 633-0275. Recently renovated hotel on Upper West Side. Inexpensive.

Manhattan East Suite Hotels, tel. 744-5660. This group of hotels features comfortable all-suite hotels with fully equipped kitchens and convenient locations. Moderate.

Mayfair Regent, 610 Park Avenue, tel. 288-0800. Elegant hotel on fashionable Upper East Side. Chic Le Cirque restaurant on ground floor. Expensive.

Mayflower on the Park, 15 Central Park West, tel. 265-0060. Comfortable hotel convenient to Lincoln Center and midtown. Directly across from Central Park. Moderately expensive.

Milford Plaza, 270 West 45th Street, tel. 869-3600. Large hotel convenient to theaters. Moderate.

New York Hilton, 1335 Avenue of the Americas, tel. 586-7000. Enormous, active hotel in Rockefeller Center. Moderately expensive.

Plaza, Fifth Avenue at 59th Street, tel. 759-3000. Glamorous hotel across from Central Park recently beautifully restored. Expensive.

Regency, 540 Park Avenue, tel. 759-4100. Luxury hotel known for its dining room's "power breakfast" scene. Expensive.

Roosevelt, Madison Avenue at 45th Street, tel. 661-9600. Midtown location convenient to Grand Central Station. Moderate.

United Nations Plaza, 1 United Nations Plaza (44th Street at First Avenue), tel. 355-3500. Across street from the UN; indoor pool and tennis court. Moderately expensive.

Vista International, 3 World Trade Center, tel. 938-9100. The first hotel built in Lower Manhattan in this century. Convenient to Wall Street, Battery Park City, South Street Seaport. Expensive.

Waldorf-Astoria, 301 Park Avenue, tel. 355-3000. Perhaps New York's most famous hotel. Midtown, convenient to offices and shopping. Expensive.

YMCA: Sloane House, 356 West 34th Street, tel. 760-5850; Vanderbilt, 224 East 47th Street, tel. 755-2410; West Side, 5 West 63rd Street, tel. 787-4400. All conveniently located, the latter two have a pool and exercise facilities. Inexpensive.

Museums

Manhattan

American Museum of Natural History, Central Park West at 79th Street, tel. 769-5650. Major museum for natural history and ethnography. Naturemax theater features four-story-tall movie screen for IMAX movies. The Hayden Planetarium adjoins the museum.

Asia Society, 725 Park Avenue, tel. 288-6400. Exhibits of Asian art and culture.

Cloisters, Fort Tryon Park, tel. 923-3700. This is the center for the Metropolitan Museum of Art's medieval art collection, including medieval gardens.

Cooper-Hewitt Museum, Fifth Avenue at 91st Street, tel. 860-6868. The Smithsonian's design museum, housed in Andrew Carnegie's former mansion.

Frick Collection, 1 East 70th Street, tel. 288-0700. Henry Clay Frick's magnificent art collection, housed in his equally magnificent and enlarged mansion.

Guggenheim Museum, Fifth Avenue at 89th Street, tel. 360-3500. Modern art housed in Frank Lloyd Wright's elongated snail-shaped building, with recent addition.

Intrepid Sea-Air-Space Museum, Pier 86, West 46th Street at Twelfth Avenue, tel. 245-0072. Retired aircraft carrier *Intrepid*, now a museum of military technology and retired guided-missile submarine *The Growler*.

Jewish Museum (temporarily housed at New-York Historical Society while its Fifth Avenue home is being renovated), tel. 399-3430. Museum of Jewish history and culture.

Metropolitan Museum of Art, Fifth Avenue and 82nd Street, tel. 879-5500. Over 5,000 years of the world's culture, including many of its artistic treasures, is represented in one of the world's leading museums.

Morgan Library, 29 East 36th Street, tel. 685-0008. J. Pierpont Morgan's renowned collection of illustrated and rare books, as well as his art collection.

Museum of Modern Art, 11 West 53rd Street, tel. 708-9400. The museum that introduced the world to modern art.

Museum of the American Indian, Broadway at 155th Street, tel. 283-2420. One of the world's largest collections of artifacts of the Indians of the Americas.

Museum of the City of New York, Fifth Avenue at 103rd Street, tel. 534-1672. Collections show the history of New York. Special collections on the theater and children's toys.

New-York Historical Society, Central Park West at 77th Street, tel. 873-3400. Collection on New York and early American history includes outstanding collection of Tiffany lamps.

Studio Museum in Harlem, 144 West 125th Street, tel. 864-4500. Collection highlights the works of black artists.

Whitney Museum, Madison Avenue at 75th Street, tel. 570-3676. Collection includes modern and contemporary art.

Other Boroughs

American Museum of the Moving Image, 35th Avenue at 36th Street, Astoria, Queens, tel. (718) 784-4520. Museum devoted to film technology and cinematic art.

Brooklyn Children's Museum, 145 Brooklyn Avenue, Brooklyn, tel. (718) 735-4400. Wonderful "hands-on" museum experience for children. Check the museum's activity programs.

Brooklyn Museum, 200 Eastern Parkway, Brooklyn, tel. (718) 638-5000. Major art museum known especially for its Egyptian art collection. Adjacent to the beautiful Brooklyn Botanic Gardens.

Bronx Zoo, Fordham Road and Southern Boulevard, Bronx, tel. (718) 220-5100. More than 4,000 animals live in naturalistic indoor and outdoor environments. Children's zoo May–October.

New York Botanical Garden, Bronx Park, Bronx, tel. (718) 220-8700. One of the world's largest botanical collections, including forty acres of original New York forest.

New York City Transit Exhibit, Boerum Place and Schermerhorn Street, Brooklyn, tel. (718) 330-3060. The history of New York City transit, including vehicles that can be entered.

Richmondtown Restoration, Staten Island, tel. (718) 351-1617. Three centuries of local history are on display at this living history museum.

Bookstores

West Village

Three Lives & Co., 154 West 10th Street, 741-2069 (art and fiction).

Biography Book Shop, 400 Bleecker Street, 807-8655 (biographies).

Books of Wonder, 132 Seventh Avenue, 989-3270 (children's books; current, rare, and collectible).

Foul Play, 10 Eighth Avenue, 675-5115 (mystery, suspense, and espionage).

A Different Light Bookstore, 548 Hudson Street, 989-4850 (gay and lesbian literature).

Oscar Wilde Memorial Bookshop, 15 Christopher Street, 255-8097 (gay and lesbian literature).

Central and East Village

Tower Bookstore, 383 Lafayette Street, 228-5100 (general books).

Shakespeare & Co., 716 Broadway, 529-1330 (general books).

Strand Bookstore, 828 Broadway, 473-1452 (eight miles of new and used books).

Cooper Square Books, 21 Astor Place, 533-2595 (general books).

St. Mark's Bookshop, 12 St. Mark's Place, 260-7853 (literature, politics, art).

Wall Street Area

Classic Bookshop, 133 World Trade Center, 221-2252 (general books, especially on investment and computers).

Waldenbooks, 57 Broadway, 269-1139 (general books, especially business and fiction).

Chelsea

Barnes & Noble Main Store, 105 Fifth Avenue, 805-0099 (general books, especially college textbooks).

Barnes & Noble Annex, 128 Fifth Avenue, 633-3500 (bargain books).

Midtown

Brentano's, 597 Fifth Avenue, 826-2450 (a landmark building with a must-see decor).

Doubleday Bookshops, 724 Fifth Avenue, 397-0550 (general books).

Coliseum Books, 1771 Broadway, 757-8381 (general books).

Rizzoli Bookstore, 31 West 57th Street, 759-2424 (art, architecture, and design).

Drama Book Shop Inc., 723 Seventh Avenue, 944-0595 (theater books).

Gotham Book Mart, 41 West 47th Street, 719-4448 (famous literary center since 1920).

McGraw-Hill Bookstore, 1221 Avenue of the Americas, 512-4100 (professional books of all publishers).

Travellers Bookstore, 22 West 52nd Street, 664-0995 (books on travel, including guides, maps, and literature).

The Complete Traveller Bookstore, 199 Madison Avenue, 679-4339 (books on travel).

Upper West Side

Shakespeare & Co., 2259 Broadway, 580-7800 (general books).

Eeyore's Books for Children, 2212 Broadway, 362-0634; and 25 East 83rd Street, 988-3404.

Murder Ink, 271 West 87th Street, 362-8905 (mystery and suspense books).

Black Books Plus, 702 Amsterdam Avenue, 749-9632 (books by and about African Americans).

Barnard Book Forum, 2955 Broadway, 749-5535 (scholarly books and university press books).

Applause Theatre Books, 211 West 71st Street, 496-7511.

Endicott Booksellers, 450 Columbus Avenue, 787-6300 (literature and the arts).

Storyland, 379 Amsterdam Avenue, 769-2665 (children's books).

Upper East Side

Madison Avenue Bookshop, 833 Madison Avenue, 535-6130 (current fiction and nonfiction).

Canterbury Book Shop, 1045 Lexington Avenue, 737-7525 (fiction with emphasis on art and literary criticism).

Burlington Book Shop, 1082 Madison Avenue, 288-7420.

Corner Bookstore, 1313 Madison Avenue, 831-3554 (general bookstore with emphasis on art).

Kitchen Arts & Letters, 1435 Lexington Avenue, 876-5550 (cookbooks and other books on food).

Storyland, 1369 Third Avenue, 517-6951 (children's books).

Books & Co., 939 Madison Avenue, 737-1450 (current).

Bookberries, 983 Lexington Avenue, 794-9400 (current & children's books).

Foul Play, 1465B Second Avenue, 517-3222 (mystery, suspense, espionage).

Harlem

Liberation Bookstore, Malcolm X Boulevard at 131st Street, 281-4615.

Gourmet Foods
and Greenmarkets

INTERESTING AND GOURMET
FOOD SHOPS

Dean & Deluca, 560 Broadway, tel. 431-8230 (delicacies deluxe).

Orwasher's Bakery, 308 East 78th Street, tel. 288-6569 (handmade bread and rolls).

Zabar's, 2245 Broadway, 787-2000 (food and kitchenware and a unique shopping experience—quintessential New York).

Cheese of All Nations, 153 Chambers Street, 732-0752.

Godiva Chocolatier, 701 Fifth Avenue, 593-2845, and other locations.

Balducci's, 424 Avenue of the Americas, 673-2600 (greengrocer, bakery and pastry, fishmonger, butcher, and delicacies).

GREENMARKETS

Farmers from New York, New Jersey, and Pennsylvania come to sell their own homegrown produce in these various locations:

Manhattan

City Hall (Park Row), Tuesday and Friday year-round.

World Trade Center (Church and Fulton streets), Tuesday, June–Dec.; Thursday year-round.

Federal Plaza (Broadway and Thomas Street), Friday year-round.

Washington Market Park (Greenwich and Reade streets), Wednesday and Saturday year-round.

St. Mark's Church (10th Street and Second Avenue), Tuesday, June–Nov.

West Village (Gansevoort and Hudson streets), Saturday, June–Nov.

Union Square (17th Street and Broadway), Wednesday, Friday, Saturday year-round.

Roosevelt Island (Bridge Plaza), Saturday, June–Nov.

Sheffield Plaza (57th Street and 9th Avenue), Wednesday and Saturday, year-round.

IS 44 (77th Street and Columbus Avenue), Sunday, year-round.

West 102nd Street (at Amsterdam Avenue), Friday, June–Dec.

West 125th Street (Adam Clayton Powell Blvd.), Tuesday, July–Nov.

West 175th Street (Broadway), Thursday, June–Dec.

Brooklyn

Cadman Plaza West (Montague Street), Tuesday and Saturday, year-round.

Emergency Health and Travel Information

HOSPITALS

Beth Israel Medical Center, First Avenue and 16th Street, tel. 420-2000.

Columbia Presbyterian Medical Center, 622 West 168th Street, tel. 305-2500.

Hospital for Special Surgery, 535 East 70th Street, tel. 606-1000.

Memorial Sloan-Kettering Cancer Center, 1275 York Avenue, tel. 794-7081.

Mount Sinai Medical Center, 100th Street and Fifth Avenue, tel. 241-6500.

New York Hospital, Cornell Medical Center, 525 East 68th Street, tel. 746-5454.

St. Vincent's Hospital, Seventh Avenue and West 11th Street, tel. 790-7000.

FOREIGN GOVERNMENT
REPRESENTATIVES

Austrian Consulate General, 31 East 69th Street, tel. 737-6400.

British Consulate General, 845 Third Avenue, tel. 745-0200.

Canadian Consulate General, 1251 Avenue of the Americas, tel. 768-2400.

French Consulate General, 934 Fifth Avenue, tel. 606-3600.

German Consulate General, 460 Park Avenue, tel. 940-9200.

Greek Consulate General, 29 Broadway, tel. 425-5764.

Israeli Consulate General, 800 Second Avenue, tel. 351-5200.

Italian Consulate General, 690 Park Avenue, tel. 737-9100.

Japanese Consulate General, 299 Park Avenue, tel. 371-8222.

Spanish Consulate General, 150 East 58th Street, tel. 355-4080.

AIRLINES

Air France, 666 Fifth Avenue, tel. 247-0100.

Alitalia, 666 Fifth Avenue, tel. 582-8900.

American Airlines, 100 East 42nd Street; 1 East 59th Street; 18 West 49th Street, tel. (800) 433-7300.

British Airways, 530 Fifth Avenue, tel. (800) 247-9297.

Delta Airlines, 100 East 42nd Street; 1 East 59th Street, tel. 239-0700.

Northwest Airlines, 100 East 42nd Street, tel. 736-1220.

United Airlines, 100 East 42nd Street, 1 East 59th Street; tel. (800) 241-6522.

USAir, 100 East 42nd Street; 1 East 59th Street, tel. (800) 428-4322.

USEFUL ADDRESSES AND
TELEPHONE NUMBERS

Fire, Police, Ambulance dial 911

American Express has the following services: pick up personal mail, traveler's checks, replace lost American Express cards, traveler's checks refunds, cash personal checks for cardholders. 150 East 42nd Street, New York, NY 10017, 687-3700.

New York Public Library, 42nd Street and Fifth Avenue, tel. 340-0884.

Jacob K. Javits Convention Center, 11th Avenue between 34th and 39th streets, tel. 216-2000.

New York City Transit Authority subway and bus travel information, tel. (718) 320-1234.

Index

Index

Index

Index

Index

About the 92nd Street Y

The 92nd Street YM-YWHA, founded in 1874, is a New York City treasure with an international reputation. At once a community and cultural center, it is the only institution that houses under one roof a seventy-five-foot swimming pool, an acclaimed professional orchestra, a residence for four hundred young people, and one of the world's most distinguished literary forums, The Poetry Center at the 92nd Street Y. From its inception, it has pioneered programs—for families, for the disabled, for the elderly, in arts education, recreation, and Jewish life—that have become national models. These programs are open to all.

The renowned Tours and Talks Program at the 92nd Street Y was founded in 1978 by Batia Plotch, the editor of this volume. The tours cover the gamut of New York's riches, including museums, architecture, neighborhoods, food, natural beauty, history, the arts, and Jewish heritage. Most take place on weekends during the day, although the extremely popular July 4th all-night walking tour begins at 2:00 am, and the visit to the Fulton Fish Market begins at 5:45 am (that's when the place comes alive). The program has recently been expanded to include weekend trips and longer journeys to domestic and international destinations.

You are most welcome to call the Y to find out more about the tours within and outside of New York. Trips are open to all, and there are no membership dues. The Y is located at 1395 Lexington Avenue, New York, New York 10128. Phone: (212) 996-1100.

THE HENRY HOLT WALKS SERIES

For people who want to *learn* when they travel, not just see.

Look for these other exciting volumes in Henry Holt's best-selling Walks series:

PARISWALKS, Revised Edition, by Alison and Sonia Landes
Five intimate walking tours through the most historic quarters of the City of Light.
288 pages, photos, maps $12.95 Paper

LONDONWALKS, Revised Edition, by Anton Powell
Five historic walks through old London, one brand-new for this edition.
272 pages, photos, maps $12.95 Paper

VENICEWALKS by Chas Carner and Alessandro Giannatasio
Four enchanting tours through one of the most perfect walking environments the world has to offer.
240 pages, photos, maps $12.95 Paper

ROMEWALKS by Anya M. Shetterly
Four walking tours through the most historically and culturally rich neighborhoods of Rome.
256 pages, photos, maps $12.95 Paper

FLORENCEWALKS by Anne Holler
Four intimate walks through this exquisite medieval city, exploring its world-famous art and architecture.
208 pages, photos, maps $12.95 Paper

VIENNAWALKS by J. Sydney Jones
Four walking tours that reveal the homes of Beethoven, Freud, and the Habsburg monarchy.
304 pages, photos, maps $12.95 Paper

RUSSIAWALKS by David and Valeria Matlock
Seven intimate tours—four in Moscow and three in Leningrad—that explore the hidden treasures of these enigmatic cities.
288 pages, photos, maps $12.95 Paper

NEW YORKWALKS by The 92nd Street Y, edited by Batia Plotch
One of the city's most visible cultural and literary institutions guides you through six historic neighborhoods in New York.
336 pages, photos, maps $12.95 Paper

BARCELONAWALKS by George Semler
Five walking tours through Spain's cultural and artistic center—synonymous with such names as Gaudí, Miró, and Picasso.
272 pages, photos, maps $12.95 Paper

JERUSALEMWALKS, Revised Edition, by Nitza Rosovsky
Six intimate walks that allow the mystery and magic of this city to unfold.
304 pages, photos, maps $14.95 Paper

BEIJINGWALKS by Don Cohn and Zhang Jingqing
Six intimate walking tours of the most historic quarters of this politically and culturally complex city.
272 pages, photos, maps $15.95 Paper

Available at your local bookseller or from Special Sales Department, Henry Holt and Company, 115 West 18th Street, New York, New York 10011, (212) 886-9200. Please add $2.00 for postage and handling, plus $.50 for each additional item ordered. (New York residents, please add applicable state and local sales tax.) Please allow 4–6 weeks for delivery. Prices and availability are subject to change.